THEORY AND INTERPRETATION OF NARRATIVE
James Phelan, Peter J. Rabinowitz, and Robyn Warhol, Series Editors

Feminist Narrative Ethics

Tacit Persuasion in Modernist Form

Katherine Saunders Nash

THE OHIO STATE UNIVERSITY PRESS • COLUMBUS

Library of Congress Cataloging-in-Publication Data
Nash, Katherine Saunders, 1973–
    Feminist narrative ethics : tacit persuasion in modernist form / Katherine Saunders
Nash.
        pages cm — (Theory and interpretation of narrative)
    Includes bibliographical references and index.
    ISBN 978-0-8142-1242-4 (cloth : alk. paper) — ISBN 0-8142-1242-5 (cloth : alk.
paper) — ISBN 978-0-8142-9345-4 (cd-rom) — ISBN 0-8142-9345-X (cd-rom)
    1. Feminist literary criticism. 2. Feminism and literature. 3. Fairy tales—Great Brit-
ain—History and criticism. 4. English literature—19th century—History and criticism.
5. Persuasion (Rhetoric) I. Title. II. Series: Theory and interpretation of narrative series.
    PN98.W64N37 2014
    801'.95082—dc23
                                    2013028288

Cover design by Mia Risberg
Text design by Juliet Williams
Type set in Adobe Sabon
Printed by Thomson-Shore, Inc.

9   8   7   6   5   4   3   2   1

For Frances Josephine and Penelope,
hoping the fourth wave will learn from the first

∽ CONTENTS

✎ ACKNOWLEDGMENTS

FOR PERMISSION to quote from Sayers's holograph manuscripts, I thank David Higham Associates, Ltd., and the Marion E. Wade Center in Wheaton, Illinois. I especially appreciate the gracious support given me at the Wade Center by Marjorie Lamp Mead, Associate Director, and Laura Schmidt, Archivist.

For permission to quote from Virginia Woolf's holograph manuscript of *The Years*, I thank the Society of Authors as the literary representative of the estate of Virginia Woolf, as well as the Henry W. and Albert A. Berg Collection of English and American Literature, the New York Public Library, Astor, Lenox and Tilden Foundations. I am grateful to Anne Garner, the librarian who facilitated my visit to the Berg Collection, and to Isaac Gewirtz, Curator of the Berg Collection, for granting me access to Woolf's original manuscript.

For permission to reproduce, in chapter 4, a revised version of the essay I published in *Narrative* 15, no. 1 (2007): 4–23, I thank The Ohio State University Press.

For the benefit of research leave, which permitted me to write this book from scratch instead of revising my dubiously advantageous single-author dissertation on John Cowper Powys, I thank the English department at Virginia Commonwealth University. For their help in my making the most of that research leave, I thank my friends and colleagues at VCU and in the International Society for the Study of Narrative.

Many friends have lent me their particular expertise and special assistance. I am grateful to all of them. A long string of adverbs amplifying that gratitude would never be sufficient. I appreciate especially the generosity and insights given me by Steve Arata, Beth Barr, Alison Booth, Gretchen Comba, Nick Frankel, Jerry McGann, Alan Palmer, Salvatore Pappalardo, Pat Spacks, Lauryl Tucker, and Jean Wyatt. They have helped me shape and hone, reshape and rehone these chapters with admirable patience. They are the village I could not do without.

I also have the pleasure of being in debt to Jim Phelan and Peter Rabinowitz, because they, too, helped me develop this book as well my career. Since the day I met them at the 2005 Narrative Conference in Louisville, Peter and Jim have supported me as a reader, writer, and teacher of narrative theory. They have encouraged me generously, giving me opportunities to establish myself as a scholar, offering me guidance that no junior scholar could rightfully expect and few young people in any profession actually encounter. Jim's constructive editing of my first publication, in *Narrative,* as well as his leadership during his six-week NEH seminar on narrative ethics, grounded my investment in the rhetorical theory of narrative. They have been exemplary series editors. At every step of the way they have helped me, giving me a model of mentorship I hope to emulate in the years ahead.

I thank my parents, my sister, my daughter, and Andrea Laue for supporting me unconditionally. And, with a very full heart, I thank my husband, collaborator, colleague, editor, and best friend, Jason Coats.

THE FOLLOWING have graciously allowed permission to reprint from Dorothy L. Sayers and Virginia Woolf manuscripts:

> "Detectives in Fiction." 6 pp in 6 lvs. with revisions, DLS MS-66. Wheaton, IL: The Marion E. Wade Center, Wheaton College, n.d.; "Strong Poison." 371 pp in 371 lvs. with revisions, signed, DLS MS-211. Wheaton, IL: The Marion E. Wade Center, Wheaton College, n.d. By permission of Sarah Burton, Society of Authors.
>
> "[The Years] The Pargiters; a Novel-Essay Based Upon a Paper Read to the London National Society for Women's Service." M42 volumes 1–8: The Berg Collection of English and American Literature, New York Public Library, Holograph, unsigned, dated 11 Oct. 1932–15 Nov. 1934. By permission of the Henry W. and Alfred A. Berg Collection of English and American Literature, The New York Public Library, Astor, Lenox and Tilden Foundations.

✍ INTRODUCTION

STUDIES of British modernist prose fiction tend to celebrate indirection as one of a novelist's most valuable resources. Ambiguity, lambency, irony, and linguistic indeterminacy are hallmarks of modernist narrative, crucial assets for modernist writers, and touchstones for their readers. These qualities of a narrative's *telling* (its transmission through narrative voice, or discourse), as distinct from that which is *told* (its characters and events, or story), are often given special consideration as accomplishments in themselves. Although both telling and told typically feature indirection in modernist literature, a long tradition of scholarship focuses primarily on innovative acts of telling.

Integral to indirect telling and a major site of innovation, especially in this period, is the construction of impersonality.[1] Not only do many modernist narrators lack the humanist characteristics conventional in Victorian narration, but authors tend to disappear inside their own discourses. Authorial stances are typically difficult to discern in modernist fiction, even in the rare cases when the narrator's opinions are clear and/or consistent. Many scholars readily concede that overt authorial judgments went out of fashion with the "intrusive" narrator and thus the goal of distilling acts of telling, of distinguishing the implied author's views from those of the narrator (let alone those of the inferential reader), is frequently either dismissed outright or deflected into considerations of structure, technique, or theme. It is not easy to distinguish between aesthetic impersonality on the one hand and the true absence of authorial judgments on the other. For a number of interpretive and theoretical purposes, making such a distinction might not even be necessary. But when the act of telling in a narrative has ideological and even ethical ramifications—when impersonality and indirection mask a persuasive argument—traditional approaches to structure, technique, and theme may overlook that argument altogether.

Recent investigations of fiction from this period have sought to broaden the purview of the modernist canon by undermining divisions between rarified and popular forms (a vertical expansion) and by discovering new works written during the period by heretofore underappreciated authors (a horizontal expansion).[2] Both moves attempt to lessen the evaluative register of classifying prose as modernist. The novelists studied in this book include two authors securely within the high modernist canon (Virginia Woolf and E. M. Forster) as well as two who are typically considered either low modernist or not modernist at all (Dorothy L. Sayers and John Cowper Powys). I find in modernist indirection evidence of a pervasive cultural response to first-wave feminism, one of many influences on modernist authors. But I am much more interested in studying tacit arguments about women's rights and gender constructions made within modernist fiction than I am in literary cultural studies. I posit that the novels in this book are more than glyphs that represent unconscious responses to societal pressures. They are, in fact, paradigmatic examples of oblique authorial strategies to persuade a readership that has developed a taste for indirection to think differently about women's rights and prerogatives.

This is a book about feminist novels written in modernist-era Britain. Most of them, though, have little to do with feminism as a theme, as a way of life for characters, or as a subject directly addressed by the narrator. Rather, these novels establish ethical standards and rhetorical strategies that guide audiences toward particular judgments about gender. I concentrate on works in which the implied author's stance on feminism seeks not to make readers become activists but rather to cultivate an experiential effect for the reader. Those attentive to rhetorical cues in these works will provisionally accept certain progressive attitudes toward gender and inhabit them for the duration of the novel. These attitudes, though various and contingent on each individual author's formal strategies, all stem from a common understanding of feminism: that gender roles are constructed; that such roles place systematic, inequitable constraints on women and men, to women's especial disadvantage; and that gender relations can and must be revised to eliminate that disadvantage.[3]

Much of this book is devoted to interpreting authorial stances, rhetorical purposes, and implied readerly experiences in modernist novels, highlighting the way dynamics among these three elements promote particular feminist beliefs and critique normative gender constraints in a politically fraught moment of British history. This sort of analysis cannot prove how effective such indirect promotion of feminist principles might be for any individual reader. But it does identify potent undercurrents in novels that seem to have no overt ideological agenda—undercurrents that make the dangers of gender inequity vividly real for the attentive reader and that suggest the urgency of social change. In fact, the novels' conspicuous focus on topics other than feminism gives them unusual force. They endorse feminism not as a special, separate topic but as an integral dimension of ordinary social relations. Instead of merely denaturalizing patriarchy and misogyny, they provide constructive alternatives within realistic story-worlds. They encourage the practice of feminism in lived experience, not just theory. By casually yoking feminism and crime detection, for example, or feminism and class struggle, novelists avoid didactic exhortation and portray equitable gender relations from the inside out.

Theory, too, can work from the inside out. A rhetorical approach to narrative ethics operates this way. "The rhetorical theorist, in other words, does not do ethical criticism by applying a preexisting ethical system to the narrative, however much he may admire the ethics elaborated by Aristotle, Kant, Levinas, or any other thinker; instead the rhetorical theorist seeks to reconstruct the ethical principles upon which the narrative is built," as James Phelan explains.[4] The practice of rhetorical narrative ethics is one that accounts for the ethical principles implied by individual works as well as the judgments those narratives prompt readers to make. This theoretical method attends to dynamics rather than structures or themes. Accordingly, the feminist arguments I am identifying are not mere subtexts; they are integral to the way these novels function on the multiple levels of narration, characterization, point of view, and narrative progression. My metaphor of undercurrents (as opposed to subtexts or subliminal messages) suggests a fluent, pervasive integrity or cohesion that permits us to trace meaningful connections among feminist aspects of otherwise apparently non-feminist narratives. As undercurrents, they are *influential* in both senses of the term. Although interpreting rhetorical and ethical dynamics is one of my main priorities in this study, establishing a new theory of feminist narrative ethics is my primary goal. My theory helps explain how novels may be designed to shape readers' reimagination of gender relations.

I propose this theory by way of four paradigms: the ethics of distance, the ethics of fair play, the ethics of persuasion, and the ethics of attention. These paradigms represent four distinct ways novelists may promote feminist principles as well as prompt their reciprocal acceptance by the rhetorical reader. I examine works by E. M. Forster, Dorothy L. Sayers, Virginia Woolf, and John Cowper Powys in order to illustrate as well as test the utility of these paradigms. Before I explain how each of these paradigms works, I will outline my methodology in this book, including first its theoretical basis and then its contribution to scholarship on modernism and the history of the novel. I suspect that the paradigms I am positing may be useful for understanding indirect persuasion in narratives written in other historical periods, as well, based as they are on centuries-old techniques and strategies. But I will suggest why their use at the intersection of modernism and suffragism is especially notable for scholars of feminism, novel history, and narrative theory. Following in particular Alison Case and Harry Shaw,[5] I argue that a historically aware narratology allows us to understand more precisely both the motivations for and the effects of certain innovations in novelistic form characteristic of decisive moments in history. These paradigms can shed valuable light on certain novels by each of these authors, but they can also, more broadly, help define a new dimension of rhetorical narrative ethics.

Taking Wayne C. Booth's work in *The Company We Keep* as a model, rhetorical theorists posit three dimensions of narrative ethics, including the *ethics of rhetorical purpose* (the ethical quality of the final, complete work, as well as ethics in a larger sense: an assessment of how narrative literature contributes to humanist progress), the *ethics of the told* (ethics as dramatized in the story by characters and events) and the *ethics of the telling* (the values endorsed by narrator and/or implied author in the act of narrative transmission). I propose four paradigms that offer new ways of understanding in particular the ethics of the telling. I examine narrative techniques for what they reveal about the relative ethical positions held by author, narrator, and audience.

A narrative theorist more invested than I am in tracking how efficacious narratives can be for permanently converting readers into feminists might be inclined to emphasize the ethics of rhetorical purpose in novels of this period. But for my purposes, the ethics of the telling matters most because it arises from specific, singular acts of socially progressive intervention and reimagination. Even if these acts have only temporary or provisional effect on flesh-and-blood readers, they are interesting to me for what they reveal about authorial strategies, generic conventions, and social norms, as well as their innovative adjustments. Peter Rabinowitz, David Richter, Phelan, Booth, and others have convincingly interpreted the ethics of rhetorical purpose in a wide variety of narratives by providing close readings in service of holistic assessments. My study relies on close reading as well, but of (for the most part) individual words, phrases, and techniques, so that my attention primarily focuses on means more than on final ends.

Questions about whether a book can or cannot be defined holistically as feminist or antifeminist pertain to overall purpose.[6] Such questions have fueled debate among scholars and critics for decades; much if not most feminist literary criticism answers them in one way or another. The task of answering usually includes accounting for any given novel's ending, the conventionally privileged position for final meaning or purpose. While I value such questions about wholes, I think they often occlude our appreciation of the parts. As I will show in chapters 2 and 4, analysis that devotes particular attention to narrative progression, step by step, allows us to account for the whole without granting undue influence to the ending.[7] But how do we assess the ethical significance of internally inconsistent narratives, which may, for example, feature a few potentially feminist scenes but then come to a stunningly misogynistic conclusion, as does D. H. Lawrence's *The Rainbow?* My point is not that Lawrence's novel should be recuperated as any kind of feminist work based on a few early scenes (it should not) but that reading the ethics of the telling is not necessarily pursuant to reading the ethics of rhetorical purpose.

The best demonstration of the four paradigms I am proposing draws on a wide range of novels whose final rhetorical purpose is multifarious at best, incoherent at worst. And yet, these novels feature narrative techniques that enact compelling and potentially radical feminist arguments. The difference between *The Rainbow* and the novels I examine is that the latter have integrity in their ethics of the telling. *The Rainbow* contains passages that could be construed as feminist but, to invoke my metaphor once more, those passages are not tributaries to an ideological undercurrent; they are not elements of an integral feminist conviction. The word *conviction,* of course, suggests human agency. As I will argue, the source of ethical undercurrents is the implied author.

In short, even if the final rhetorical purpose of the novels in this study is not feminist in nature (for some it is, for others it is not), assessing the implied author in each case permits a nuanced reading and interpretation of the feminist ethics of the telling. For all their inconsistencies these novels are deliberately crafted, finely nuanced, ethical texts that both acknowledge the urgency of changing gender politics and strive to effect that change through readers' ethical judgments of and within narratives.

If the ethics of the telling pertains to local rather than global relations among reader, text, and author, so, of course, does the ethics of the told (ethics as dramatized by story-level instabilities). A great number of narratives with feminist investments create very powerful effects through imagery and dialogue. The author of a narrative about domestic abuse, for example, might choose to make her boldest feminist statements through the vivid depiction of cruelty and its consequences. Moreover, most narratives convey ethical arguments through a combination of telling and told. In this study, though, I have isolated novels that selectively privilege telling over told. Their strongest, most ethically influential aspects consist in tensions between reader and narrator, on the one hand, and reader and implied author, on the other.[8] As I noted above, this makes the novels under consideration interpretively similar in that they do not (for the most part) thematize gender conflict. It also makes them historically remarkable for their formal innovations. And finally, it puts them into conversation with one another theoretically.

THE PATTERN of prioritizing telling over told may be explained in part by three major historical and generic factors impinging on novelists of this period who strove to make ideological arguments in fiction. The most prominent factor, as I have already noted, is the aesthetic influence of British modernism. British modernist narratives characteristically subordinate story to discourse: how something is rendered (telling) tends to attract more of the reader's attention than what is rendered (told). Although the famous dictum "show, don't tell" would seem, on the contrary, to prioritize the told over the telling, modernists tend to craft their "showing" with such exquisite care that to "record the atoms as they fall upon the mind in the order in which they fall" (as Woolf recommends) means that the act of recording has far more significance than the atoms themselves. In other words, narratives that purport to be unmediated are in fact thoroughly, if covertly, mediated.

Moreover, modernist narratives tend to demand reader participation, rendering textual details in some significant disorder and requiring their assembly by the reader in the conspicuous absence of a centralized narrator. They emphasize subjectivity, depicting disparate impressions (atoms) rather than dictating cohesive observations. Form and content mirror one another: the quandary of interpretation troubles both the telling and the told. Although British modernism at its apex purported to be apolitical, touting art for art's sake in direct repudiation of Victorian social conscientiousness, it is by now common knowledge that many modernist authors covertly integrated politics with aesthetics.[9] Most of the novels in this study—with the exception of Forster's, a man ahead of his time in most ways—were written late in the modernist period, when strategies for weaving ideological strands into covertly mediated narratives had been practiced and honed for thirty-plus years.

The first few decades of the twentieth century concurrently marked a second crucial factor: the peak of first-wave feminism. Moral, ethical, and political dimensions of women's lives were under intense discussion, both publicly and privately. Women's citizenship, economic status, reproductive and sexual lives, employment, access to healthcare, education, and reading habits—to name a few—circulated as topics of public discourse, making audible a variety of conversations previously hushed in polite company. Visible dimensions of political activism gained prominence as well: as activists pressured lawmakers and citizens to support women's suffrage, they staged dramatic and increasingly violent demonstrations. Such conspicuous audible and visible modes of persuasion influenced a counteractive movement in fiction, so that some novels employed a nuanced and indirect approach to the telling and downplayed their depiction of the told.

Especially after 1918's partial victory and 1928's achievement of full adult suffrage, a cultural backlash against loud and spectacular political argumentation gained strength. Women now had the vote. What more, it was asked, could they possibly demand? Most of the novels I am considering—again, with the exception of Forster's—postdate 1928, when backlash was in full force. Their use of relatively oblique argumentation through narrative technique does not suggest diminished aspiration or capitulation to antifeminism. On the contrary, it corresponds to a sea change in the feminist movement. Although activists in the women's movement considered it politically productive for several decades to focus on discrete goals—most prominently, women's suffrage from 1860 to 1928—the broader movement, from its inception in the eighteenth century onward, was and continues to be for gender equity: for equal civic and personal rights as well as responsibilities.[10] I see narrative ethics as a powerful next stage of feminist argumentation in 1930s Britain: one of many tactics adopted after the vote was won for gaining wider public participation in comprehensive gender equity. Certain novels of this period encouraged readers to replace feminism-as-political-tactics with feminism-as-ethical-worldview, and to replace adversarial impatience with the lived experience of feminist beliefs. These beliefs, I will argue, can be inculcated through an ethics of the telling.

The third factor particularly influential at this moment consisted in certain generic conventions that seemed especially valuable and stable in this period. Whereas experimentation was and is a commonplace of modernist prose fiction, the innovations of Forster, Sayers, Woolf, and Powys stand apart from most because they revolutionize generic standards many of their contemporaries did not even think to question.[11] Sayers's violation of the detective fiction genre's precious cardinal rules of the Golden Age, for example, and Woolf's creation of a novel-essay hybrid capable of non-coercive persuasion in a totalitarian era are ambitious efforts to transform generic convention peculiar to a specific moment of literary history. Powys's inventive variation on narrative progression replaces hermeneutic plotting with a sensuous, digressive, even random narrative dynamics, radically departing from the relatively streamlined cerebration so fashionable in modernist stream-of-consciousness narrative. (For instance, James Joyce's *Ulysses* is certainly digressive and, in parts, sensuous, but every word of it is deliberately placed—which makes it exemplary of canonical modernist prose fiction and quite unlike Powys's novel.) Finally, in an era famous for its irony, Forster's irony magnificently distinguishes itself. He camouflages his cagey implied author with the ironic indirections of a nimble, chatty narrator, blurring the line between these two slippery figures almost beyond recognition. In his hands, ordinary modernist irony becomes an especially sophisticated vehicle for humor and social critique, a virtuosic spectacle of voice.

Although the novels in this study have in common the historical forces of modernism, suffragism, and generic trends, in most senses, Forster, Sayers, Woolf, and Powys are mighty strange bedfellows. Aesthetically, their styles are incongruous with one another. Woolf's high modernist techniques are a far cry from Powys's stubbornly retrograde, yet self-consciously radical, adaptation of Victorian realism. Their purported audiences vary widely. Sayers wrote to attract a genre-fiction audience intent on measuring her wits against those of other crime fiction novelists, while Forster attracted a cosmopolitan readership conversant if not well-educated in domestic and international, racial, and sexual politics. They also represent four distinct points on a spectrum, as far as their personal lives are concerned, from liberal feminism (Woolf) to qualified support (Sayers) to studied indifference (Forster) to outspoken misogyny (Powys). And yet, while as flesh-and-blood writers they had very different private attitudes toward the women's movement, as implied authors they have produced analogous, complementary ethical projects. The fact that, with all their differences, they all employed feminist narrative ethics leads me to place them in theoretical and critical conversation.

As it happens, all four of them created, in the novels under consideration, implied authors with significant ethical and aesthetic differences from the implied authors of their previous works. One way in which they promoted their narrative ethics was to highlight that departure from the established career author,[12] to destabilize readers' assumptions about what they would find in the book ahead. To read each of them in these particular works is to encounter an authorial mind self-consciously extending, adapting, tempering, or repudiating previous stances on gender relations taken in her or his earlier works. Because rhetorical effects in each of these novels depend to a striking extent on the reader's recognizing features of the implied author and contrasting them with those of the career author, this project gives me the opportunity to revisit one of narratology's enduring disagreements: the utility of the implied author concept. In particular, I wish to argue its utility for feminist narrative theorists, who have preferentially analyzed narrators, flesh-and-blood writers, and historical context.

Feminist theorists and critics tend to concentrate more on politics than on ethics, by which I mean they correlate literary analysis with real-world power and authority in texts and institutions. Without any doubt, feminist politics is an ethical enterprise: the struggle to better women's lives and opportunities is rooted in a conviction that women deserve the dignity and respect denied them by patriarchal exploitation. Likewise, the ethics of feminism has political ramifications and consequences, because conferring dignity and respect on women on a large scale means changing the way texts and institutions, literary canons and civic governments define women's citizenship and therefore distribute power. But I contend that feminist critics and theorists have much to gain by leavening their investment in narrative politics with a more thorough consideration of narrative ethics. Feminist scholarship's traditional focus on the dynamics among real writers, narrators, and real readers might broaden to include a greater consideration of implied authors and their audiences.[13]

Because I examine works whose major feminist contributions occur locally, within the ethics of the telling, I need a theoretical construct that can countenance discursive multiplicity (and even incoherence) and the provisionality of ethical judgments. The degree to which these efforts succeed in guiding readers to feminist ethical judgments on a case-by-case basis depends in large part upon the creation of an ethical rapport between novelist and reader through narrative dynamics. The implied author concept allows me to attribute rhetorical purposiveness to a person, someone proximate but not equivalent to the novelist, a figure located outside the text, who attempts to guide readers' imaginative ethical judgments.

The implied author concept, coined by Booth in *The Rhetoric of Fiction* (1961), was contested long before its official coinage, as it has been ever since. The question of how to define and evaluate a writer's intentions long precedes the New Critics' attack, in 1946, on the intentional fallacy. Acknowledging the long literary history of efforts to understand authorial purposes, Booth gives readings of poetry and prose fiction from the eighth century B.C.E. forward that all feature authorial efforts to communicate through deliberate aesthetic, rhetorical, and ethical choices. While the New Critics described authorial intentions as hidden, private motives, irrelevant and in fact distracting to pure literary analysis, Booth warmly defends the idea that implied authors are not only immanent but accessible in most fiction. As instantiations of authors' "conscious and unconscious . . . freely chosen and socially or psychologically imposed self-fashionings," they are the "friends" we make, the "company we keep" as we read novels.[14]

A SIGNIFICANT NUMBER of distinguished critics have questioned the need for the existence of the implied author concept. Why not, using Occam's razor, cut out an extraneous humanist construct (Genette)?[15] Why rely on a concept so ill-defined, even incoherent (Nünning, Kindt and Müller)?[16] Is the implied author a summation of the text's purposes (the "textual whole") or a figure outside the text who conceived of those purposes (Chatman, Rimmon-Kenan)?[17] If a variety of different readers see different implied authors in the same text, should we not think instead of an inferred author (Abbott)?[18] What do we make of internally inconsistent or multiple implied authors (Hogan)?[19] Why not replace the defeasible implied author concept with hard evidence from cognitive science

(Herman)?[20] If poststructuralists can discuss the notion of designedness without a designer, what advantage does the implied author concept lend to rhetorical theorists (Serpell)?[21]

I answer all of these questions briefly in the remainder of this introduction and more fully in the course of the book. My response in brief, however, is that the notion of the implied author gives rhetorical narrative ethics a rich explanatory power it would otherwise lack. A poststructuralist model succeeds mightily at explaining some texts and their cultural contexts. But language without agency privileges indeterminacy, and ethically potent fiction deserves to be explicated, not merely labeled *indeterminate*. To decide that a text is constructed in one way rather than another way because someone designed it that way provides powerful explanatory results. In particular, I find the implied author vital in texts that feature moments of provisional but influential ethical persuasion in their narrative discourse. An implied author can provide a reader (be she resistant, or amenable, or casually ludic) with insights that neither an inferred author, nor a textual whole, nor distributed intentionality can offer. The implied author concept, which Rabinowitz freely admits is both "*easily* defeasible" (emphasis in original) and "fundamentally and profoundly a heuristic device,"[22] is also the concept that helps explain one way readers in a vexed political moment could internalize tacitly persuasive ethical arguments in the fiction they read. These arguments may be all the more persuasive for being represented by a friend.

In a 2011 issue of *Style* devoted to the implied author concept, over a dozen prominent narratologists retest existing debates and map new applications for the concept. In his introduction, Brian Richardson emphasizes the scholarly disagreements featured in that volume, but he also neatly summarizes the narrow ground of critical consensus:

> We may reasonably conclude that any attempt to simply equate the implied author with the totality of the text is ultimately untenable and should be abandoned. Likewise, attempts to situate the implied author within the communications structure of the text, as Booth's and Chatman's well-known diagrams attempt to do, are doomed to fail: the implied author does not communicate. At the same time, we can predicate values of an inferred author based on the material of the given text. It is also the case that the implied author remains a very useful heuristic construct. Published narratives are intentional acts, and it is a helpful interpretive practice to assume that a narrative is purposive, as if from a single sensibility: if one doesn't notice a reason for a segment of a text, it is beneficial

to assume that an overarching purpose exists and that the reader or critic would do well to continue to seek the justification of its presence.[23]

(Please note that Richardson's specification that *published* narratives are intentional acts begs the question of how to assess intentionality in drafts and revisions. I propose an answer to this question in chapter 3.)

Richardson's summary postdates the resolution of one of the most important debates over the implied author concept, and the one most applicable here: whether the implied author is located inside or outside the text. If the implied author is inside the text, he says, then the communications model is based on a contradiction, because a figure whose voice does not appear in the text—a figure said to be everywhere seen but never heard—does not communicate. But to locate it outside the text means anthropomorphizing a textual element, which many reject as redolent of authorial intention. Of the twentieth-century animus against authorial intention too much has been written already. Ansgar Nünning's productive contribution to the debate in 1997 began by temporarily setting aside the inside-outside controversy and focusing instead on imprecision in Booth's original definition of the concept. In *The Rhetoric of Fiction* Booth defined the implied author at some points as the real author's "second self" and at others as "the completed artistic whole." Nünning thus proposed, to widespread (but by no means universal) critical agreement, that the implied author concept be replaced by the term "structural whole."

But Nünning's second major contention, that the structural whole is a readerly construct and thus varies from reader to reader, contravened one of the fundamental tenets of rhetorical narrative theory. Phelan, objecting to the inconsistency between looking for signals in the text and ascribing all power to the reader, redefined the implied author. In *Living to Tell about It* (2006), Phelan argued that the implied author is properly situated *outside* any given text, fiction or nonfiction alike. That is, the implied author, as a streamlined version of the flesh-and-blood writer, is responsible for creating a text, not for being one. Even more importantly, he demonstrated—in keeping with the consistent conviction of all rhetorical theorists, including myself—that the implied author *does* communicate. As a creative figure responsible for deploying all rhetorical resources at her disposal, the implied author communicates indirectly, using dialogue, narrative voice, characterization, and any number of other linguistic materials to shape a particular design for readers to appreciate. Phelan's redefinition, which I will test in chapter 3, satisfied Nünning and many others, and allowed the ongoing debates over the concept's utility to proceed based on a new, though limited, degree of consensus.

Locating the implied author outside the text has ramifications for the study of narrative ethics. Lanser, firmly agnostic on the implied author debate, grants that "surely the notion of an author reconstructed from the text could be useful whenever there is dissonance or simply difference between the assumed authorial purposes and the received performance that is the text. Implied authorship in this sense becomes not simply a redundant marker, as Gérard Genette would have it, but a reminder that we don't have to—and sometimes can't—square a text's norms with what we know of its historical author's putative values."[24] Lanser then quotes a useful insight by Wolf Schmid:

> The implied author cannot be modeled as the mouthpiece of the real author. It is not unusual for authors to experiment in their works with their world-views and to put their beliefs to the test in their works. In some cases, for example, authors use their works to depict possibilities that cannot be realized in the context of their real-life existence, adopting in the process standpoints on certain issues that they could not or would not wish to adopt in reality. In such cases, the implied author can be more radical than the real author ever really was or, to put it more carefully, than we imagine him or her to have been on the basis of the evidence available.[25]

Even those who outright reject the implied author concept appreciate the importance of distinguishing the flesh-and-blood author from the figure who created the text.[26] Many of these critics call the figure an inferred author (someone construed by the reader, as opposed to the implied author, who is created by the writer). The vast majority recognize that interpreting unreliable narration, collaborative authorship, and fraudulent texts requires positing either an inferred or implied author as distinct from the writer. (In chapter 1, I suggest how we might expand the list to include other categories of narrative that make the same requirement.) These types of narrative often feature an ethical component in the relationship between real author on the one hand and either inferred or implied author on the other. The recent ethical turn in literary criticism and narrative theory has helped foreground the importance of that component, productively altering the way one can interpret, and theorize, novels' arguments and readers' judgments.

The paradigms I am proposing in this study make clear that rhetorical narrative ethics requires the implied author concept as opposed to that of the inferred author. Obviously, readers can infer what authors imply. But if we must choose either one model or the other, the implied author model has greater explanatory power for novels that offer readers information and perspectives they did not already possess. A novel with an inferred author at the helm is far less likely to persuade readers of concepts the latter disagree with, because ethical authority in that case would be generated by the reader. If values in the text are imputed to the real and inferred authors (the latter having no existence beyond that which the reader constructs), then novels have far fewer chances to teach ethics, to surprise readers out of their assumptions, or to undermine errors in readerly judgment. The didactic or pedagogical value of novels that employ the paradigms described in this book depend on the existence of an implied author whose purposes influence, but are not constructed or determined by, the reader's inferences. In short, again, implied authors can teach readers things that inferred authors cannot.

The fact that, with all their aesthetic, political, and personal differences, the four authors in this book all employed feminist narrative ethics suggests that their efforts may represent a variety of repeatable paradigms, not just singular instances. Even though their paradigmatic solutions to representing feminism differ, all four were calculated always to avoid overt didacticism and to provide covert representations that compelled readers to participate in the meaning-making process. These calculations, considered in the long history of prose narrative, are hardly unique to these four authors. They are notable, as I have said, for their productive coordination of historical moment and generic innovation, but my hypothesis is that they represent opportunities authors in previous and subsequent eras have seized as well. They are special for this time period in part because, while most authors publishing during this period were content to depict cultural change in terms of the ethics of the told and of rhetorical purpose, these four devoted substantial energy to developing entirely new ethical idioms of the telling by which they conveyed their complex stances on feminism. The paradigms I derive from their examples are contingent upon the precise historical moment from which they spring, but arguably supple enough to be applied to narratives of other historical moments.

As I elaborate each of my four paradigms in the chapters that follow, I will first situate the novel in question in terms both of the author's biographical existence and career authorial persona; I will then pose the generic, aesthetic, and ethical challenges they tackled in the novels under consideration; and finally, I will theorize the unique strategies each employed to prompt feminist understanding within their novels. First, though, to conclude this introduction, I will outline the four paradigms, clarifying how and why these four authors make exemplary use of narrative ethics at this moment in literary history and how we might extrapolate, from the examples they have provided, certain feminist and literary theoretical principles.

I BEGIN with *the ethics of distance,* which affects the rapport between reader and implied author when the latter seeks to make an ethical argument and guide readerly judgments while yet effacing his or her own ethical convictions. Narratives representative of this paradigm feature implied authors who communicate value judgments but do so from a significant remove from the telling and/or the told. They may well, as in Forster's instance examined in chapter 1, feature a prominent narrator whose ethical stances are so vivid, ubiquitous, and even contradictory that it is difficult to derive a sense of the implied author's "real" beliefs. But it is the implied author, not the narrator, whose rhetorical designs define this paradigm.

The most common axes for measuring distance in narrative are emotional, intellectual, temporal, spatial, physical, psychological, and ethical. In *The Rhetoric of Fiction,* Booth teases out permutations of distance among implied authors, narrators, characters, and audiences. One notion he develops in this and later works is that irony is a particularly suitable technique for establishing distance in a narrative. When irony is juxtaposed or conjoined with an ethical stance, the interpretive and theoretical stakes are usually especially high. This is why, as I observe in chapter 1, the instances of unreliable narration most attractive for close readings are the ones that entail ethical disjunction. Although not all unreliable narrators are ethically deficient, most of the celebrated ones are: Jason Compson, Robert Lovelace, and Humbert Humbert, to name just three. Forster supplies a sterling opportunity to consider an ethics of distance in a constellation of pervasively ironic—but wholly reliable—statements. His characteristic use of what Trilling calls his "double turn" manipulates the distances between reader and character, between narrator and character, and between narrator and implied author. This chapter examines all three relationships, but prizes the last one above all. For the enigmatic rapport between reliable narrator and implied author is at once the hardest and the most important to interpret if one is to deduce Forster's ethical stance(s). His ethics of the telling is saturated with ironic distance, and yet it manages to convey a keen deprecation of conventional gender roles. I argue that he uses distance to critique gender inequity—however obliquely—as well as slyly to endorse new models for feminist relations among women and men.

The ethics of fair play obtains when an implied author gives her readers all the clues they need to make certain ethical deductions. The "solution" is revealed overtly at the story's end, but it is available before that point to discerning, participatory readers. Ideological questions such as the ones Sayers poses, examined in my chapter 2, are ethical in nature. Three of the novels in her popular Lord Peter Wimsey mystery series pose questions such as, How should one balance feminist principles with marriage in early-twentieth-century Britain? and How may a woman maintain the integrity of her career when faced with responsibilities to husband and children? Sayers presents a range of answers to these questions, just as she exhibits an array of murder suspects, motives, and opportunities. Her primary narrative technique in service of fair play is focalization. Whereas the books early in her Wimsey series achieve fair play through what I call methodological and affective varieties of focalization, after she introduces a love interest in the character of Harriet Vane, focalization takes on ethical purposes as well. By this I do not mean that the focalization is necessarily ethically admirable, but rather that its ethical dimension predominates. Crucially, Harriet's ethical convictions, especially about gender relations, do not always match Sayers's. But her methods of solving problems—be they matters of criminal detection, judgment of character, romantic conduct, or other myriad puzzles she negotiates—always evoke (if sometimes indirectly) the implied author's norms about gender. The reader is asked to make ethical judgments, not only about events but also about Harriet's own evaluations.

This chapter examines Sayers's successful challenge to one of the supposedly immutable, cardinal rules of Golden Age detective fiction: that adding a major love interest to a mystery spoils the mystery. Although most experimental blends of romance and detection tend to impoverish one or both plot lines, Sayers accomplished a balance between the two in her Wimsey series. Unlike E. C. Bentley or Margery Allingham, two other novelists whose detectives fall in love while sleuthing, Sayers requires the reader's attention to the romance plot as part of a feminist argument, thereby preventing the detective plot from subsuming the love interest in the novels featuring Harriet. Gender politics here combines with ethics and aesthetics in service of detective fiction's hallmark convention of fair play. Analysis of Sayers's rhetorical purposes in her Harriet Vane novels can allow a fresh understanding of the ethics of fair play, not just as a professional responsibility, or as a recipe for a good mystery, but also as a mechanism by which detective fiction can make ideological arguments and prompt its readers to make a wider variety of deductions than the Golden Age rules of detective fiction anticipated.

The ethics of persuasion applies to an implied author's effort to influence without coercing a reader. In any time period, such a challenge would be difficult. In the early 1930s, though, the global encroachment of fascism made coercion an especially nasty specter. Readers and writers alike recognized that political argumentation could and often did slide too easily into propaganda. Woolf met this formal and ethical challenge by melding prose fiction with ideological essay. She set out to write what she called a novel-essay "about the sexual life of women . . . Lord how exciting!" which would contain "millions of ideas but no preaching—history, politics, feminism, art, literature—in short a summing up of all I know, feel, laugh at, despise, like, admire, hate and so on."[27] Succeeding in this endeavor would mean an unprecedented coordination of two seemingly incompatible genres as well as a triumph of feminist humanism.

Whereas in chapters 1 and 2 I concentrate on the rhetorical and ethical strategies of narrators, implied authors, and career authors, in chapter 3 I propose a new model of authorship: the project author. As Woolf wrote and rewrote her novel-essay in a series of strikingly dissimilar drafts, both her narrative techniques and the nature of her ethical authority changed. The ethics of persuasion in Woolf's eventually published novel *The Years* is virtually unrecognizable unless we posit an authorial figure that is dispersed beyond the bounds of the published text. It is therefore necessary to seek an alternative to the implied author concept, because the usual techniques for recognizing authorial purpose that are employed in a rhetorical approach to narrative are largely thwarted by this novel's particular kind of difficulty. Its conspicuously unsettling formal characteristics—false starts to inconclusive instabilities, strikingly banal diction—are surface-level indications of an authorial figure not only unfamiliar (for readers acquainted with the career author) but also dispersed (regardless of readers' previous reading experience). The implied author seems, literally and colloquially, scattered, and one is hard pressed to assemble evidence for any coherent argument, ideological or otherwise.[28] Once we begin to assess rhetorical and ethical purposes distributed among holograph manuscript, revisions, and publications, however, the subtler effects of her urgent ethical paradigm in the project are revealed, and an intense, persuasive argument takes shape.

Finally, *the ethics of attention* figures prominently when an implied author explores the ethical ramifications of observation, receptivity, and reading itself. In an early-twentieth-century context of feminism, this paradigm illuminates ways narratives could respond to contemporary anxieties about young women's vulnerabilities to mental influence and suggestion, particularly as readers of fiction, but also as subjects of mesmerism, hypnotism, and spiritualism. For centuries women had been construed as susceptible to control by people and ideas due to their supposed innate sympathy as well as their putative psychological, mental, and biological frailty. Although such chauvinism operates even today, its prevalence slowly diminished in nineteenth- and twentieth-century Britain, and as Kate Flint has shown, large numbers of novels published as early as the 1860s "mock within themselves the belief that women read uncritically, unthoughtfully. . . . they stimulate, simultaneously, their readers' capacity for self-awareness and social analysis and judgment."[29] As I demonstrate in chapter 4, however, the ethics of attention can also obtain in less straightforwardly pro-woman narrative dynamics. The feminist implications here have little to do with the women's movement for political opportunity, but much to do with the transformation of gender constructs. Specifically, one of women's supposed weaknesses is transformed into an admirable strength.

Powys's notion of "young-girl-like receptivity" implies a state of curiosity that anticipates a pleasant revelation, free of the menace of corruption. He diverges radically from the equation of receptivity with passivity. Receptivity here is an extraverted, proactive collection of experiences, an absorptive quest, but it is also a state in which the quester's perspective is chaste, innocent, and fresh. I argue that this concept is key to the way Powys revolutionized plot dynamics in his most important novel, *A Glastonbury Romance*. He replaced conventional hermeneutic plotting (the gradual resolution of narrative instabilities) with what I call an erotics of progression, in which instabilities circulate freely and readerly attention is receptive (a mental state he associated with women) rather than goal-directed. Powys applied conventions of the occult, especially radically suggestive states of mind, to narrative dynamics in his fiction, undermining contemporary assumptions about the natural stability of gender.

THE FORMAL innovations of Forster, Sayers, Woolf, and Powys stand apart from other forms of modernist experimentation because they depend in part on narrative ethics, as determined by feminist politics, for their rhetorical effects. They acknowledge women's burgeoning civic power and revolutionize the way fiction prompts ethical judgments by readers. As these authors pressed the formal limits of their genres, they established significant, even paradigmatic authorial rapports with their readers. Because of their political context, those rapports had—and still have—persuasive ideological power.

This study brings critical assessments of modernist narrative innovations into conversation with rhetorical and feminist narrative theory. I hope it will contribute some critical vocabulary and theoretical underpinnings to extant scholarship on rhetorical narrative ethics. I hope it may be useful to graduate students and scholars of modernist novels, narrative theory, gender theory, and the history and theory of the novel. To my mind, a full appreciation of an ethical rapport between author and audience must be informed not only by evidence of the flesh-and-blood writer's decisions (that in some cases includes archival evidence of manuscript revisions), but also by the implied author's rhetorical strategies, which are subtly but powerfully influenced by historical and cultural context. I believe that practicing historically sensitive narratology is the best means of gaining insight into feminist narrative ethics.

CHAPTER 1

The Ethics of Distance

"I grudged her nothing except my company."

—E. M. Forster[1]

O NE MAY AS WELL begin with E. M. Forster, who—as a flesh-and-blood writer, as a Liberal humanist, as a queer man, as a member of Bloomsbury—had the most ambivalent relationship with feminism of any of the novelists this study considers. A glance at his professional personae and personal life reveals clear positions both for and against feminism. "It is historically true," he noted in his 1910 lecture "The Feminine Note in Literature," "that women have had a miserable chance as human beings," and that the practice of chivalry degrades both women and men.[2] In the same year, he expressed misgivings about the suffragists' tactics ("It is difficult for an outsider to settle at what point physical force becomes justifiable") yet troubled himself to attend a speech by Christabel Pankhurst (deeming her "very able, very clever and very unpleasant").[3] Years later, Forster described his attitude toward suffrage-era feminism as having been "false enthusiasm [for] women's rights. She shall have all she wants. I can still get away from her, I thought. I grudged her nothing except my company."[4] But his description may have been distorted by retrospection, as his unswerving commitment to humanism went hand-in-hand with a conscientious regard for women's dignity both before and after they gained suffrage. His biographer, P. N. Furbank, suggests that "[h]e supported women's rights, in a general way, but rather out of abstract justice than because he thought the vote would do women much good."[5]

It is no easier to recognize any fixed attitude toward feminism by looking at Forster's private behavior. He both loved and resented being surrounded by female relatives and friends. He lived with his mother for the first sixty-six years of his life, yet his personal papers and reports of his behavior suggest some significant aversion to women, especially "clever" and "up to date" women, as Virginia Woolf complained.[6] Then again, one of his enduring confidants, Florence Barger, was a militant feminist.

Since feminism was an uncomfortable topic for him, it's unclear why he returned to it repeatedly in his fiction.[7] If he did support women's rights, it's curious that he obscured his support so assiduously. Attentive reading of his novels does not reveal *why* Forster distances himself from feminism in his fiction, but it does suggest how he uses distance to make ethical arguments through narrative form. Interpreting the *how* suggests both advantages and disadvantages of the ethics of distance, as well as why the affordances of this kind of narrative ethics would be especially appropriate for Forster's articulation of feminist principles.

Scholarship on Forster has acknowledged two main benefits of distance as a formal strategy: as a characteristically Victorian feature of extradiegetic narration and as a necessary component of (modernist) irony. Distance has also been noted for its usefulness to a closeted queer writer, who privately expressed some impatience with the obligation to write heterosexual romances. But it has not yet been adequately considered as a rhetorical strategy for ethical ends. What Lionel Trilling has called Forster's "double turn"—his characteristic strategy of first positing and then inverting or contradicting an idea[8]—relies heavily on distance for its meaning. He employs the double turn in his other novels to propose and test a wide variety of ethical stances: ethics as it pertains to Anglo-Indian relations, to courtship, to marriage, to pedagogy, to familial obligations, to class conflict, to violence. In all of these instances, the implied author's distance from the telling and told is crucial. I contend that Forster employed an ethics of distance to make feminist arguments in certain of his novels.

Forster's closeted attraction to men has been retrospectively identified as a source of his ambivalence toward women.[9] The majority of Forster scholarship since 1971 has mentioned this personal factor, often in order to account for his careful detachment and pervasive irony. His "confusion" over his gender identity, so the argument goes, arose from the "fear of the feminine in himself" based on a Victorian notion of male homosexuality as *anima mulieris in corpore virile inclusa* ("a woman's soul trapped in a man's body").[10] Leonard Woolf, with affectionate rue, used to call him "a perfect old woman."[11] Readers of his novels as well as Forster himself have acknowledged a "feminine" dimension to his narrators' voices and even the personae of his implied authors. More than one book reviewer mistakenly referred to "Miss Forster's" discerning treatment of female characters; F. R. Leavis (less benevolently) noted his "characteristic spinsterly touch."[12] As George Piggford observes, "It is not insignificant that 'The Feminine Note' was composed by a man labeled 'feminine,' even, mistakenly, female. Forster's notoriety, at a peak in late 1910, rested in part on his uncanny ability to . . . write in some sense like a woman."[13]

Forster's unique amalgam of feminine and masculine qualities, however, does not necessarily betray any confusion. On the contrary, one finds in his writing his strikingly lucid understanding of gender identity, and though he personally wavered on the subject of feminist activism, the position he takes on gender identity in any given novel entails a political stance. Nor should his ambivalence be taken for lack of interest; on the contrary, all of his novels demonstrate deep, complex investments in both gender identity and gender politics. Much of the best Forster scholarship—most of it, in recent decades, by queer theorists—has attended more to his gender politics than his ethics of gender relations.[14] Queer theory, like most feminist theory, attends more closely to politics than ethics. As I explain in my introduction, for my purposes in this book the difference between the two hinges on the presence or absence of an investment in real-life social change. To study politics in narrative is to examine correlations between literary artifacts, on the one hand, and the power and authority of texts and institutions, on the other. To study narrative ethics is to theorize and interpret the way narratives can guide their readers, within the act of reading but not necessarily beyond it, to certain ethical judgments. Like many, I use the term *gender politics* to refer to real-life sensibilities and power struggles over gender roles. Gender politics, one might say, pertains to citizens; the ethics of gender politics pertains to readers reimagining public and private gender roles and expressions.

Most of Forster's most ambitious constructions of gender identity and politics may be found in his novels *The Longest Journey* (1907), *Maurice* (written 1914), and *A Passage to India* (1924)—the three novels that center on intimacy among men. The ethical arguments of these novels are not within the scope of this study. Moreover, in some ways a study of Forster's attitude toward women would seem a step backwards to an earlier phase of scholarship on gender.[15] As I will demonstrate, however, Forster's engagement with feminism in *A Room with a View* and *Howards End* permits him to articulate sophisticated arguments about gender-role constraints that he would not have dared to publish were they about men.[16]

Of the novels with both women and men at their center, only *Howards End* has been explored as potentially feminist. Elizabeth Langland points out that Forster's "desire for something other than the classical opposition between male and female, masculine and feminine, . . . initiated his embattled relationship with patriarchy" inscribed in the formal strategies of *Howards End*. With its epigraph "Only connect . . . ," Langland argues, *Howards End* endorses "not the old androgyny, a merging or blurring of terms and traits; [but] a condition that preserves difference."[17] Robert K. Martin concurs, going on to observe, "Whatever Forster's personal misogyny,[18] [*Howards End*] is feminist in its concern for spiritual inheritance and continuation and against unnatural, or male, ownership."[19] While gender identity is certainly complicated in Forster's fiction, an assessment of its ethical ramifications indicates much more integrity than confusion in the implied author's politics.

One purpose of this chapter is to demonstrate that Forster employs narrative ethics to criticize patriarchal politics in two of his novels, *A Room with a View* and *Howards End*. The feminism of the latter has received scant critical recognition, while the former has rarely been analyzed as having a political dimension at all.[20] But the broader purpose of this chapter is to theorize one of the four paradigms of narrative ethics this study incorporates. I begin with an ethics of distance, in which the implied author's political beliefs are partially obscured by a carefully constructed, stable, ironic detachment. Each of the paradigms in this book represents one historically situated effort to engage feminist politics in suffrage-era Britain through narrative ethics. I begin with Forster's ethics of distance because it presents its audience with the greatest challenge to construing a coherent political stance. The relative radicalism of subsequent paradigms is clearer in light of this fairly conservative—albeit virtuosic—engagement with politics through narrative ethics.

The most common axes for measuring distance in narrative are emotional, intellectual, temporal, spatial, physical, psychological, and ethical. In *The Rhetoric of Fiction*, Wayne C. Booth teases out these permutations of distance among implied authors, narrators, characters, and audiences, giving special attention to the varieties of unreliability that result from distance between implied author and narrator. Unreliability, as James Phelan has demonstrated, does not necessarily entail an ethical axis. But several of the most compelling theoretical insights into unreliability, including Phelan's, have cited cases of ethical unreliability—not surprisingly, since ethical disparity can have such high stakes.[21] In short, the usual purpose theorists have for studying what I am calling an ethics of distance, particularly in the relationship between implied author and narrator, is to explore a narrator's unreliability. Forster supplies a sterling opportunity to consider an ethics of distance in a constellation of wholly reliable statements.

The continual indirections of his frisky, chatty, unpredictable narrators make it difficult to discern their attitudes, let alone those of the implied author. "The unexpected whimsy, the sideways shuffle, the dangling disclaimer" make his narrators "as slippery as a fish," explains Kenneth Graham.[22] Trilling observes that "Forster's insistence on the double turn" often "suggests forgiveness" but just as often "makes the severest judgments. And even when it suggests forgiveness it does not spring so much from gentleness of heart as from respect for two facts co-existing."[23] Moreover, he points out, both implied severity and implied forgiveness are leavened even after the "double turn" by the accretion of more and different ironic statements by the narrator. These statements have a wide variety of potential targets or "victims." Furthermore, implied readers may or may not be required to tag the statements as provisional. Graham offers a succinct description of Forster's quintessential double turn: "[It is] one of these moments where a totally different register suddenly declares itself within the bland or witty cadences of his prose, jolts our attention to a quite different line of thought or feeling, and casts a new light of suggestiveness on everything that has gone before, hinting at contradictory combinations or ramifying echoes in the text that has been already unfolded."[24] This move in the discourse tends to increase the distances between reader and character, between narrator and character, and between narrator and implied author.[25]

Rhetorical theory assumes that narratives are deliberately shaped from raw materials that might have been shaped otherwise, but were not. Rhetorical theorists examine the advantages and disadvantages of particular acts of shaping. For Forster, one major advantage of distance as a rhetorical strategy is the privacy it affords him as implied author. He adopts strategies that make it difficult to discern his positions. As one critic remarks, "It is a dangerous game to try to pin E. M. Forster down."[26] He is the sort of person who can look one straight in the eyes and deadpan ironic statements one after another: an enigmatic person, sophisticated, intelligent, relentlessly secretive, and self-controlled.[27] Forster's manipulation of distance through a number of narrative techniques, including but not exclusively irony, allows him to maintain those qualities of secrecy and control. His narrator, or nonfictional speaker, guides readers to ethical judgments while the implied author of either fiction or nonfiction remains in the background, his ethical convictions mysterious if not entirely indeterminate. Whereas the narrator shows his hand, the implied author keeps his cards close to his chest. One obvious disadvantage of this approach, of course, is that Forster's various subtleties may be lost on the reader. Like Nabokov, whose authorial audience is exponentially smarter than his actual audience,[28] Forster deploys so many sleights of hand that he risks underestimation and misunderstanding.

To establish an ethics of distance in Forster's fiction, it is necessary to answer at least two central questions. First, given such rich and multidirectional irony, how is it possible to establish Forster, as Booth confidently claims he is, as a "stable ironist," a voice whose covert meanings are consistently determinate?[29] Second, how might one determine what those "meanings" are? While nearly everyone can agree that Forster's rhetorical techniques are pervasively ironic, very few critics have distilled from those techniques any core convictions.[30] Evaluating his uses of distance in the relationships among narrator, characters, and readers permits a limited number of deductions about the implied author's convictions, which are otherwise almost completely concealed. Recognizing distance not as a symptom of ambivalence, closeted diffidence, or bottomless irony but rather as Forster's rhetorical and ethical resource in each of these relationships ultimately points to his feminist commitments in *A Room with a View* and *Howards End*.

ALTHOUGH the novels will receive the majority of my attention in this chapter, the notion of an ethics of distance may best be introduced through consideration of a less complicated text. Forster's 1925 essay "Me, Them and You," mounts a scathing liberal-humanist critique of class privilege. All good Liberals, regardless of their feminist beliefs, know what to say about class inequality, and the implied author here seems to be uncharacteristically straightforward in his rhetorical purpose. His formal strategies in achieving this purpose, however, are characteristically unstraightforward. Forster deploys a nimbly ironic voice separate from his own to address one audience ("You," the working classes) that overhears another being criticized ("Them," the privileged classes). Although You is ostensibly the noun of direct address, the satire in this piece is clearly directed at

Them, and the audience is easily construed as being uneasily allied with Them.

Distance is crucial in this essay, not only to its subtlety, but also to its persuasive efficacy. First, Forster's speaker is distinct from the implied author of this personal essay (a genre that pretends to collapse the two figures),[31] but the degrees of distance between speaker and author change as the essay progresses. The essay's first lines underscore this distance analogically: "I have a suit of clothes. It does not fit, but is of stylish cut. . . . Underneath the suit was a shirt, beneath the shirt was a vest, and beneath the vest was Me. Me was not exposed much to the public gaze; two hands and a face showed that here was a human being; the rest was swathed in cotton or wool. Yet Me was what mattered, for it was Me that was going to see Them."[32] Although the suit may not fit the speaker precisely, it conceals and protects him from exposure to the public. Likewise, although the speaker may not "fit" the implied author precisely, it serves its analogous purpose. Stylishly cut clothing and the ability to pay an admission fee permit Me to enter a portrait gallery along with other leisured members of the public. Pictures of Them hang on the walls, demanding obeisance. While the speaker is the one who obtains access to the spectacle, however, the implied author is the one who "matters," as he is the source of critical judgment. The implied author's critique takes the form of the speaker's oblique argument through analogy (letting his response to Their portraits in a gallery articulate his resentment of Their privilege). The speaker "drift[s] from Them to Them, fascinated by the hands and faces which pee[p] out of the costumes," and even talking to the portraits "civilly" as though they are alive. Repeatedly, he chastises himself for repeatedly making the "very serious mistake" of trying to discern, let alone talk to, real people beneath their elaborate clothing. "How cheap did my own costume seem now, and how impossible it was to imagine that Lord Curzon continues beneath his clothes, that he, too (if I may venture on the parallel), was a Me" (26, 27).

Nearly every aspect of this performance is ironic: the efforts at civil conversation, the pretense at being rebuffed by portraits, the self-chastisement, the annoyance at those who cloak their authentic selves, the curiosity felt about the "real" (or rather, triply unreal) people. Even his denigration of his own costume as "cheap" is arguably ironic. Although we may assume that the speaker really does feel his suit is shabby in comparison to Their fine clothing, the analogy between speaker and suit is ironically inverted: even while the speaker feels ashamed of his suit, the implied author is confident in being well served by his carefully, finely constructed speaker. As both a narrator and a character in the story, the speaker is hardly cheap; in fact, he is extremely valuable. He permits the implied author to make a series of cutting remarks while remaining safely cloaked by the speaker's witty, canny persona. The statement "Me was what mattered" stands alone as unironic, providing a stable platform on which a variety of ironies are constructed.

Near essay's end, however, both analogy and irony recede as speaker and implied author draw closer together. The essay turns toward this conflation at the moment when Me happens upon a portrait of You. This turn occurs just as the distances between speaker and author, on the one hand, and speaker and Them, on the other, are at their maximum extent: "[M]y clothes fitted worse and worse, and there seemed in all the universe no gulf wider than the gulf between Them and Me—no wider gulf, until I encountered You" (28). "You," who lacks both suitable clothes and enough money and leisure to enter the portrait gallery, is depicted in a group of Yous: miserable wartime refugees, blinded by mustard gas, yet gracefully and heroically calm, clean, and attractive. At the first mention of You, irony diminishes as righteous anger builds. At the same time, distance between implied author and speaker recedes until a distinction between them is no longer meaningful. Anger is inversely proportional to rhetorical distance here.

The other kind of distance that matters most in this essay, the one between speaker and his double audience, likewise varies in the course of the essay. The speaker admits and even initially enjoys his own economic privilege. He first describes paying his admission price as a way of getting inside, out of the snow. He later disparages this sense of advantage: after the argument's turn, his first observation is that "You had been plentiful enough in the snow outside (your proper place)" (28). The parenthetical irony marks the first of many changes in tone. For example, it is a weakly sarcastic statement, clumsy in comparison to the subtler irony found earlier in the essay. Moreover, as soon as he calls attention to the physical distance between Me and You, the speaker diminishes the ethical distance between them. Finally, although the speaker has never been ethically close to Them, both ethical and intellectual distances between these figures increase after the essay's turn.

[T]here you were, though in modified form, and in mockery of your real misery, and though the gulf between Them and Me was wide, still wider yawned the gulf between us and You. For what could we do without you? What would become of our incomes and activities if you declined to exist?

You are the slush and dirt on which our civilization rests, which it treads under foot daily, which it sentimentalizes over now and then, in hours of danger. (29)

The conflation of Me and Them into "us" or "we" is Forster's strongest persuasive stroke. By erasing the distance between those two figures, by never again mentioning either Me or Them as separate entities, the speaker eliminates the reader's comfortable sense of moral superiority to Them. The reader is made to feel complicit in class privilege by association. The speaker reviles the society that treats You as slush and dirt, he deplores the misery You feel, and he anticipates, in the essay's final words, a "new dawn" that will correct this injustice. The political ramifications of this essay result directly from the way Forster manipulates rhetorical distance to make an ethical argument about political inequity.[33]

"You," like "Me," functions as both a rhetorical figure and a character. "You" is, of course, by default a way of addressing the audience. This makes the move to "us" even more nuanced. Direct address of "You" initially pulls the reader into an uncomfortable recognition of her own privilege: the misery that defines You as a character is trenchantly juxtaposed with the freedom from misery that defines You as audience. As direct address shifts from "You" to "us," that discomfort grows more intense. The ethics of this rhetorical situation hinges on how Forster manipulates distance between Me and Them, speaker and covert audience. The effect demanded of the reader by essay's end—extreme discomfort with being conflated with "us"—depends primarily on Forster's choice to posit and then suddenly erase a crucial distance.

In *A Rhetoric of Irony,* Booth considers Forster's peculiar persuasive tactics in "Me, Them and You": "[H]is message is deflected from direct exhortation to a kind of wry, almost mystifying allusion. . . . It is almost as if he were refusing to be involved in any implicit message his essay contains: 'You comfortable readers may infer from this that you ought to disentangle your souls and bodies from the "snobbery and glitter," but don't expect me to help you. Or even to become deeply involved in your inevitable doom.'"[34] Even in this authoritative study of rhetorical irony, however, note Booth's uncharacteristic equivocation: the speaker's rhetoric is "kind of wry, almost mystifying." It is "almost as if" Forster's persona "were refusing to be involved" in his own *implicit,* let alone any explicit, argument. The persona offers the audience neither "help" (in the form of a clearly explicit argument to a single audience) nor sympathy for being "inevitabl[y] doom[ed]" to ethical shortcoming.

Booth devotes most of his attention in this brief explication to interpreting the speaker's relationship with his audiences. As I did above, he also observes variations in distance featured in the essay between clothing and man. But Booth's unease in defining the relationship between speaker and implied author in this essay points to how difficult Forster has made that task. Earlier in *A Rhetoric of Irony* he asserts that, in general, Forster is one of the "reliable but ironic authors who convince us that they are pretty much the real man or woman speaking to us."[35] For those who are not already convinced that speaker and author are in fact one and the same, however, Booth supplies no evidence. The unusually hesitant tone of his subsequent analysis—and even the "pretty much" of his original claim—suggest not that Forster's irony is unstable but that Booth is not entirely clear on where one figure ends and the other begins in Forster's work.

In texts by Forster that present much more complicated rhetorical situations than the one in this essay, of course, the challenge only increases of discerning speaker from implied author. This is the case with all of his novels, for example. He obscures his implied authors by thoughtful design. The whimsical and multidirectional pyrotechnics of his narrators make it impossible to fathom full portraits of the implied author. Although one may have the *sense* that his ironies are stable, one is hard pressed to prove with methodical explication precisely and exhaustively what the implied author actually believes.

Because Forster's speakers are not explicitly and consistently distinguished from his implied authors, because they are not, as Booth says, "radically distinct mask[s]," Booth suggests we may as well regard them as "pretty much [equivalent to] the real man."[36] This is why cases of unreliable narration supply the best opportunities for validating the implied author concept: explicit distinction makes room for interpretation of both figures. I want to create room, though, for making more than a technical distinction between reliable narrator and implied author in this case. I suggest that, while the narrator deadpans ironies, the implied author asks deadly serious ethical questions and places high stakes on particular answers. Herein lies the essential difference between them. The narrator never contradicts the implied author on any ethical issue, but his rhetorical prowess casts real doubt on what, if anything, the narrator really believes. His proliferation of conflicting statements may make him seem dilettantish at best and casuistic at worst. But the implied author offers a corrective for the presumptive inconsistencies of the narrator: taken together, the narrator's spectrum of judgments suggest an implied author committed to the complexity of his ethical position, as well as to a few consistent ethical principles. While we cannot construe full portraits of the implied authors of *A Room with a View* and *Howards End*, we can look for patterns in their reliable narrators' ironic indirections, including patterns in the way they manipulate distance, to find the implied authors' ethical endorsements.

THE DOUBLE TURN that honors "two facts co-existing" serves as Forster's first and most fundamental premise: it creates the predominant pattern in his indirections. It appears in every novel, every short story, every essay he wrote; it is indispensable to his writing style. It manifests in an incessantly shifting speaker or narrator, one whose opinions are presented, inverted, retracted, and reasserted with a difference. "Two facts co-existing" represents Forster's respect for complexity, for philosophical dialogism. It underlies his choice to use irony in the first place. It is integral to a queer sensibility (which gender theorists assert "prevents any easy binaristic demarcation between the 'straight' Forster and the 'gay' Forster[37]). Conscious multiplicity of perspective, deliberate self-contradiction, respectful attentiveness to two (or more) sides of a vexing question—these are all characteristic traits of a responsible, intellectual Liberal. Their striking prominence in all of his narrators' voices does much to define the relationship between narrator and implied author.

A Room with a View is much more comfortable to read than "Me, Them and You" because its forms of distance produce humor, not rebuke. The ethical and ultimately political critique it offers can easily be overlooked. The premise of this critique—chivalry stifles the individual potential of both women and men—is simple to recognize in both the telling and the told, but the nuanced exploration of that premise, including the implied author's oblique endorsement of feminism, is a great deal further to seek. The narrator presents a wide spectrum of answers to a single, fraught question: How may a young woman achieve personal fulfillment in spite of patriarchal social constraints? While the ethics of the told offers a limited set of answers to that question, the ethics of the telling suggests a wide array of answers.

In a rather cheerful satire of drawing-room dynamics, the young woman in question, Lucy Honeychurch, is "repressed" by her self-righteous and ludicrous spinster chaperone, Charlotte, during their visit to Florence. Charlotte, "skilled in the delicacies of conversation," rebuffs the friendly generosity of two unfamiliar men, whose ingenuous disregard for social niceties makes Lucy "perplexed," "bewildered," and enticed by "the sense of larger and unsuspected issues" latent in the conversation. The narrator satirizes Charlotte as well as the equally "clever" Miss Lavish for their stuffy and foolish misinterpretation of the Emersons as "brutal," "gross," and "impertinent."[38] The two spinsters' conventionality is depicted as unpleasant, short-sighted, reflexive, self-denying. Integral to the Emersons' unconventionality is their progressive attitude toward women's personal and civic opportunities. The ethics of the told is simple: the Emersons offer Lucy truer companionship than her original social set because they honor her as a person instead of an ornament. Their habit of thinking critically about social interactions lends them an appealing humanist candor, whereas Charlotte and Miss Lavish uncritically perform self-defeating, sexist scripts. The intellectual and social distance between Lucy and the Emersons is superficial and temporary, and Lucy's education promises to close that distance. Her potential for becoming fulfilled as a person in her own right is depicted as her chief asset, and a judicious marriage will be the best protection of that asset. She will either marry the chivalrous, ideologically "medieval" Cecil or the enlightened social outcast George Emerson. As George's father puts it, succinctly: "By understanding George you may learn to understand yourself. It will be good for both of you" (26).

This simple equation is never disputed overtly in the ethics of telling or told. By the last chapter, "The End of the Middle Ages," Lucy and George are happily married. But the chapter's title refers to a passage, located early in the novel, that comments on gender politics in a way that is neither simple nor succinct.

Why were most big things unladylike? Charlotte had once explained to her. . . . It was not that ladies were inferior to men; it was that they were different. Their mission was to inspire others to achievement rather than to achieve themselves. Indirectly, by means of tact and a spotless name, a lady could accomplish much. But if she rushed into the fray herself she would be first censured, then despised, and finally ignored. Poems had been written to illustrate this point.

There is much that is immortal in this medieval lady. The dragons have gone, and so have the knights, but she still lingers in our midst. . . . It is sweet to protect her in the intervals of business, sweet to pay her honour when she has cooked our dinner well. But alas! the creature grows degenerate. In her heart also there are springing up strange desires. She too is enamoured of heavy winds, and vast panoramas, and green expanses of the sea. She has marked the kingdom of this world, how full it is of wealth, and beauty, and war—a radiant crust, built around the central fires, spinning towards the receding heavens. (39)

The passage begins as Lucy's paraphrase of Charlotte's explanation, thus doubly marked as provisional by Charlotte's discredited gender politics and Lucy's inexperience. Up to this point in the novel, the narrator has emphasized his sympathy for Lucy while underscoring his distance from her, particularly in terms of her gender and youth. His attitude toward her has been benevolently avuncular, and the type of sympathetic response he has prompted from the reader has suggested that we, too, are expected to be older and wiser than Lucy. But the narrator's distance from his character increases considerably when he shifts to extradiegetic commentary, suddenly expanding his domain from a drawing-room farce to a thousand-year span of human history, worldwide activity, and planetary motion. The dragons have vanished (and along with them the most obvious threat to the medieval lady); the knights are obsolete (which condemns Cecil's chivalry before he even appears in the novel); and paternalism and sexist homage are "sweet" (suggesting their sweetness to the practitioner, though not necessarily to the lady who is perforce excluded from "business" and consigned to cooking "our dinner"). Wry, distanced caricature continues through the turn ("alas!"), but then the irony changes direction, as the medieval lady is suddenly a "creature [who] grows degenerate." This suggests not only decrepitude and retrogression but also moral or sexual taint. The demise of the medieval lady means, at this moment, not uplifting liberation but rather a dirty, visceral decline to the subhuman. Of course, "degenerate" can easily be read in the same ironic key as "alas!," poking fun at those who would perceive ambition in women as sexually ruinous. But the word "degenerate" has more gravity than the whimsical dragons and knights do. As an epithet, it has more potential to do serious damage to a woman's reputation in a patriarchal culture than, say, "unladylike." Thus it seems likely that, though "degenerate" is ironic, its tone implies a slightly harsher critique of patriarchal control than is found earlier in the passage.

"In her heart *also* are springing up strange desires" (my emphasis). The irony has shifted again, this time to include at least two possible meanings. On the one hand, the transition from medieval lady to modern woman may be due to her decrepitude but "also" her heart's desire for change. Such a shift in gender roles—especially one desired by the lady herself—would indeed appear "strange" in a patriarchal society. On the other hand, "also" may signal a growing similarity between women and men: her heart as much as any man's gives rise to "strange desires." The next sentence seems to support this latter reading: "She too is enamoured of heavy winds, and vast panoramas. . . . " Such ambitions have led men through the centuries to believe that "wealth, and beauty, and war" are their special province, theirs to make and dispose of at will. The two possible interpretations of this segment ambiguously suggest both feminist and sexist sympathies.

The most remarkable sentences of this passage appear at its end: "Men, declaring that she inspires them to it, move joyfully over the surface [of the earth], having the most delightful meetings with other men, not because they are masculine, but because they are alive. Before the show breaks up she would like to drop the august title of the Eternal Woman, and go there as her transitory self" (39–40). Because the last sentence of this passage is sympathetic to women who would rather be treated as people than symbols, the whole ending may appear feminist. But the penultimate sentence casts serious doubt on this reading. If only women could be alive and have delightful meetings! Patriarchal privilege isn't restricted to men, according to this narrator; it's restricted to the living, and by definition, only men are alive in a patriarchal context. Why, one wonders, don't women simply come alive? Is degeneracy any closer to life than immortality? Is the end of the medieval lady a step in the right direction, or a wrong one? Is discarding her august title—so that neither women nor men would pay homage to that obsolete gender role—the action that will finally allow her "transitory self" to move more joyfully and to associate more freely?

In little more than a paragraph, Forster's narrator jokes about dragons; notes the sweetness of patriarchal subjugation; makes an ambiguous reference to degeneracy; acknowledges that ambition is human, not masculine or feminine; comfortably naturalizes patriarchal privilege by figuring it as equivalent to life itself; and suggests the advantage to women of being perceived as "transitory" instead of "eternal." He is arch but conscientious. This narrator evidently knows that women who work outside the home—who join "the kingdom of this world"—are all too often castigated as degenerate, both because they might be said to diminish a society's fertility rate if reproduction is not their first priority, and because public presence can be construed as promiscuous. In context of this passage, it is clear that he has appropriated the word "degenerate" in order to castigate such castigation: he uses "degenerate" as a catchword.

Forster first builds a rapport with his reader through the narrator's humor ("Poems had been written to illustrate this point" jokingly gives moral authority to the likes of Coventry Patmore) and uncontroversial logic (implying that "strange desires," perfectly commonplace for men, should not be considered so strange for women). The second half of the double turn—the moment in which a particular feminist response is indicated—appears in the final sentences. Moving joyfully cannot but be a good thing; women's exclusion from that movement and joy cannot but be unfair. All it takes to move joyfully is to be alive. If men are unique in being alive, something is terribly wrong. The reader's ethical judgment in response to this entire passage, especially its final lines, is strongly guided toward feminist awareness of gender inequity, as well as of the arbitrary nature of that inequity.

Forster's ironic distance—archness superimposed on conscientious protest—defines this particular paradigm of narrative ethics. Feminist argumentation through humor and simple logic is one component of his ethical endeavor; his characteristic double turn is another such component; but irony gives Forster's ethical rapport with his reader a special and important quality by emphasizing the role of distance. By employing an ironic narrator Forster creates space around both implied author and reader. He keeps the implied author at least partially aloof while also prompting the reader to make critical and ethical judgments without too much intervention from that narrator. The reader's navigation of irony means that her judgments remain provisional, wary, partially unsupported by textual cues. In other words, neither Forster nor his narrator provides the reader with many comfortable or easy interpretations.

Forster manipulates distance to ensure the reader's deliberation and judgment. First, distance between narrator and character—found especially in the sudden move from free indirect discourse to extradiegetic narration—calls attention to the narrator's privileged understanding of the characters' plights. As the narrator increases the distance between himself and the story he tells, he prompts the reader's expectation that he will use that superior vantage for interpretations and evaluations that shed light directly on the characters' problems. But by thwarting that expectation the narrator generates a second kind of distance, between himself and the reader. Because that expectation of elucidation is never met, the reader has to synthesize conflicting sets of opinions and produce her own evaluations.

The third type of distance I am concerned with, that between narrator and implied author, is subtler. The narrator, here as elsewhere in the novel, articulates a range of conflicting positions on suffrage-era feminism. He celebrates women's ambitions and yet hints at blaming them for being the victims of patriarchal control. Underlying these conflicts is at least one stable notion: that the constraints a patriarchal system puts on women look different depending on one's vantage. The two facts co-existing, one might say, are the vantage of those with social privilege in a patriarchal system juxtaposed with the vantage of those without it. Both perspectives are represented in the narrator's voice. The distance between those two perspectives creates a parallax.[39]

The ethics of the telling prompts the reader to correct for this parallax. Reading this way is, of course, challenging since the reader him- or herself brings to the text one of the two perspectives in question and is compelled to read ethically, outside of either set of presuppositions. The question of how a young woman can achieve personal fulfillment looks different to those with power and those without it in a patriarchal system. If the ethics of the told answers this question rather simply—shed empty social obligations and marry a feminist man—the ethics of the telling teases out many uncomfortable permutations without directly answering the question at all. The absence of any answer, especially in the context of a generally lighthearted book, has suggested to many that Forster himself has no answer; that the indirections of the narrator simply point to the political apathy of the implied author. The ethics of the told is, after all, pleasant enough; it is easy to let the happy ending supersede the difficult divagations of the telling in one's experience of the novel.

Paul Armstrong's more generous but still cynical interpretation proposes that what I am calling a parallax is, in effect, both question and answer. He claims that Forster's liberalism itself was ironic; that, though he posited certain values, he recognized their contingency and used his narrator's equivocation to undermine their stability.[40] He makes a strong case that the narrator's playful inconsistency is *in itself* the core conviction we may glean Forster upholds:

> Forster's contradictory liberalism imagines a mode of non-consensual reciprocity that is represented nowhere in the text itself but that defines the narrator's relationship to the reader. . . . Instead of being persuaded by Forster's narrator or unifying our position with his, we are invited to see through and across his winking gestures to play a complicated game based on the premise that neither of us is in the position we seem to occupy.[41]

It is tempting to see Armstrong's model of non-coercive play, a rhetorical performance that engages with ideas without seeking to convert

or persuade its audience, as fitting the narrator. He asserts that the inces-
sant rhetorical reversals of Forster's narrator "reflec[t] his recognition of
the impossibility of reconciling different ways of seeing, a recognition he
attempts to bring readers to share by his subtle play with narrative authority and point of view. . . . [O]scillation, manifested primarily in the formal
qualities of his narratives, is the ultimate meaning of his politics."[42]

Oscillation may be the narrator's main rhetorical strategy, but it is not
the ultimate meaning of Forster's politics. The narrator does wink, but it
is not because Forster has no designs on persuading us of anything. Armstrong's reading is appealing because it absolves us of struggling to read
around or behind the narrator. But it ignores the traces of authorial conviction that supersede the irony.[43] In other words, although Armstrong
makes a technical distinction between Forster and his narrator, his analysis depends on—and is undermined by—the fact that he conflates narrator
with implied author. Especially in Forster's work, the distinction between
narrator and implied author is both theoretically and interpretively indispensable. Richard Walsh has advanced the theoretical position that no
such distinction exists; that any and all acts of narration are accomplished
either by authors or by characters.[44] Walsh systematically undermines
narratology's assumption of the narrator concept by way of a pragmatic
theory of relevance.[45] His first premise for the case against the narrator
concept, however, seems to me inapplicable to the narratives considered
in this book, especially those by Forster (including both his essay and his
novels). Walsh's premise is that "the narrator, as an inherent structural
principle, functions primarily to establish a representational frame within
which the narrative discourse may be read as report rather than invention.
In other words, it defines the extent to which we can set aside our knowledge that the narrative in hand is indeed fictional" (69).

On many levels—intellectually, practically, rhetorically—Forster's representation of narrative requires the distinction Walsh wants to argue out
of existence. Like most if not all writers of his caliber, Forster compresses
two, three, or more dimensions of a given idea into each sentence. Pars-
ing those dimensions, in part by assigning them to different voices (or fictional minds) within the act of representation, yields interpretive results
that are far richer and more valuable than deciding merely whether those
statements are "report" or "invention." The referential and ontological
qualities of Forster's narration have very little to do with his narrator's
"primary function." That function, as I have been arguing with my close
readings of "Me, Them, and You" and *A Room with a View,* is primarily
to articulate a shifting, challenging, yet reliable perspective that contrasts

implicitly with that of the implied author and often explicitly with those of the characters. In order to articulate compressed, multidimensional ideas, Forster employs a narrator with significant perspectival difference from implied author, on the one hand, and characters, on the other.[46]

The distinction between narrator and implied author in Forster's work has substantial interpretive consequences, as well. We have already glanced at one stable position inherent in the narrator's equivocation: that gender constraints look different according to how much social privilege one has. A second stance may be detected as well: that gender roles are social constructions that can be—are being—altered through time and human effort. Lucy's femininity is depicted as mutable, culturally relative, and dependent on her strategic choices as she matures. "Lucy does not stand for the medieval lady," subjoins the narrator hastily; but of course, without endorsing the comparison, Forster still makes it inevitable (40). The logic of the plot hinges on the assumption that gender roles are constructed and mutable. Being Cecil's wife promises to entail a radically different sort of female experience than does being George's wife. Cecil is consistently associated with the past; George with society's future. Cecil is freighted with British conventionality, while George's freedom from convention is repeatedly associated with a putatively equitable Italian culture. Both marriages would fit within a heteronormative system, but George's weaknesses and errors make him more appealing for being unmasterly.

These two constants—the parallax of gender constraints and the mutability of gender constructions—are perhaps easily overlooked more than eighty years after full adult suffrage was granted in Britain. But they entail a positive, highly charged, debatable gender politics in their historical moment. They do not constitute a feminist stance because Forster does not endorse in this passage, even from a distance, the belief that gender roles *ought to* be changed. But they are also definitive evidence against Armstrong's bottomless irony argument.[47]

Moreover, the bottomless irony argument cannot account for passages in which Forster foregrounds the urgency of resolution. In this urgency we find the *ought* that makes Forster's equivocation finally legible as feminist. Before turning to *Howards End,* I will juxtapose two passages from *A Room with a View* that, taken together, illustrate the way Forster manipulates distance in the ethics of both telling and told to endorse the resolution of gender inequity. His use of distance prompts the reader to take on feminist beliefs, even if provisionally, for the remainder of the novel.

In the prelude to *A Room with a View*'s celebrated bathing scene, Forster employs character-character dialogue to suggest a need for resolution of inequity. Although the bathing scene mainly concentrates on men in relation to each other, it is preceded by a short conversation among men about women:

> "'How d'ye do? how d'ye do? Come and have a bathe,' [Mr. Beebe] chuckled. 'That's the best conversational opening I've ever heard. But I'm afraid it will only act between men. Can you picture a lady who has been introduced to another lady by a third lady opening civilities with 'How do you do? Come and have a bathe'? And yet you will tell me that the sexes are equal."
>
> "I tell you that they shall be," said Mr. Emerson, who had been slowly descending the stairs. "Good-afternoon, Mr. Beebe. I tell you they shall be comrades, and George thinks the same."
>
> "We are to raise the ladies to our level?" the clergyman inquired.
>
> "The Garden of Eden," pursued Mr. Emerson, still descending, "which you place in the past, is really yet to come. We shall enter it when we no longer despise our bodies. . . . In this—not in other things—we men are ahead. We despise the body less than women do. But not until we are comrades shall we enter the garden." (126)[48]

This dialogue functions, in Phelan's phrase, as "narration by other means":[49] characters are Forster's primary rhetorical resource here, not the narrator. Mr. Emerson, whose outspoken ethical positions throughout the novel seem authorially endorsed, is perhaps the only unironic element of the work as a whole. His position is refreshingly clear and straightforward, especially in comparison to the narrator's gyrations.

Mr. Beebe begins the exchange by recognizing the pleasures of male companionship. Such pleasures, he notes, are not available to women, whose inhibitions would get in the way. Although Mr. Beebe jokingly refers to gender inequality, Emerson responds seriously. He believes it is wrong that women are excluded from uninhibited pleasure. He takes a qualified feminist position, the only one explicitly made in the novel. Because he fails to acknowledge any systemic reason why women would "despise the body," Emerson's explanation could be read as victim-blaming. Even if he is not blaming the victim, the simplicity of his statement hardly does justice to the question at hand. Moreover, his response to Mr. Beebe's question does not indicate whether or not Emerson thinks men could (let alone should) take any part in changing women's attitudes toward the body. In these two regards, he is positioned at a calculated distance from women. He states no sense of obligation to contribute to their well-being. He even ignores Mr. Beebe's pointed question about such an obligation.

This is, of course, a casual conversation among acquaintances, at least one of whom wants to keep the conversation frivolous (Freddy feels "appalled at the mass of philosophy" Emerson has heaved onto to the conversation [126]). But even in a casual situation, and perhaps more admirably *because* of the casual context, Emerson claims his fair share in inequity's consequences by stressing its disadvantages for both men and women. He could let an inopportune occasion pass for voicing this unpopular opinion, but he does not. Or he could assert his distance from the consequences, but he does not. His conclusion—"not until we are comrades shall we enter the garden"—states that until the problem is rectified neither women nor men can progress toward the desired goal. His moral authority, obvious sincerity, and seriousness of purpose make that goal inherently appealing, regardless of whether the reader believes intervention is possible, necessary, or sufficient. His distance from the problem does not undermine the rhetorical force of his observations.

Forster's use of distance for ethical ends is best exemplified by a passage near the end of his novel. Perhaps it should come as no surprise that this prime example is an analogy rather than anything more direct: "It is obvious enough for the reader to conclude, 'She loves young Emerson.' A reader in Lucy's place would not find it obvious. Life is easy to chronicle, but bewildering to practice, and we welcome 'nerves' or any other shibboleth that will cloak our personal desire. [Lucy kept saying to herself that] she loved Cecil; [and that] George made her nervous; will the reader explain to her that the phrases should have been reversed?" (142). Harry Shaw observes that the passage anticipates our frustration that we can't talk to Lucy, it reminds us that such frustration is pleasurable as well as a convention in the novel genre, and it "make[s] us feel *akin* to Lucy, not distant from her. . . . Lucy can't understand her feelings and we can understand her feelings, but then we can't explain them to her. By the same token, if we were in Lucy's place and she in ours, our superior knowledge would vanish, but she'd then be unable to help us. For that matter, the narrator can't talk to Lucy either."[50]

For Shaw's purposes, Forster is an author who, because of his "immediate designs on the reader," has foregrounded "how insurmountable are the boundaries between story space, discourse space, and the world of the reader."[51] His effort to evoke a particular response from the reader, according to Shaw, depends on distance—in this case, a frustratingly insuperable spatial distance and a collapsed affective distance. For my purposes, this passage provides an exemplary analogy for the parallax considered earlier. The analogy is not about separate space, but about separate epistemologies of gender roles. Those with social privilege ("superior knowledge") and those without it view privilege differently. Those with relatively few gender-based constraints perceive constraint itself differently. Lucy's society severely circumscribes her opportunities to show emotional, let alone sexual, interest in men. If "nerves" are her recourse for concealing that interest from herself and others, she is bound to be quite nervous. If she were granted the social privilege of expressing her desire, Lucy's knowledge would be "superior" but, according to this analogy, she would be unable to help those on the other side of the divide.

This scene tempts us with crossing the border but does not permit it. Our feeling of sympathy for Lucy is accompanied by a recognition that we cannot intervene in her plight. At the same time, as readers, we are participating in, and enjoying, the very system that functions according to the circumscription of her knowledge. As Shaw says, "[R]emember that your pleasure in novels like this one—including the pleasurably disturbing exasperation you're feeling now—depends upon abiding by certain rules in this fictional game of ours."[52] In his conversation with Beebe, Emerson is sympathetically observant but does not intervene; here, the reader's sympathy only highlights her inability to intervene. The reader and Emerson are doing ethical work of a sort, but it is not the kind that directly reduces other people's disadvantages. Neither Beebe nor Emerson seems to want to intervene in reducing women's inhibitions. They seem only too glad to have the privilege of bathing parties outdoors on a warm summer afternoon. Perhaps they are even prevented from intervention, not only by conventional inertia but by a lack of urgency to enact social change. But Emerson's heartfelt aspiration for Eden, and his idea that Eden will remain unavailable to both women and men until they become equitable "comrades," suggests a quiet urgency, an ongoing problem that requires eventual resolution.

This analogy is mine, not Forster's; I do not propose that Forster has tucked an elaborate feminist metaphor into his teasing aside. And yet, Forster very evidently perceives, and dramatizes in *A Room with a View*, a gulf between people who see women's sexual and social constraints from a position of privilege, and those who experience those constraints firsthand. He simultaneously perceives, and dramatizes, a difference between the comfortable vantage of narrator and reader, on the one hand, and the limited vantage of character, on the other. In one scene he depicts the rather abstract urgency of Edenic reward; in the subsequent scene he underscores a very concrete and frustrating urgency. By dramatizing the distance between narrator and character in the latter scene, he directs the reader's attention to the pleasures and frustrations of being on one side of a divide. He evokes the reader's feminist awareness without advocating activity or intervention. Through covert double turns and ironic echoes in this funny, cheerful novel, Forster obliquely suggests a growing need for social change.

IN HIS 1939 pamphlet *What I Believe,* Forster insists: "I hate the idea of causes, and if I had to choose between betraying my country and betraying my friend, I hope I should have the guts to betray my country."[53] Such a statement (profoundly controversial on the eve of World War II) clearly prioritizes ethics over politics, the situational ethical encounter over any abstract social obligations. Whereas *A Passage to India* explores the tensions that arise from betrayal of both friends and countries, *Howards End* evaluates what it means to show greater reverence to a friend than to a cause. It also underscores the profound difficulty and discomfort of intervention in other people's lives: the "guts" such activity requires. Helen and Margaret Schlegel consider feminism to be more than just a cause. To them it is a worldview and the foundation for their self-definition. The Wilcoxes—self-interested, practical, wealthy, conservative, patriarchal, imperialistic—offer a competing worldview, one that so completely assumes its own normativity that any dissenting ideology is relegated to being a "cause."

This novel, like *A Room with a View,* asks a straightforward question about gender politics: How may the Schlegels and the Wilcoxes coexist? How may they not just tolerate each other but actually love? As in *A Room with a View,* the ethics of the told is more overt than the ethics of the telling. Margaret's judicious mediation between the two families and her eventual success in uniting them in a nonpatriarchal family at Howards End are both depicted as ameliorative ethical accomplishments. Also in keeping with *A Room with a View,* the narrator of *Howards End* answers the question in a dazzling variety of ways, whereas the implied author's stance is powerfully immanent and yet oblique.

The question of where the implied author stands, and the attendant challenge of knowing what the reader is expected to believe, arises whenever the narrator makes a claim that contrasts with the situational ethics dramatized by the characters. The frequency with which this contrast occurs in *Howards End* suggests that the latter novel adapts the parallax within the telling of *A Room with a View* to a larger scale, that of both telling and told. If a parallax was uncomfortable in *A Room with a View*, it is much more so writ large. In *Howards End*, the humor that cloaked *A Room with a View*'s political agenda is gone, and the narrator's divagations seem less whimsical than canny, sophisticated, even edgy. His more serious tone suggests that Forster has raised his ethical stakes and cast off some of the comforts of complacent nonintervention.

The disjunction between telling and told worries many readers. Barbara Rosecrance has noted that, in all of Forster's novels, "[t]he narrator seeks a relationship with the reader that both assumes and compels acceptance of his values, drawing the reader into the world not so much of the characters as of his own imaginative judgments."[54] But in *Howards End*, she concludes,

> despite the narrator's brilliance, his persuasion must ultimately be regarded as unsuccessful. He does not achieve a harmonious integration of ideology and dramatic representation, of content and form. His reflections are often disconnected from the action, so that the novel appears to present an uneven alternation between essay and scene, comment and action. To a degree found in no other Forster novel, the narrator's diction is abstract, metaphorical, hyperbolical; the anxiety and inflation of his tone suggest the desperation of [Forster's] attempt to harmonize and persuade.[55]

She is right that the reader is attracted more to the narrator's judgments than to the story-world, and that this novel features a considerable gap between telling and told. Note too that she assigns the reader less agency than I do. She reads the narrator as irresistibly coercive, whereas I read the gaps and blanks as his invitation to the reader to make independent judgments, ones that Forster lets her measure against his own stance with the second half of the double turn. But I am not persuaded that disharmony between ideology and representation is an unsuccessful rhetorical tactic, nor that the narrator's concerted effort to persuade need reveal any authorial desperation. Forster's double turn effected on the levels of story and discourse creates a distance between those two dimensions of his novel—a distance most can agree is uncomfortable but which I will argue is also ethically productive.

Howards End, it has often been observed, is a matrilineal home. Mrs. Ruth Wilcox inherits it from her grandmother; when she is not in residence she appoints Mrs. Avery as its guardian; and before she dies, she bequeaths it to Margaret. Not only are Mrs. Wilcox's sons and husband allergic to the place—suffering comically from hay fever—but they fail to recognize its spiritual value to her. Mrs. Wilcox's effort to share the house with Margaret during her lifetime, on an impulsive day trip from London, is abruptly prevented by the imposition of her husband and daughter. But her written bequest (conveyed, as the narrator notes three times, by the matron of her nursing home) is prevented by a much more serious familial imposition: the Wilcoxes burn the note without informing Margaret of its contents.

The decision to burn the note recalls the opposition mentioned earlier of cause versus friend; in this case the choice is between legal and personal obligations. Henry patronizingly explains to his daughter-in-law, Dolly, "Legally, I should be justified in tearing it up and throwing it into the fire. Of course, my dear, we consider you as one of the family, but it will be better if you do not interfere with what you do not understand. . . . [T]o my mind the question is the—the invalid's condition at the time she wrote" (95). This decision is literally a man's prerogative (as Mrs. Wilcox's note is addressed "To my husband"), but Forster underscores how male that decision is, too. "Evie was scowling like an angry boy. The two men were gradually assuming the manner of the committee-room. They were both at their best when serving on committees. They did not make the mistake of handling human affairs in the bulk, but disposed of them item by item, sharply" (95–96). While Henry's reverence for his wife had been explicitly gender-coded—he admired most her "unvarying virtue, that seemed to him a woman's noblest quality"—his turn against her begins when he reduces her to a genderless "invalid." He and his children construe Mrs. Wilcox's one gesture of independence as a betrayal, again overlaid with gender codes: "Yesterday they had lamented: 'She was a dear mother, a true wife: in our absence she neglected her health and died.' Today they thought: 'She was not as true, as dear, as we supposed. . . . [A]ll they could say was 'Treachery'" (97).

The characters who feel betrayed by Mrs. Wilcox are clearly the ones betraying her. Consistent with the men's businesslike treatment of each other and withering treatment of Dolly is their insulting disregard for the dead woman. "Considered item by item, the emotional content was minimized, and all went forward smoothly" (96). Lest we mistake them for monsters, the narrator assures us that "They were not callous, and they left the breakfast table with aching hearts" (91), but such a weak defense only highlights their ethical deficiency. A challenge for the reader's own ethics arises, however, when, against a conspicuously straightforward ethics of the told, the narrator offers a discordant comment.

> [T]he discussion moved towards its close.
>   To follow it is unnecessary. It is rather a moment when the commentator should step forward. Ought the Wilcoxes to have offered their home to Margaret? I think not. The appeal was too flimsy. It was not legal; it had been written in illness, and under the spell of a sudden friendship; it was contrary to the dead woman's intentions in the past, contrary to her very nature, so far as that nature was understood by them. To them Howards End was a house: they could not know that to her it had been a spirit, for which she sought a spiritual heir. (96)

"The commentator should step forward" jars aesthetically: although the narrator has opined on a number of topics earlier in the novel, he has never drawn such abrupt attention to his own commentary. The act of stepping forward suggests that he was previously holding back, standing at a remove from his story. But the comment also jars ethically. His "I think not" pushes the reader, rather forcefully, to decide several things: whether the narrator means what he is saying, whether the implied author believes what the narrator is saying, and above all, whether or not the reader herself agrees. The last question seems easiest to answer. Juxtaposed with the ethics of the told, "I think not" prompts the reader to disagree and to think critically about why the Wilcoxes owed Ruth more than they gave her. The narrator's contrary stance shows an impish delight in tweaking the reader's nose; it is provocatively insufficient under the circumstances.

The reasoning that follows the question is all borrowed from the Wilcoxes, who made a poor case for it the first time around. As with most adaptations, this one is easy to judge as inferior to the original; repetition weakens it further, and it seems strange that the narrator would take on the attitude of characters he has critiqued in the past. This portion of the passage employs free indirect discourse, juxtaposing Wilcoxian words ("flimsy," "not legal," "illness") with plausible additions on their behalf (impugning the "spell" of friendship and citing Mrs. Wilcox's "nature"). Although free indirect discourse in itself, of course, does not necessarily indicate agreement between narrator and character, it is hard to posit much distance between the two in the wake of "I think not." The narrator seems to be endorsing, at least provisionally, the painfully underdeveloped moral sensibility of the surviving Wilcoxes.

When the narrator alludes to the limits of the Wilcoxes' knowledge—
"They could not know" Mrs. Wilcox's real feeling for her family home—
he reasserts some distance between himself and them, but at first this
distance seems compatible with his ostensible sympathy. The most charitable reading of this move is that, despite his unwavering understanding that the Wilcoxes have made a grave ethical error, he acknowledges
that they cannot be other than who they are. Their treatment of Mrs.
Wilcox is consistent with their lifelong habit of incuriosity about other
people. This does not absolve them, but it does provide a sympathetic
perspective from afar on their decision to burn the note. However, such
a charitable reading cannot explain why the narrator's original question
begins "Ought the Wilcoxes . . . ?" rather than "Why would the Wilcoxes not . . . ?" Nor does it explain why Howards End is figured, in this
question, as a "home" rather than a "house." The Wilcoxes, except Ruth,
regard Howards End as merely one of many possessions; and if we somehow forget this fact, the narrator reminds us of it a scant few sentences
later: "To them Howards End was a house."

In the act of accounting for the Wilcoxes' ignorance, the narrator helps
us recognize how censorious his original question is. His answer "I think
not" is so sensational that it allows the reader to overlook the fact that the
question begged its own answer from the beginning. Thus while on a first
reading the passage might seem to minimize the ethical distance between
narrator and Wilcoxes, a second reading uncovers a vast distance between
them.

And yet, a third reading demonstrates how productive that distance
actually is. "*Why would* the Wilcoxes . . . " is pretty simple question
to answer: because they are boors. "*Ought* the Wilcoxes . . . " is much
harder—harder than the alternative question and harder than it first
appears. The ethics of the Wilcoxes' decision is quite difficult to parse,
even as their motives are not. The passage that follows "I think not" is
designed precisely to trouble a too-quick reflex to condemn the Wilcoxes
simply because we dislike them and we like Ruth and Margaret. (If Ruth
had wanted to leave the house to someone other than Margaret, would
we be this quick to deny the Wilcoxes any grounds for concern?) We may
finally decide, after the careful deliberation that Forster compels us to
engage in, that the Wilcoxes' action here is unethical, but arguably, the
passage opens up the question as a real question and asks the reader to try
to answer it as a real question, not as a foregone conclusion. The reader,
like the narrator, may acknowledge the Wilcoxes' underdeveloped moral
sensibility, and she may agree that their motivations for burning the letter

are bad, and yet may still wonder, as the narrator does, whether the action itself was wrong or right. They may have done it for the wrong reasons, but that doesn't necessarily make the action itself wrong.

The passage continues in the same vein, with virtuosic control balancing the narrator's contempt for the Wilcoxes with his respect for the ethical question at hand.

> Is it credible that the possessions of the spirit can be bequeathed at all? Has the soul offspring? A wych-elm tree, a vine, a wisp of hay with dew on it—can passion for such things be transmitted when there is no bond of blood? No; the Wilcoxes are not to be blamed. The problem is too terrific, and they could not even perceive a problem. No; it is natural and fitting that after due debate they should tear the note up and throw it on to their dining-room fire. The practical moralist may acquit them absolutely. He who strives to look deeper may acquit them—almost. For one hard fact remains. They did neglect a personal appeal. The woman who had died did say to them: 'Do this,' and they answered: 'We will not.' (96–97)

The practical moralist is condemned along with the Wilcoxes; it is no good making excuses for people who are ignorant out of incuriosity. But the "almost" leaves wiggle room for the reader willing to "look deeper." This is, I believe, an instance of Forster's ethical courage in permitting his narrator free rein to question and probe. I read Forster as believing that the personal appeal is of supreme importance. But he lets his narrator test even that conviction, asking uncomfortable questions that put the onus on the reader to think hard about a scenario that was, at first glance, rather simple.

Incidentally, the ironic concession at the very end of the passage refers to Mrs. Wilcox as just a "woman." To the Wilcoxes, of course, she should be more than just a woman, so this description highlights their sense of estrangement from her. For the reader, calling her a woman is superfluous, unless Forster's point is to remind us of how much of the family's reaction is based entirely on her gender. For if Henry had surprised his family posthumously, without doubt they would have lent him more latitude than they have given their mother.[56]

This scene marks a decisive change in the narrator's discourse. Once one has begun applying two, three, or more alternative readings to a passage, it might be hard to know where to stop. How do we establish a rhetorical reading under such circumstances? This is why Booth's insight that Forster is a stable ironist is so vital. Forster manages to reassure us that, even though the narrator is sometimes sincere, sometimes says pre-cisely the opposite of what he means, and sometimes prompts a reading in between, the novel coheres. It is also why my emphasis on the ethics of the telling, sometimes independent of the ethics of overall rhetorical purpose, helps illuminate Forster despite his cagey elusiveness. Even if the narrator is "abstract, metaphorical, hyperbolical," the implied author is never "desperate." He is always firmly in control. If we are not convinced that Forster is a stable ironist, his narrator's variability will only bewilder. But if we posit that stability, we recognize that some passages, like the one above, are sharp corrections to readers who, like the Wilcoxes, are incurious. Readers unwilling to exercise a careful ethical sensibility will fall for Forster's "I think not" trap and will miss the increasingly blatant inverse meanings of the sentences that follow. On the other hand, readers who are willing to read critically may derive pleasure from their success. Booth reminds us that "[e]very reader will have greatest difficulty detect-ing irony that mocks his own beliefs or characteristics."[57] This passage is marvelous proof of that.

The most prominent instances of ethical disjunction between telling and told in *Howards End* are ones that, like the example above, feature an outspoken extradiegetic commentator. "We are not concerned with the very poor," he sniffs, in the novel's most controversial passage. "They are unthinkable, and only to be approached by the statistician and the poet. This story deals with gentlefolk, or with those who are obliged to pre-tend that they are gentlefolk" (43). Forster's puzzling blend of condescen-sion and compassion toward Leonard Bast has been examined countless times. It seems that such an audacious statement acts as a lightning rod; minus these three sentences, Forster's attitude toward Bast would surely be a less vexed topic of debate.[58] Not surprisingly, when critics interpret the politics of this novel, they tend to give most attention to the narra-tor's bold, sweeping pronouncements. But these passages are not his finest or most interesting means for making ethically and ultimately politically efficacious arguments through narrative form. Forster contrasts the ethics of telling and told on a less conspicuous register, within free indirect dis-course and focalization.

Howards End is focalized extensively through Margaret, primarily for bonding effects, and occasionally through Henry, almost exclusively for estranging effects. Such motivated focalization—supporting Margaret's point of view, while vilifying Henry's—might seem to be self-evidently feminist. But in the midst of his focalization he inserts words and phrases that increase the ethical distance between telling and told. This is the case in a dramatic confrontation between Margaret and Henry (by now her husband), and it is even more significant in the novel's highly ambiguous final scene. The ethical import of these scenes is clearer when they are compared to some passages earlier in the novel.

The narrator establishes early on that the Schlegel sisters' commitments to feminism are equally strong, though they practice it differently. Both women care less about feminism as a cause than as a guide for ethical personal relations, but in her idealistic way, Helen tends to concentrate on who people ought to be, whereas her more realistic sister hovers between accepting people as they are and willing them to be better.[59] Margaret's proclivity for hovering tends to give the free indirect discourse that involves her peculiarly penumbral quality, as a blend of two ideologically ambivalent voices.[60] Of both sisters, the narrator remarks, "In their own fashion they cared deeply about politics, though not as politicians would have us care; they desired that public life should mirror whatever is good in the life within. Temperance, tolerance, and sexual equality were intelligible cries to them" (25). Their activism, in other words, comes in the form of daily, lived experience, rather than civil disobedience; they are not suffragists. When Ruth Wilcox misinterprets their intellectual discussion as a sign of more conventionally activist feminist politics, she politely remarks, "'I never follow arguments. I am only too thankful not to have a vote myself.' 'We didn't mean the vote, though, did we?' supplied Margaret. 'Aren't we differing on something much wider, Mrs. Wilcox? Whether women are to remain what they have been since the dawn of history; or whether, since men have moved forward so far, they too may move forward a little now. I say they may. I would even admit a biological change'" (75). Margaret's brief remark on biological change is echoed in the fact that she does not want children of her own, as well as in her participation in the spiritual matrilineage of Howards End. Taken together, these hints suggest Forster is offering an oblique challenge to normative gender roles for women through Margaret's character.

Forster's use of free indirect discourse and focalization through this slightly non-normative, feminist character offers him the opportunity to ask and answer nuanced, situation-specific questions about ethical gender relations. He does this by giving Margaret a strong ideological commitment to feminism but also a complicating factor that the narrator and reader cannot share with her: love for Henry. Forster's narrator increases tension between reader and Margaret whenever her affection overrides her self-respect, which is repeatedly equated with her feminist conviction. The narrator underscores the political implications of her self-denial.

For example, when Margaret learns that Henry has committed adultery against Ruth and ruined his mistress Jacky's chance for a respectable life, she is furious. She wonders how much of her outrage is feminist (on behalf of herself, Ruth, and Jacky, against "not only . . . her husband but . . . thousands of men like him" [329]) and how much is mere sexual jealousy—that is, how much of her resentful self-interest stems from biological imperative rather than progressive politics. As she thinks on the subject, a question arises: "Are the sexes really races, each with its own code of morality, and their mutual love a mere device of Nature to keep things going?" (237). Here is the penumbral ambivalence of free indirect discourse: it is reasonable to read both the narrator and Margaret as genuinely uncertain of an answer to the question. The reader is expected to take the question seriously and to consider possible answers.

After more consideration, Margaret's "judgment told her no," that mutual reverence transcends procreation: "Far more mysterious than the call of sex to sex is the tenderness that we throw into that call." The reader is prompted not only to evaluate whether or not this seems an adequate answer but also to consider how much her affection for Henry has influenced her thinking. In this case, Margaret has managed to balance affection and feminist self-advocacy. She neither will reject Henry on principle, as one of "thousands" of adulterers, nor will she demean herself by embracing sexual rivalry, which would be dehumanizing (she describes it as a conflict worthy of a "farmyard"). But this glimpse into her thought process shows us how difficult it is to be a feminist under these circumstances. In that moment, Margaret's disappointment in Henry prevents her from taking comfort in her intellectual insight: we are told that she "could not feel" the value of that tenderness in the face of systemic impunity (238). Because we do not love Henry, we take solace in a distanced approach to the consequences of his adultery. Because she does love Henry, she feels no solace.

The pain she feels underscores the difficulty of her ethical stance on feminism. Unlike Helen, whose idealism somewhat insulates her from painful disillusionment, "On the whole [Margaret] sided with men as they are. Henry would save the Basts, as he had saved Howards End, while Helen and her friends were discussing the ethics of salvation" (227). Although Margaret does not know it, the narrator and reader both know that Henry has already destroyed one Bast (Jacky), and, through her ruin, indirectly destroyed the other one (Leonard). The narrator knows too that Henry has invested money in, but not in any way "saved," Howards End—saving Howards End is Margaret's eventual responsibility. The reader's and narrator's "superior" knowledge allows them a "superior" ethical stance as well. They disapprove of Henry more than Margaret does because they know more about Henry's misdeeds than Margaret can. But the disjunction between narrator/reader and Margaret here should also remind us that Margaret's challenge is (like Lucy Honeychurch's) much more difficult than theirs is. It is easy to condemn Henry's wrongs from a greater distance than Margaret can (or wants to) obtain.

The climactic confrontation between Margaret and Henry could not be more explicitly feminist in both theme and form. Henry refuses to acknowledge the hypocrisy of condemning women (such as Helen) for sex out of wedlock while going unpunished (as he does) for committing the same deed. Margaret makes a thoroughly profeminist case: "I've had enough of your unweeded kindness. I've spoilt you long enough. All your life you have been spoiled. Mrs. Wilcox spoiled you. No one has ever told you what you are—muddled, criminally muddled. Men like you use repentance as a blind, so don't repent. Only say to yourself: 'What Helen has done, I've done'" (305). Henry's rebuttal is obtuse and unpersuasive; Margaret clearly wins the argument, and again, the salient dialogue apparently functions as a straightforward narration by other means. But more subtle and liminal attitude toward feminism may be found in passages focalized through Margaret before and after the argument.

When Margaret believes her sister to be ill and does not know how to help, she thinks to herself, "Henry was the only hope. Henry was definite. . . . He could not well make it worse" (278). We know that her faith in him is misplaced; that his definiteness is exactly what will make a delicate situation worse. Free indirect discourse through Henry confirms our fears: "The sick had no rights; they were outside the pale; one could lie to them remorselessly. When his first wife was seized he had promised to take her down into Hertfordshire [to Howards End], but meanwhile arranged with a nursing-home instead. Helen, too, was ill. And the plan that he sketched out for her capture, clever and well-meaning as it was, drew its ethics from the wolf-pack" (279). Even when Margaret fathoms Henry's plan for capturing Helen, she accedes to it. Here the tension between reader and Margaret increases substantially. She recognizes at some level that Henry's plan is ethically flawed, but her judgment again is clouded by her affection for her husband: "Whether Henry was right or wrong, he was most kind, and she knew of no other standard by which to judge him. She must trust him absolutely" (283).[61] Margaret cannot know about the "remorseless" nursing-home lie, but if his patently bankrupt "kindness" is the ultimate standard to which Margaret will hold Henry, the reader cannot help but despair for her, as well as believe her judgment to be seriously compromised.

Up to this point in the novel, whatever ethical distance the reader has had from Margaret has been tempered with sympathy. If the reader is antifeminist, she is nevertheless prompted to admire Margaret's many positive qualities, including (but certainly not restricted to) her marital allegiance and practicality. If the reader is profeminist, he admires her ethical probity but is frustrated by Margaret's sometimes self-compromising positions. Both kinds of readers are expected to accept some misjudgments because of the difficulty of her position, earnestly trying to reconcile feminist self-respect with love for Henry. But when Margaret acquiesces to Henry's plan, so that she is personally responsible for putting Helen's safety and dignity at risk, I believe any rhetorical reader must blame her for complicity. This seems to me the tipping point at which the reader's distance from Margaret turns from wary acceptance to ethical condemnation. Graham considers this shift in ethical assessment as a technical flaw in Forster's novel:

> [T]he ironic double turn . . . does not appease our simple outrage that Margaret has let him off and betrayed herself, quite incredibly, once again. In such an instance, cross-purposes and self-testing [in the discourse] perhaps go too far, and ignore the degree to which the reader has already been persuaded to invest his emotional and intellectual sympathy in Margaret. The line between a rich creative tension and a reader-losing incongruity, between a double turn and a false step, is often a fine one.[62]

I agree with Graham that Forster's discourse-level ethical questions contrast and eventually conflict with the story-level sympathies he has evoked. I agree as well that Forster's discourse, full of inversions, contradictions, and ironic juxtapositions, contains a few false steps. This is not one of them. Not only must we recognize how difficult her position is, we must also recognize when—and especially why—appeasement of a domineering man must stop. Forster's major ethical accomplishment, in a novel full of ethical nuance, is to prompt this very reaction, our principled, feminist objection to Margaret's generous and loving tolerance for Henry. The reader, who may in real life not have a progressive feminist outlook, is finally prompted to be more feminist than Margaret herself.

A few pages later, Margaret realizes acquiescence has been a mistake. When she glimpses her sister's pregnant form she is dazed by the shock, but goes to stand protectively between Helen and the group of curious men. "A new feeling came over her; she was fighting for women against men. She did not care about rights, but if men came into Howards End, it should be over her body" (287). The sentiment, as well as the dramatic tableau, is feminist. But why does it include the disclaimer that she does not care about rights? Margaret cares for people more than causes and she is not an activist; this much has been amply demonstrated in the novel. Moreover, she is in an emergency: would women's rights in the abstract occur to her in a crisis? Again, focalization provides Forster an opportunity to slip in a bit of ideological distance between narrator and character. Would her protectiveness seem, to some audiences, more worthy if it were purely personal rather than politically symbolic? Does a corner of the reader's mind need convincing that Margaret's feminism is based in ethics rather than politics?

This novel endorses women's rights well beyond legal and civic advances. Helen's free access to Howards End, her privacy and dignity, and her ability to support her fatherless infant are all "rights" that Margaret—and Forster—believe in absolutely. Unless the narrator intends for us to reflect on a larger sense of the word "rights," it makes little sense for him to note that Margaret did not care about them. It would seem that the narrator is again saying "no" and meaning "yes," albeit in a more muted way. Because of the reader's very recent feminist condemnation of Margaret, however, even a brief disclaimer on the subject of feminism is important. The jarring element of this short passage serves as an echo of Margaret's response to Mrs. Wilcox, quoted earlier. The rights she cares about are those that extend well beyond suffrage (75). The echo of the earlier scene in the later one offers some hope that Margaret has regained some of the feminist sensibility she possessed before falling in love with Henry. Her reconciliation with Helen would be much less satisfying, for readers and characters, if Margaret had not recovered some part of her previous feminist awareness.

And yet, by novel's end, even this modest hope is threatened. Henry, evidently permanently broken by Charles's murder of Leonard Bast, at last accedes to Margaret's wishes. He makes Howards End legally her property and lives with her there, along with Helen and Helen's son. Helen credits Margaret for having rescued both herself and Henry when they were most desperate, and her benevolent rule promises a better life for all four members of the unconventional family. Yet when Henry admits, at the eleventh hour, that he burned Ruth Wilcox's note, he is characteristically unrepentant, even "tranquil." "Margaret was silent. Something shook her life in its inmost recesses, and she shivered. 'I didn't do wrong, did I?' he asked, bending down. 'You didn't, darling. Nothing has been done wrong,'" she tells him (340). Against a backdrop of "infectious joy" on a warm June day, the final conversation of the novel chills. *Howards End* concludes with Margaret capitulating to Henry's sense of entitlement once again, so that although she is the head of her household, she has also (again) conceded much of her feminist self-respect to stay with him. She appears fully cognizant of her own concession. Even at the novel's end, the narrator's oscillation continues; the final tone is at once hopeful and dreadful. The question lingers of whether or not, even after their considerable effort, either Helen or Margaret has made any progress in clearing a space for their feminist worldview at that especially important moment in British history. It suggests Forster's sensitive recognition, in any case, of the pressures society exerts even on women who recognize the limitations of patriarchy.

A Room with a View engages with feminist principles while holding them at arm's length. The implied author's comfortable distance from the serious constraints of conventional gender mores allows him to take a philosophical, noninterventionist role in a contemporary debate, but it does not prevent him from doing some justice to the ethical significance of feminism. In *Howards End,* the implied author is more decidedly partisan. He employs a narrator who is as slippery and equivocal as the one in *A Room with a View,* but he poses profounder questions and answers them more elegantly. *A Room with a View*'s discourse contains a parallax that incorporates the vantages of those with social privilege and those without it, a parallax that prompts the reader to read critically and to consider, if not embrace, feminism. In *Howards End* that parallax expands to encompass both telling and told, so that the story dramatizes the difficulty of assertive feminist behavior while the discourse complicates that difficulty even further.

Forster's distanced approaches to feminism, characterized by layer upon layer of ironic inversion and tonal divagation, nonetheless constitute in both novels a consistent ethical position on a vexed political topic. Forster's obliquely feminist ethics found in *A Room with a View* and *Howards End* is one of the very few discernible traces in his oeuvre of a coherent implied author, one who guarantees the stability of his notoriously complex irony.

CHAPTER 2

The Ethics of Fair Play

"The less love in a detective-story, the better. . . . A casual and perfunctory love-story is worse than no love-story at all, and since the
mystery must, by hypothesis, take the first place, the love is better
left out."

—Dorothy L. Sayers[1]

A S A WRITER and theorist of Golden Age detective fiction, Dorothy L.
Sayers devoted considerable attention to the convention of fair play.
Her fiction and nonfiction provide rich records of her practical and intellectual engagement with the uses of fair play in detective fiction, with its
affordances, its limitations, and especially its relationship to the strategies adopted by authors and readers alike in pursuit of a mystery's end.
The notion of fair play has for centuries represented equitable conduct in
contests. Its adoption as a central tenet of Golden Age detective fiction
underscores practitioners' self-conscious, deliberate responsibility to both
flesh-and-blood readers and authorial audiences.[2] Scholarship on detective fiction has sometimes referred to fair play as an ethical mandate in the
relationship between author and audience, though in most cases the word
ethical has been used rather loosely. Analysis of Sayers's rhetorical purposes in her Harriet Vane novels can allow a fresh understanding of the
ethics of fair play—not just as a professional responsibility, or as a recipe
for a good mystery, but as a mechanism by which detective fiction can
make ideological arguments.

A rhetorical approach to her narrative techniques illuminates certain key reading experiences those techniques prompt in her audience. Those experiences, I will argue, are primarily ethical in nature, evoked deliberately by the author in response to a political climate marked by partisan statements on both sides of the debate over women's civic rights and responsibilities. Sayers, as one of Oxford University's first women graduates and someone who earned her living by writing, was personally invested in women's free and fair access to meaningful employment. That ethical investment, while influential for her early fiction, became a productive, decisive advantage in her later fiction, particularly in her novels featuring Harriet Vane. By applying the ethics of fair play both to her detective plot and to her feminist concerns, Sayers made the progression of her series coextensive with an ideological argument. I do not claim that Sayers perceived fair play as itself feminist; I wish to demonstrate, though, that the ethics of fair play should be compared to the ethics of the feminist argument she makes in her detective fiction. I contend that engagement with her mysteries entails a reader's serious and prolonged engagement with certain principles of feminism. In order to accomplish her distinctive blend of professional responsibility and feminist ethos, Sayers bent and eventually broke a cardinal rule of generic convention, which allowed her to overcome one of detective fiction's greatest formal challenges: coordinating a love story with a detective story.

Sayers wrote twenty-one short stories and eleven novels about Lord Peter Wimsey between 1923 and 1942.[3] Her most prevalent and versatile technique in service of fair play was focalization. Focalization is a technique that renders perspective through narration. Usually, a focalizer is a character and/or a narrator whose conceptual or perceptual point of view is rendered through the telling. Focalization pertains to who *sees*, as opposed to who *speaks*, in a given act of narrative telling. In some cases the narrator is the focalizer, whereas in others, the narrator speaks on behalf of a character whose conceptual or perceptual perspective pervades the narrator's voice. In the latter instance, the voice is attributed to the narrator while the point of view is attributed to the focalizing character.[4]

More adeptly than most of her contemporaries, Sayers exploited a variety of effects on her authorial audience by manipulating point of view. After focalizing her first four novels through Peter,[5] Sayers substantially altered her methods of engaging her audience when she created a love interest for her detective, beginning with her fifth novel, *Strong Poison*. Although Peter remains focalizer in *Strong Poison*, the novel tests the limits of his viewpoint, skewing and often occluding access to what and how he sees in the novel. As I will argue, focalization takes on a new hermeneutic purpose as well as new generic significance when Sayers combines a courtship plot with a detection plot. Moreover, whereas focalization in the first four novels helps make them end-driven—it encourages the authorial audience to anticipate the mystery's solution and the novel's conclusion, as is customary in detective fiction—beginning with Harriet's first appearance focalization prompts attention to the romance's progression and the novel's middle.[6]

When she adopted Harriet as focalizer in her novels *Have His Carcase* and *Gaudy Night*, Sayers complicated still more the consequences of her decision to introduce a love interest. Her ambitious experiments with point of view within the bounds of fair play became a formal means of promoting her feminist argument: she gave focalization in her detective novels ethical significance. Because she is a detective fiction writer, Harriet's ways of observing, interpreting, and evaluating evidence of criminal activity contrast with the previous novels' established context of Peter's habits of mind. Without essentializing gender differences, Sayers juxtaposed Harriet's mind with Peter's, not only in the substance of their thoughts but in their methods and purposes of vision, their attitudes toward their respective vocational responsibilities. She stretched the boundaries of conventional detective fiction, not by introducing a female sleuth—for Harriet is not a detective—but rather by distinguishing between the strengths of mind of a woman and a man in the wake of Britain's suffrage movement.

A social critique of gender roles in the workplace might easily be accomplished without including a romantic element; similarly, an ambitious generic hybrid need not tackle difficult ideological questions. Sayers goes yet one step further by making the romance between Peter and Harriet signify a larger question about how one balances work with love. Although Peter's professional and romantic pursuits have some setbacks, his privileges—as a noble and as a man—comprise a status quo vividly at odds with Harriet's experiences. For Peter, of course, marriage need not impinge on career. But as an independent, professional woman, Harriet faces a much more difficult balance if she is to accept Peter's marriage proposal. Her investigation of both love problems and detective problems leads her back innumerable times to the same question, which is never explicitly stated but is fundamental to the series: whether or not feminist marriage is practicable. Can married couples in early-twentieth-century Britain be "fellow-creatures," each with the freedom to pursue an occupation and a variety of interests?[7] Or must one spouse's vocation and interests always be subordinate to the other's? Sayers never pairs the terms *feminist* and *marriage,* and yet her series of Harriet Vane novels requires its audience to develop a stance on both concepts as well as their interrelation.

Sayers explores the ethics of fair play in her achievement of two difficult balances. The successful integration of feminism and marriage proves just as intriguing, and challenging, as the generic blend of love story with detective story. The reader is prompted early on to adopt a set of feminist beliefs, at least for the duration of the series, as an extension of fair play. While Harriet frequently makes mistakes, changes her mind, or feels uncertainty, I will argue that the implied author endorses a more consistently feminist stance, and that she asks the reader to evaluate Harriet's judgments and actions accordingly.

In letters and essays Sayers qualified her attitude toward feminism. Addressing a women's group in 1938, she explained that "[w]hat is repugnant to every human being is to be reckoned always as a member of a class and not as an individual person. . . . What is unreasonable and irritating is to assume that *all* one's tastes and preferences have to be conditioned by the class to which one belongs. That has been the very common error into which men have frequently fallen about women—and it is the error into which feminist women are, perhaps, a little inclined to fall into about themselves."[8] She went on to distinguish between the "right and the wrong kind of feminism," the "right" kind being the belief that all people deserve "an interesting occupation, reasonable freedom for their pleasures, and a sufficient emotional outlet"; the "wrong" kind being "aggressive" competition with men simply for the sake of dramatizing grievances, with no practical gain (138; 132–33).

Critics who cite her distaste for political activism as evidence that she was not a feminist seem to assume that feminism must be political in nature; they do not leave room for feminism as an ethical position. Ethical treatment of all people, for her, must include granting each individual's right to choose and pursue a vocation. "'A woman is as good as a man' is as meaningless as to say . . . 'a poet is as good as an engineer' or 'an elephant is as good as a racehorse'—it means nothing whatever until you add: 'at doing what?'" (129). She continues:

[S]ome of them (though not all) know more about children than the majority of men, and their opinion, *as women,* is of value. In the same way, the opinion of colliers is of value about coal-mining, and the opinion of doctors is valuable about disease. But there are other questions—as for example, about literature or finance—on which the "woman's point of view" has no value at all. In fact, it does not exist. No special knowledge is involved, and a woman's opinion on literature or finance is valuable only as the judgment of an individual. I am occasionally desired by congenital imbeciles and the editors of magazines to say something about the writing of detective fiction "from the woman's point of view." To such demands, one can only say, "Go away and don't be silly. You might as well ask what is the female angle on an equilateral triangle." (137)

In both fiction and nonfiction, Sayers consistently upheld this practical, anti-essentialist feminist stance. She peopled her fictional world with characters who articulate nearly every point along a wide political spectrum on women's rights, but as an implied author she endorses a consistent position. She not only validates women's rights to education and vocation, she also castigates a patriarchal system (in a wide variety of guises) that squanders women's potential. Because Harriet herself is not consistently feminist, these authorial positions have sometimes gone unnoticed. Sayers's choice to endow Harriet with some of her own personal traits—the two share a profession as detective novelist, a distinguished alma mater, and (as some have overemphasized) an affection for Peter—speaks to her skills as a sophisticated thinker and accomplished novelist. Their similarities allow Sayers to comment implicitly on her own activity as a writer, but the distinctions between Sayers's and Harriet's ethical judgments are more interesting, because they provide the basis for the reader's engagement with a feminist argument. Differences between Sayers and Harriet suggest that Harriet is no mere avatar; rather, she is one of many rhetorical resources at Sayers's disposal.

Although many have criticized Sayers's generic blend, few have theorized about it, and only one study adopts narrative theory as a methodology. In *Why We Read Fiction*, which takes a cognitive approach to narrative theory, Lisa Zunshine validates the rule against integrating romance with detective fiction, asserting that "the kind of mind-reading expected from the reader of the detective novel is indeed not particularly compatible with the kind of mind-reading expected from the reader of the story focusing on a romantic relationship."[9] According to Zunshine, Sayers gets away with combining the two genres only because "we understand early on that Harriet Vane either will marry Lord Peter Wimsey after a requisite amount of soul-searching or will not, but we don't particularly care anyway," since she has not asked her reader to invest cognitively in the romance as much as in the detection plot.[10] One way of testing Zunshine's claim is to examine the kinds of readerly investments prompted not just by romance and detection but by fair play itself. I will argue that she requires the reader's attention to the romance as part of her feminist argument in the Harriet Vane novels. Delineating how Harriet and Peter think—about both crime and each other—allows Sayers the opportunity to make an ethical argument through focalization and narrative progression.

THE PRACTICE of fair play posed a challenge to detective fiction writers in relation to two types of progression. First, that challenge exists in real time, over the historical progression of the genre. All genres of fiction assume some overlap between real readers and authorial audiences, but the principle of fair play in Anglo-American detective fiction of the 1920s and '30s depends on that overlap. Because detective fiction relies on writerly innovation and readerly surprise, and because authorial audiences by definition know thousands of secrets revealed by previously published stories and novels (even if their flesh-and-blood counterparts have not themselves read so widely), as the Golden Age advanced, authors had to anticipate audiences' ever-increasing knowledge and sophistication in order to succeed rhetorically.[11]

Fair play likewise challenges authors in terms of the narrative progression of any given story or novel. It dictates that authors use narrative progression to reveal pertinent clues, not merely forestall closure through divagation. As G. K. Chesterton puts it, "The true object of an intelligent detective story is not to baffle the reader, but to enlighten the reader; but to enlighten him in such a manner that each successive portion of the truth comes as a surprise."[12] Flesh-and-blood readers engage with detective fiction in myriad ways, spanning a spectrum from utterly passive observation of the detective in action to vicarious detection to competition with the sleuth. But the authorial audience of any given detective fiction, as a participant in the narrative progression itself, must be surprised and enlightened through the progression, according to pacing and opportunities painstakingly constructed by the implied author.[13]

Over the course of the twentieth century, both theory and practice established the principle of fair play as the sine qua non of Golden Age detective fiction. Repeatedly, practitioners and theorists reiterated its precepts, honing to a remarkable degree the genre's conformity to certain conventions. Prominent among these conventions was the mandate that

romance had no place in detective fiction. The question of why love stories and detective stories were conventionally treated as incompatible during the early twentieth century may be answered by a close examination
of narratives that attempt to bridge the divide. A rhetorical approach to
Golden Age novels that work to integrate love and detection can yield a
rich understanding of that generic friction at that historical moment as
well as a fuller appreciation of a novelist's accomplishment—both theoretical and technical—when the integration succeeds. If, as in the Gon-
court brothers' reading of Poe, the genre of detective fiction is one that,
by definition, requires "love giving place to deductions. . . . [T]he interest
of the story mov[ing] from the heart to the head . . . from the drama to
the solution,"[14] the prohibition against integrating romance into detective
fiction would seem to be based on a fundamental, generic incompatibility,
and one potential locus of that conflict, as I will explore in this chapter, is
authorial use of fair play.

As late as 1929 Sayers avers in print that she objects to mixing
romance with detection in fiction.[15] Yet her 1930 novel, *Strong Poison,*
depicts Lord Peter Wimsey falling in love with Harriet Vane, a novelist of detective fiction on trial for murdering her former lover. Sayers's
stated objection to the generic mixture is not that it violates fair play;
rather that, with very few exceptions, love in detective fiction tends to be
"irrelevant to the action and perfunctorily worked in . . . the less love in
a detective-story, the better. . . . A casual and perfunctory love-story is
worse than no love-story at all, and since the mystery must, by hypothesis, take the first place, the love is better left out."[16] Here her objection
is aesthetic, not ethical. Elsewhere—before and even after beginning her
Harriet Vane series—Sayers identifies other arguments against combining the two genres, but her various objections to mixing the two genres
always come back to the same idea: that such mixtures violate one or
more of the obligations authors have to their audiences, be they aesthetic,
formal, or ethical obligations. Her lively and evolving interest in authorial
responsibilities to the reader, responsibilities in which fair play was integral, figures prominently in her solution to this generic problem. Although
her nonfiction tends to stress the implied author's aesthetic obligations
according to the rules of fair play, Sayers's fiction makes clear her commitment to ethical obligations: both the implied author's ethical responsibilities to the reader, and the latter's responsibility to think through the
ethical ramifications of the narrative—to read ethically.

One popular contention against blending romance with detection
that Sayers never endorsed assumes that detective fiction should be the-

matically unified. It is an aesthetic argument, but one more extreme than Sayers could countenance. "A detective novel should contain no long descriptive passages, no literary dallying with side-issues, no subtly worked-out character analyses, no 'atmospheric' preoccupations," claims S. S. Van Dine. "Such matters have no vital place in a record of crime and detection. They hold up the action, and introduce issues irrelevant to the main purpose, which is to state a problem, analyze it, and bring it to a successful conclusion."[17] Roger Caillois puts the matter even more starkly: "[T]here is no essential difference between a detective novel and a mathematical problem. . . . Its interest, its value, and even its originality increase with the limitations it accepts and the rules it imposes on itself. . . . It is cold and sterile, perfectly cerebral. It gives rise to no feeling and evokes no dream."[18]

Whereas Caillois explicitly approves of "mechanical" fiction, Sayers appreciates the challenge of humanizing the detective novel. "The modern evolution in the direction of 'fair play' is to a great extent a revolution. It is a recoil from the Holmes influence and a turning back to *The Moonstone* and its contemporaries. . . . *The Moonstone* is probably the very finest detective story ever written. By comparison with its wide scope, its dove-tailed completeness and the marvelous variety and soundness of its characterization, modern mystery fiction looks thin and mechanical."[19] From the beginning of her career, she strove to write novels that transcended mere puzzle-solving exercises. Although she recognized the genre's limitations, noting that it "rarely touches the heights and depths of human passion,"[20] she applauded efforts in the early 1930s—when publishers grew amenable to novels and longer stories[21]—to realign detective fiction with "the tradition of the English novel," with its "profound treatment of the larger emotions . . . and the great interests of humanity." The "most important development" of detective fiction in those years, for Sayers, was the "return—this time with the improved fair-play technique—to the Victorian conception of the detective story that should at the same time be a novel of characters and manners."[22] Chesterton voiced a similar view: "I will add that for this reason, despite the sneers at 'love-interest' there is a good deal to be said for the tradition of sentiment and slower or more Victorian narration."[23] In their essays, both Sayers and Chesterton acknowledge that Victorian narrative conventions such as rich characterization, atmospheric detail, multiplot progression, and sentimentality—although perceived by many detection aficionados as "literary dallying" and by modernist aesthetes as embarrassingly obsolete—may be a salutary correction to the detective novel's "heartless" mechanism.

Sayers's admiration of Collins's techniques in *The Moonstone* affected not just her theories about detective fiction but her writing of it. *The Moonstone* famously coordinates narration by and focalization through a wide range of characters, a formal technique that allowed him to depict, as Collins explains in his preface, "the influence of character on circumstances" as opposed to circumstances on character.[24] In her 1928 essay, Sayers devotes considerable attention to the "Importance of the Viewpoint." She analyzes a sample text by one of her contemporaries, distinguishing the authorial audience's varying degrees of "privileged" access to the detective's perceptual point of view and his deductions. She demonstrates that even subtle shifts in point of view, even minute differences in the reader's access to a detective's mind, have consequences for their reading of the implied author. For her purposes in the essay, Sayers's interest in that rhetorical rapport consists largely in the way it maximizes and sustains suspense. But the rapport in her own detective series hinges on a richer, more significant set of expectations for her authorial audience.

From the beginning of her series, but particularly after 1930, Sayers narrated her novels using various and multilayered perspectives. *Strong Poison* employs a greater variety of focalizers than any of her previous novels, so that pivotal clues are rendered through the perceptual and conceptual frames of several characters besides Peter. *The Documents in the Case* (1930) replaces Peter with an entirely new detective and is epistolary in form, allowing Sayers to juxtapose multiple first-person narrative perspectives. Although her next Wimsey novel, *Five Red Herrings,* reserves its ambition for intricacy of plot and does little with point of view, all of her subsequent novels feature experimentation with narrative voice.

EARLY in her Lord Peter Wimsey series, Sayers's focalization through Peter is a form of fair play. She allows sufficient access to his mind so that the vital clues of a case are available to the detecting reader, but she prevents access to Peter's deductions until the novel's end, so as to let the reader match wits with the detective. Focalization, then, is used primarily as a way of suggesting, and prompting vicarious emulation of, Peter's *methodology* in the act of detection. As Sayers remarks in her 1928 essay, "The reader must be given every clue—but he must not be told, surely, all the detective's deductions, lest he should see the solution too far ahead."[25] She lists a few popular solutions to the problem—endowing the detective with arcane knowledge that permits him to make extraordinarily sophisticated deductions, for instance—but concludes that manipulating narration of viewpoint is the optimal strategy by which an author can be both fair and discriminating in the revelation of clues—without resorting to tricks or revelations of esoteric knowledge. Focalization prompts readers to inhabit a particular experiential frame, be it that of the detective, a witness, or even an extradiegetic narrator. Whereas Arthur Conan Doyle focalizes his Sherlock Holmes tales almost exclusively through the companionate Watson, Sayers prefers varying her focalizers, and thus the reader's sources of information, as often as several times in a single scene.

In her essay, Sayers distinguishes among four degrees of focalized narration, listed in order of the reader's access to the detective's mind. In narratology's terms, these degrees are external focalization from without (by a character or narrator witnessing the detective in action), external focalization from without along with audible remarks by the detective (again, by a witness), external focalization from within (by a narrator who reports the detective's silent observations but not his deductions), and internal focalization (by the detective himself, featuring both observations and deductions).[26] One advantage of shifting viewpoint is that it conspicuously affords the reader access to some information while covertly occluding other information. If transitions among the degrees of focalization are effected smoothly, the reader is prompted to appreciate insights available through, for instance, the detective's muttered commentary in one portion of the scene, rather than wishing for more direct access to his thoughts. As long as enough of the detective's methodology is supplied to allow the reader to emulate it, the reader will be busy enough generating her own insights that she may not notice that the detective's deductions are only selectively available. Alternatively, shifting focalization may give the reader access to observations that the detective misses, and thus can give the reader a competitive advantage over the detective in their race to solving the crime.

A fictional detective's methodology typically consists of two components: his strategic creation of opportunities to obtain information and his characteristic reasoning skills. Agatha Christie's Poirot, for example, strategically relies on his outsider status as a Belgian in England, as well as the harmless appearance of his physical person, to defuse the suspicion of potential informants. His "little grey cells," in which he has supreme confidence, allow him to reason by imagination. As one critic notes, "Not for Poirot the fingerprint or the cigar ash. . . . [He refuses] to go Holmes-like on all fours in pursuit of clues. . . . Not quite an arm-chair detective, Poirot nevertheless spurns the aid of science. He is the champion of theory over matter."[27] Holmes may do his share of crawling after clues,

but the most famous dimension of his methodology is, of course, his dazzling power of deduction. His sharp eye for casual detail allows him to
make a wealth of deductions about people's personal habits, from which
he then creates larger inferences. Holmes describes his process of inference
in "The Musgrave Ritual": "I put myself in the man's place, and having
first gauged his intelligence, I try to imagine how I should myself have pro-
ceeded under the same circumstances."[28]

By contrast to these two standard-bearers, Peter Wimsey's methodology is dependent on his class and social privilege. As a British peer, Peter
uses his privilege to create information-gathering opportunities. Physical
evidence is almost always retrieved by his middle-class assistants: Bunter,
Inspector Parker, Miss Climpson and her employees at the Cattery.[29] But
he conducts his interviews in person. Unlike Holmes and Poirot, who
charge fees, Wimsey detects for a leisure-time hobby, which means that
his conversations with suspects and witnesses are always unofficial, and
not coincidentally often more productive than Scotland Yard's interviews.
The people he interviews frequently know his detection skills by reputation, but even if they do not, they are nearly always deferential to, if not
awed by, the nobleman. They usually share information with him out of
some mixture of politeness, respect, and unguarded surprise. As an aris-
tocrat he reaps the benefits of being both insider—a symbol of British
excellence—and outsider—able to reason about people's personal affairs
dispassionately from his social elevation. Focalization through Peter
allows the authorial audience—which is, like most of the suspects and
witnesses, solidly middle class—to emulate his methodology by enjoying a
vicarious assumption of social privilege.[30]

But focalization serves other purposes for Sayers as well. With each
successive novel in Sayers's series before Harriet's appearance, Peter's dis-
position, hobbies, relationships, and characteristic reasoning skills increase
the authorial audience's sense of admiration and even affection for him.
The implied author's fondness for her protagonist,[31] which is obvious, for
example, in descriptions of his postwar, shell-shocked vulnerability, pervades the authorial rapport with the reader. Focalization is a means of
prompting an *affective* reading of Peter's personality, as the novels progress from puzzles to subtler, more psychologically realistic studies of the
detective in action. The affective dimension of focalization contributes
directly to Sayers's goal of blending the detective novel with the "novel of
manners."

It's important to note that initially, Peter's romantic encounters with
women do not contribute to an affective reading of his character; in fact,

those encounters are focalized in such a way to prevent a reader's sentimental response. As the result of heartbreak early in life, Peter's relations
with women in the first four novels, though always gallant and respectful, remain emotionally shallow. Sayers pointedly demonstrates that her
detective's heart is unreadable, both to other characters and to the reader.
Peter's relations with his manservant, family members, and friends are
warmer, and Sayers narrates them more revealingly, which helps humanize Peter to a certain extent. But Peter's emotional capacity is most evident in the context of detection. Sayers treats the ethical challenges of
crime detection—questions of mercy, justice, retribution, and the class
consciousness of an aristocratic sleuth—in part as occasions for suggesting that moral and emotional riches lie just beneath Peter's rather vapid
surface. Focalization through Peter prompts an affective response to his
character when this internal complexity is partially revealed. But because
Sayers tends to reserve those revelations for moments of crime detection,
the affective consequences of focalization early in the series include the
reader's increased investment in the mystery plot.

When Harriet becomes the dominant focalizer in *Have His Carcase*
and *Gaudy Night,* Sayers's project takes a significant turn. Her use of
focalization becomes more *ethical* than affective or methodological. By
this I do not mean that the focalization is necessarily ethically admirable,
but rather that its ethical dimension predominates. As I have said, Harriet's ethical convictions do not always match Sayers's. But Harriet's methods of solving problems—be they matters of criminal detection, judgment
of character, romantic conduct, or other myriad puzzles she negotiates—always evoke (if sometimes indirectly) the implied author's norms
about gender. The authorial audience is asked to make ethical judgments,
not only about events but also about Harriet herself.[32] Harriet's job as
a detective fiction writer lends her competence and problem-solving
skills. She does not need to be a detective in order to assess situations
and resolve dilemmas effectively. Peter applies his skills as detective to the
very same situations and dilemmas, but to different ends. The authorial
audience is asked to inhabit the separately competent judgments of both
male and female focalizers and to adopt a feminist ideology through, and
occasionally in spite of, Harriet's viewpoint.

REMARKABLY, Sayers refuses to focalize through Peter throughout the
first three chapters of *Strong Poison.* Although earlier novels contain
a few passages focalized through characters other than Peter, as well as

some that are presented purely from the narrator's perspective, those passages are exceptions to the rule. *Strong Poison*'s opening chapters make the focalization itself a mystery, as the narrator stresses the visual details of the setting and teases her reader into trying to deduce, by process of elimination, whose eyes we are looking through.

> There were crimson roses on the bench; they looked like splashes of blood. The judge was an old man; so old, he seemed to have outlived time and change and death. His parrot-face and parrot-voice were dry, like his old, heavily-veined hands. His scarlet robe clashed harshly with the crimson of the roses. He had sat for three days in the stuffy court, but he showed no sign of fatigue. He did not look at the prisoner as he gathered his notes into a neat sheaf and turned to address the jury, but the prisoner looked at him. (1)

Mixed in with the visual details are interpretations and feelings, characterizing the atmosphere as ominous—"they looked like splashes of blood," "his scarlet robe clashed harshly with the roses"—but such fearful receptivity does not sound like it belongs to Peter Wimsey, the suave expert in crime detection. The prisoner herself, who sits looking at the judge, seems a more likely focalizer. But Sayers rules out this possibility with her next sentence: "Her eyes, like dark smudges under the heavy square brows, seemed equally without fear and without hope. They waited." As soon as the prisoner is described from outside herself, the reader casts about for a character-focalizer who would be both oppressed by the courtroom's atmosphere and motivated to interpret the expression in the prisoner's eyes. The next sentence supplies a clue: The judge intones, "Members of the jury—." Immediately, though, the jury members are described from outside themselves, again in judgmental and speculative terms that eliminate them as possible focalizers.

Sayers makes her use of focalization conspicuous; she calls attention to the acts of looking and evaluating while compelling her reader to wonder which character is doing those things. For twenty-five long pages Sayers suspends that question as the judge (who is blatantly unsympathetic to the prisoner) addresses the courtroom, summarizing the story of the prisoner's alleged crime. Her former lover was found poisoned to death just a few hours after they argued, and the prisoner had been researching that particular poison for a detective novel she was writing at the time. The details of the case, which normally would be leavened by Peter's internal reactions, are instead directly quoted as a monologue by the crotchety, sexist judge, interrupted only briefly and occasionally by the ambiguously focalized commentary. Sayers clearly designed this presentation to prompt certain reactions from her authorial audience. For instance, a middle-aged woman on the jury seems at first innocuous enough, but as soon as she is characterized as taking notes "vigorously" the reader familiar with other novels in the series deduces (on the basis of only one adverb) that this juror is Miss Climpson, a minor character and ally of Peter's in other books (7). Moreover, the judge's sexism interferes with his objectivity, gradually prompting the reader to find his summary of the case partially unreliable. In the guise of dispassionate description he implies value judgments that the careful reader—feminist or not—recognizes as unfair. Sayers expects her reader's ability to pick up on her cues, not just to recognize minor characters but also to make certain ethical evaluations before Lord Peter Wimsey makes his entrance in the novel.

At last he does turn up: he has been sitting silently in the courtroom all this time, unnarrated and unnoticed. "The judge paused for a moment, and Freddy Arbuthnot jerked an elbow into the ribs of Lord Peter Wimsey, who appeared to be a prey to gloom" (5). Sayers's choice of the word "appeared" again prompts her reader to wonder who is doing the focalizing. One also wonders why Peter looks gloomy—normally he is chipper, energetic, fairly superficial—and Sayers gives no evidence besides this hint that the trial has any special meaning for him. By the chapter's end, we are provided with only one other suggestion that the narration is staying well away from Peter's thoughts precisely because whatever is on his mind has a lot of significance. Peter contradicts his friend's casual assumption of the prisoner's guilt with "unusual acidity," and that is all we are told (18). The word "unusual" again gestures toward knowledge the reader familiar with the other books in the series would have, while teasingly withholding the accustomed focalization.

Sayers never resolves the mystery of who focalizes the first three chapters. Instead, she uses its extended indeterminacy to heighten the impact of Peter's precipitate and completely unexpected proposal of marriage to the prisoner (whom he has never met before the moment of his proposal). Peter's proposal to Harriet takes place early in the fourth chapter. In that meeting and in all other private meetings between them in this novel, focalization is suspended; the scenes are conducted exclusively through dialogue. And although the characters' dialogue implies some of their thoughts and emotions, for the most part, the scenes between Harriet and Peter keep the reader guessing as to how their romance is progressing, if at all. In their first meeting, when Harriet is less than delighted by being proposed to by an awkward and slightly funny-looking stranger in prison, the narrator remarks merely that "his voice sounded hurt" as Peter concedes that the specter of impending execution may be dampening her enthusiasm for matrimony (44). He ascertains that he himself does not "positively repel" her and gains her permission to keep visiting, hoping that her answer will eventually change (46). Peter continues to propose marriage to Harriet, at respectful intervals, for the rest of the novel, and she keeps politely but firmly turning him down, naming her circumstances as the reason. We infer from dialogue that Harriet is ashamed by the way her former lover treated her in life, mortified by her sudden notoriety, appalled by the misogynistic press coverage, and above all, in a position of absolute helplessness. She feels more acutely than Peter does the power imbalance between them: he purports to be her knight in shining armor, but she wants only to be left alone with dignity. She seems to like Peter, but her circumstances loom larger than his appeal.

The novel's scenes devoted to solving the mystery, which contain plenty of both focalization and direct report of Peter's thoughts, offer the usual benefits of understanding Peter's methodology and gaining insights into his character. This makes the lack of focalization in the scenes between Harriet and Peter more conspicuous. The prolonged estrangement from Peter's thoughts achieves multiple purposes. First, especially in the initial proposal scene, lack of mental access heightens surprise. Second, it helps signal that the series has become a serial narrative. It suggests that in order fully to understand Peter's behavior in this novel, one must infer his feelings and thoughts based on prior knowledge of his character. This effect is heightened by the novel's frequent references to characters from earlier in the series, particularly those from the first Peter Wimsey novel, creating an undertone of authorial retrospection meaningful primarily to the experienced Sayers reader. Focalization in *Strong Poison* is more aptly termed *contextual* focalization, since the full effect of focalization in this novel relies on one's first having read one or more other novels in the series.

The third consequence of denying focalization when Harriet and Peter are together ensures that the romance plot remain subordinate to the mystery plot. Although later in the series Sayers works hard to make the two plots interdependent, at this early moment there are good reasons for keeping them separate. In *Strong Poison*, the global instability consists in the detective plot: Peter's need to find out who poisoned Harriet's former lover. The sought-for resolution of this instability is not merely serving justice but, of course, saving Harriet from the gallows. Peter's high personal stake in his own success lends more suspense to the plot's progression, but we are well aware that even if Harriet were to reject Peter's marriage proposal definitively, once and for all, he would continue to function as a detective. The secondary end-directed conflict in the novel is actually not very much about the instability between characters—will Peter end up winning Harriet's heart or won't he?—even though that, of course, is precisely what one would expect in a romance plot. Despite the fact that the proposal scene seems to launch that sort of instability between characters, the scenes that follow it do not progress toward resolution. Peter keeps proposing, Harriet keeps declining; familiarity makes them a bit fonder of each other, but the reasons for Harriet's refusal do not go away, nor are they very likely to anytime soon. The romantic frisson between them certainly qualifies as an instability, but it promises to be long-term if not endless.

Keeping Peter's feelings about Harriet largely concealed maintains the precedent set in earlier books of depicting Peter's heart as unreadable. But punctuating that discreet privacy with his repeated marriage proposals creates an imbalance between what the reader knows of Peter and the way he is rendered in *Strong Poison*. In short, narrative progression in this novel depends primarily on an instability (Peter working to detect who the real poisoner is) and on a tension (why Peter is acting so oddly, and more generically, why the detective in a detective story would be deeply invested in something other than detecting). Contextual focalization contributes extremely little to the global instability but a great deal to the global tension, helping generate the novel's progression. The very fact that Sayers refuses to employ focalization in service of the instability *itself* contributes to the global tension and through it the novel's progression.

One cannot explain away that tension simply by saying that Peter is in love, and that people in love act unpredictably. Sayers expects her reader to use prior knowledge of Peter to recognize that he is in a crisis. His customary poise has disappeared. His healthy sense of self-deprecatory humor has taken on a bitter edge. Abandoning his usual deductive powers, Peter intuits that Harriet is not guilty before he ever sees her, and he acts confidently on the strength of that intuition. Also, because Peter has previously claimed to have no interest in marriage or even in dating, we are compelled to wonder what it is about Harriet Vane that makes him act this way. Since Harriet's character and appearance are never focalized through Peter, any evidence of his reasons for falling for her must be inferred rather than seen. Moreover, it is clear that falling in love has triggered much self-doubt in Peter: he starts to feel his age (he's nearing forty), he worries that he won't detect the real murderer before Harriet is convicted, he recognizes that his titled privilege is not the kind of power that will help him win Harriet's heart. All of these worries have the potential to revolutionize Peter's character; they all suggest a complex subjectivity lacking in the previous books. This wealth of potential is not exploited in *Strong Poison,* but it makes character development in subsequent books more plausible.

Again, Sayers had good reasons for keeping the romance plot subordinate to the mystery plot. She renders Peter falling in love in order to create distance between him and the reader, to upset the reader's expectations based on previous novels, and to emphasize this novel's relation to the rest of the series. What this added up to was an opportunity to test the limits of her genre.

By her own account, Sayers had yet another reason for rendering Peter as she did in this novel. In an essay, she attests that she had intended to end her series by marrying Peter off at the end of *Strong Poison,* but found in the course of writing it that "I had landed my two chief puppets in a situation where, according to all the conventional rules of detective fiction, they should have had nothing to do but fall into one another's arms; but they would not do it, and that for a very good reason. When I looked at the situation I saw that it was in every respect false and degrading; and the puppets had somehow got just so much flesh and blood in them that I could not force them to accept it without shocking myself."[33] If this account is accurate, my hypothesis is that Sayers originally designed the novel to progress through two instabilities: the mystery plot and the romance plot. She could have ended her series by letting the romance plot supersede the mystery plot in this final novel. When she realized that she had put Harriet and Peter into a "false and degrading" position, however, she deemphasized the romantic instability and created a tension with her implied reader. She kept the initial launch—Peter's abrupt proposal in the jail cell—but then instead of letting the romance plot progress, she developed tension through her narration, particularly by disrupting her normal patterns of focalization, thus destabilizing one of the customary strategies of her career author.[34]

My examination of the only extant manuscript of *Strong Poison* supplies a bit more information. Sayers revised her handwritten manuscript very sparingly, and neither of the first two meetings between Harriet and Peter reveal any revisions whatsoever.[35] The most substantial changes in the early chapters are in service of fair play. She heightens the precision of details about the murder victim's last dinner ("poured the wine" becomes "decanted from a fresh bottle at the table," for example) and endows a typewriter with some obligatory, distinctive flaws ("a Woodstock machine, with a chipped lower-case p and an A slightly out of alignment").[36] At the point of Harriet and Peter's third meeting, however, the manuscript reveals a dramatic revision. "Wimsey ground his teeth and went down to Halloway Gaol, where he very nearly made a jealous exhibition of himself. . . . 'What is it you really want?' he dem"[37] The rest of the page has been torn away. The following page begins, in smooth penmanship with no revisions, with Peter and Harriet's conversation exactly as it appears in the printed book. If the manuscript reveals any truth to Sayers's claim that she changed her mind mid-novel, this is surely the moment of revelation, but with the majority of the page missing, the evidence is scant. The deleted line of dialogue adumbrates an emotionally fraught scene, but the printed text provides a rational and relatively poised conversation, again free of thought report and focalization. The chapter ends with an emphatic return to the detection plot, with an overt gesture of fair play: "He read the letter again, mechanically noting that it was typed on a Woodstock machine, with a chipped lower case p, and a capital A that was out of alignment. Suddenly he woke up and read it a third time, noticing by no means mechanically, the chipped p and the irregular capital A. . . . For the first time, in this annoying case, he felt the vague stirring of the waters as a living idea emerged slowly and darkly from the innermost deeps of his mind" (129–30). In this brief passage, Sayers temporarily employs focalization in the method customary of previous books in her series, though in short supply in this novel: external focalization from within provides Peter's observations without having to reveal his deductions.

A rhetorical reading of the published novel (which is identical to the holograph manuscript) reveals that the global tension cooperates with the global instability from the novel's outset; Sayers did not evidently go back and revise either mechanism of progression after penning her lovers' third meeting. But notably, after Harriet and Peter's third meeting the tension between implied author and authorial audience over Peter's unaccountable behavior gains greater prominence, as well as hermeneutic significance. The tension's new prominence suggests that Sayers may well have changed her mind, deciding not to force competition between her two instabilities and preferring instead to enhance her authorial audience's appreciation of the generic experiment by emphasizing tension.

Seeking corroboration for Sayers's "infanticidal" intentions, many scholars have pointed to two scenes in which Sayers efficiently summarizes the love story's potential to unseat the detective story's primacy:

"For the first time, too, he doubted his own power to carry through what he had undertaken. His personal feelings had been involved before this in his investigations, but they had never before clouded his mind. He was fumbling—grasping uncertainly here and there at fugitive and mocking possibilities. He asked questions at random, doubtful of his object, and the shortness of the time, which would once have stimulated, now frightened and confused him" (90). A few chapters later, we find Peter "[grinding] his teeth and [raging] helplessly, striding about the suave, wealthy, futile room," feeling tempted to smash his own reflection in a grand mirror because, unless he acts quickly, Harriet will likely soon be convicted of murder (168). These scenes are typically paired and quoted as evidence of Sayers' acknowledgment that the love story in *Strong Poison* was designed to end the series. Gayle Wald makes much of Peter's frustration and self-doubt as signals of the "excesses of desire," worrying that, "[t]hough the murder mystery has a solution that can be arrived at through careful reasoning, the love story remains dangerous because unsolvable, frightening because its origin is in the individual psyche, beyond even the lover's conscious control." Thus, romance is at odds with detection because detective fiction "cannot exist without the repression or containment of desire in a simple exchange between detective and criminal."[38] Although the moment of self-doubt is certainly unusual for Peter, and his disorientation is clearly attributed to his love for Harriet, my reading of the novel's progression leads me to believe that the scene is less momentous, less indicative that Peter's career is on the brink of collapse, than it has been perceived to be. Wald and others extrapolate from it to claim that Peter makes methodological mistakes, but *Strong Poison* offers no evidence of any actual mistakes—merely his worry about their potential.

Peter's self-doubt has much more in common rhetorically with the deleted conversation than it does with anything subsequent to the deletion. Histrionics, such as smashing mirrors and demanding "What is it you really want?" belong to an end-driven romantic instability, one that speeds towards its conclusion of either joyous reconciliation or heartbreak. In choosing to downplay the romantic instability in favor of the detection instability and the global tension, Sayers belies her purported "infanticidal" intentions. Peter's recognition of the chipped lowercase *p* at the conclusion of his third meeting with Harriet reinvigorates the global instability (the detection plot), and although Sayers's hero does not regain his self-assurance until she resolves the global tension in the last lines of the novel, after the deleted scene Sayers heightens the importance of the tension through unconventional focalization. Of the remaining twelve chapters in *Strong Poison,* only one contains any focalization by Peter. Seven chapters are focalized by Miss Climpson and Miss Murchison, two employees of the Cattery who perform all the essential legwork to detect and trap the murderer, using opportunities impossible for Peter to exploit by himself. Miss Climpson's detection is so esteemed by the implied author, in fact, that at the crucial moment of discovery her deductions are elided (221), although her observations are supplied incessantly by either internal focalization (in her letters) or external focalization from within by the narrator. All revelations pertinent to the mystery's solution are delivered exclusively through dialogue except for one last instance of perceptual focalization, as Bunter reads the titles of the books that have prompted Peter's solution of the mystery. Again, Sayers reveals what a character sees without revealing what he deduces.

Strong Poison culminates in a dramatic resolution of the mystery plot. With truly virtuosic self-assurance Peter detects the murderer and traps him in a nefarious web of lies. In between chapters devoted to Peter's solution of the mystery and the springing of his cunning trap, Sayers sandwiches a very brief interview between Harriet and Peter, in which she declines his proposal one more time. "'All right,' said Wimsey, 'I won't worry you. Not fair. Abusing my privilege and so on.'" Although he says it lightly, the fact of his privilege manifests as the source of the new primary instability between the two of them. He is a peer and she a middle-class writer. But more importantly, Harriet can't stand the inequity in their relationship caused by her debt to him. As soon as he saves her from the gallows, this debt looms larger than their class difference. Although both characters theoretically aspire to a marriage of equals—Peter has remarkably egalitarian views despite the conservative nature of his titled ancestry—neither of them can see a way of getting past this inequity. By the novel's end, Sayers has maneuvered so that at last her romance plot has the potential to compete with future mystery plots.

The resolution of the tension between implied author and authorial audience, in the final lines of the novel, manifests in Peter's revelation to the duke that he is in love with a middle-class woman. The conversation marks his decision to stop hiding his feelings, from the Duke and likewise the reader, and to continue trying to win Harriet's heart—"If she'll have me," says Peter (261). His willingness by novel's end to pursue both love and detection openly and simultaneously is a resolution to *Strong Poison*'s tension as well as the long-deferred launch of the romantic instability with global proportions. The duke is appalled by Peter's news, but Peter is unapologetic. He reasserts his customary self-confidence, displaying the wit and good humor absent earlier in the novel. With her light touch in this brief scene, Sayers offers closure to that line of tension, giving the romance plot the opportunity to mature in future novels.

THE SECOND NOVEL featuring Harriet Vane is internally focalized through Harriet, and that fact announces the novel's bold departure from its six predecessors in the novel's first lines. Harriet is on holiday, having slipped away from London without notifying Peter, depriving him of the chance to offer his point of view to her or the authorial audience. She soon discovers a dead body on a deserted stretch of beach. Because we have never had access to her mind, we treat this scene as a prime opportunity to learn something about her character. Just as Sayers's focalization in previous novels habitually emphasizes Peter's methodology, focalization here initially prompts us to compare Harriet's untested methodology with Peter's well-established one. Harriet first thinks, "What would Peter do?" and then instantly squelches that thought. The reader is denied a direct comparison for the same reason Harriet has rejected Peter's proposals of marriage: Sayers's regard for Harriet's self-respect will not let her subordinate Harriet to Peter. Harriet is determined to observe and interpret this scene competently, but she does it in a way that Peter would not. Her career as a mystery writer has taught her to appreciate certain details that might, at least in a novel, be clues, so those are the details she looks for.

Harriet deliberately turns her attention from wondering how Peter would handle discovery of a dead body to imagining how the fictional protagonist in her detective series (Robert Templeton) would behave. But repulsed by the sight and "horrid halitus of blood," she realizes that, unlike her protagonist, she may not have the stomach for examining a corpse. "Harriet felt that she had never fully appreciated the superb nonchalance of her literary offspring. Of course, any ordinary person, who was not a Robert Templeton, would leave the body alone and run for the police" (8–9). Thought report followed by internal focalization suggest that Harriet is no "ordinary person," since her professional knowledge leads her to see and think about crime in an experienced and informed manner—and yet, we realize, as Harriet does, that experience does not make her a detective. Although she regrets in this moment not knowing what a detective knows, she is spurred to action by something she does know, as a novelist: the tide is coming in, which means the body will soon be swept out to sea. Experienced as she is with coordinating plot details such as time of death and timetables, she works against the clock collecting as much evidence as she can. Later, she continues her investigation in town: "Harriet wondered why she was asking about the trains, and then suddenly realized that, with her professional interest in time-tables, she was instinctively checking up the ways and means of approaching the Grinders. Train, car, boat—how had the dead man got there?" (24).

Here Sayers uses focalization primarily to demonstrate methodology, just as she does when Peter is focalizer. But whereas Peter's deductions are typically elided, Harriet's deductions are all narrated. Like Holmes's Dr. Watson or Poirot's Captain Hastings, Harriet's amateur status allows her deductions to be shared freely with the reader, on the assumption that they must be in some important way inaccurate. And like that of Watson and Hastings, Harriet's focalization provides clues not only about the crime but about her relationship to the detective. But whereas Watson and Hastings cannot possibly compete with Holmes and Poirot—their focalization underscores their subordination to the detective—Harriet's focalization represents her independence from Peter, emphasizing her alternative form of competence.

At this point we can readily see focalization serving at least three purposes. First, because it foregrounds different methodological approaches to investigative work, focalization furthers the mystery plot. Second, as many have noted, fostering access to Harriet's point of view helps Sayers achieve her goal of writing psychologically richer novels. Third, by lending dignity to Harriet's alternative competence, focalization through her character advances Sayers's feminist argument. Although Peter has largely earned his reputation as a great detective, previous novels depict his access to crucial information as a product of his privilege as a man, and a rich man at that. He interviews key witnesses in elite clubs open only to wealthy men. He recognizes a murder weapon as one of only a few straight-edge razors produced by an exclusive West End men's hairdresser.[39] He frequently makes deductions that a woman who works for her living could not possibly make. And yet, whereas focalization in the pre-Harriet novels allows Sayers to exploit the methodological *opportunities* Peter's gender and class privilege afford him as a detective, when Sayers introduces her love story she begins using focalization to suggest Peter's methodological *limitations,* particularly as they relate to class and gender.

In *Strong Poison,* Katharine Climpson, Miss Murchison, Marjorie Phelps, Eiluned Price, Sylvia Marriott, Mrs. Pettican, Hannah Westlock, and a female manicurist all have access to valuable information, access that is a direct product of their vocations.[40] Sayers leaves no doubt that without these women's help, Peter could not have solved the case. As noted above, two of them—Miss Climpson and Miss Murchison—are focalizers, by virtue of the fact that they do some key investigative and deductive work that Peter cannot do himself. Their viewpoints are valuable not because they are women but because they are individuals informed by their particular vocations. However, the fact that they are all women calls attention to itself in the first Harriet Vane novel; previous novels in the series feature a more even distribution of female and male witnesses. The women in *Strong Poison* have specialized knowledge by virtue of their so-called women's work, and without that knowledge Peter could not make his case. In *Have His Carcase,* Sayers takes her point a step further, using predominantly internal focalization through Harriet to underscore her opportunities as well as her limitations, both of which are often consequences of her vocation.

At a crucial juncture in *Have His Carcase,* Harriet and Peter interview the same suspect. By juxtaposing these two scenes I wish to demonstrate a different way in which Sayers uses focalization to promote her feminist argument, and further, to prove that she requires the reader's attention to the romance as part of her ethical argument.

Peter and Harriet separately interview Henry Weldon. Weldon's mother was engaged to be married to the murder victim, a sleazy, Russian-born lounge lizard much younger than herself. Weldon's mother has latched onto the notion that Bolsheviks killed her fiancé. Her weepy fondness for the deceased and the foolishness of her Bolshevik theory leave her open to the sexist, condescending pity of other characters—an attitude that Harriet secretly indulges and that Peter finds tempting but appears to avoid on principle. Henry Weldon shows no such scruples. To Peter he says, "Thought I'd better push along and cheer Mother up. Stop all this nonsense about Bolsheviks. Won't do to have her wasting her time with these tom-fool notions. Enough to send the old dear clean off her rocker, you know. Once they get these notions in their heads it's a job to get rid of 'em. Form of mania, don't you think, like women's rights and crystal-gazing?" (145). In most of the previous novels, Peter is regularly given opportunities to bond with murder suspects through sexism: when a suspect makes a sexist or even misogynistic remark, Peter responds sympathetically with a view to eliciting information. Before this novel, sexism is just one among many themes Peter uses to talk to people on their own level, seemingly equivalent to discourses about motorcars, foreign policy, first editions, and fine art. This scene marks the first time in the series

Peter refuses to engage with a suspect on sexist terms, even at the risk of losing valuable information by alienating the suspect. His awareness of Harriet's politics, and the effect of those politics on his chances of marrying her, directly influences his methodology as a detective, though this fact is left up to the reader's inference. Ignoring Weldon's jab at women's rights, Peter returns to the Bolshevik theory, agreeing "cautiously that an unreasonable conviction might, in process of time, amount to an obsession." When Weldon pursues his offensive theme, "Lord Peter delicately raise[s] his eyebrows" and says nothing (146). Because Weldon is a suspect Peter considers quite unlikely to be guilty, given his alibi for the time of the murder, we might assume Peter's non-engagement with Weldon is a signal of his disinterest in Weldon's testimony. To prevent that mistake, Sayers shows Peter a few minutes later drawing Weldon out through a politically neutral discourse, man-to-man: that of hunting and fishing (147). This scene is rendered mostly through dialogue, depriving us of direct access to Peter's thoughts, which gives it even greater contrast to the later scene in which Harriet interviews the same suspect.

As Harriet's scene opens, an unusually coy, tongue-in-cheek narrative voice reports that she has purchased an afternoon frock specially for the purpose of talking with Henry Weldon during a picnic.

> The curious inhibitions which caused her to be abrupt, harsh, and irritating with Lord Peter did not seem to trouble her in dealing with Henry Weldon. For him she produced a latent strain of sweet womanliness which would have surprised Wimsey. She now selected a slinky garment, composed of what male writers call "some soft, clinging material," with a corsage which outlined the figure and a skirt which waved tempestuously about her ankles. She enhanced its appeal with an oversized hat of which one side obscured her face and tickled her shoulder, while the other was turned back to reveal a bunch of black ringlets, skillfully curled into position by the head hairdresser at the Resplendent [Hotel]. High-heeled beige shoes and sheer silk stockings, with embroidered gloves and a handbag completed this alluring toilette, so eminently unsuitable for picnicking. In addition, she made up her face with just so much artful restraint as to suggest enormous experience aping an impossible innocence, and, thus embellished, presently took her place beside Henry in the driving-seat of Mrs. Weldon's large saloon. (227–28)

Focalized through Harriet, this passage uses Sayers's usual mode (external focalization from within) to indicate Harriet's detective method—she vamps Henry Weldon to get information out of him—by describing her anticipation of what kind of feminine look will please Weldon. The first two lines of the passage also suggest that Harriet is considering how Peter and other people would perceive her dressing up for Weldon. At first it may seem that the first two lines are focalized from without, and that the adjectives belong to the narrator, not Harriet. Why would Harriet describe her principled resistance to Peter's overtures as "curious inhibitions"? Certainly this and the next line are dissonant elements in a paragraph that offers an otherwise straightforward account of Harriet's thought process. My reading, though, is that Harriet is ventriloquizing other people's criticism of her. Although she is the focalizer, she's imagining the way other people would focalize her.[41] Harriet knows that people who have seen her with Peter might well consider her resistance to his courtship as nothing but "curious inhibitions," rather than a serious feminist stance. She adds to this her uncomfortable awareness that trafficking in sexist stereotypes with Henry Weldon, using her feminine wiles to get information from a man inferior to Peter in every way, would make her resistance to Peter seem even more curious, not to mention compromise her reputation as an independent woman. Although this passage concentrates on her detective strategy it crucially demonstrates preoccupation with her relation to Peter Wimsey. It contributes more directly to the mystery plot than the romance, but it suggests that both romance and politics affect the fundamentals of the mystery plot: in this case, interviewing a suspect.

As the scene progresses Harriet flirts openly with Weldon, massaging his ego and encouraging his confidence in order to elicit information. She deliberately encourages his sexist condescension, deprecating her own abilities as she lavishly praises his, making references to how much more manly he is than Lord Peter Wimsey, pretending to agree with Weldon's contempt of his mother's foolish female ways. Unlike in the scene between Peter and Weldon, we have the advantage of free indirect discourse:

> No—Henry was really too easy. Surely even his colossal vanity could not suppose that he had really made a conquest. Yet there he sat, smiling away and almost audibly purring. No doubt he thought that Harriet Vane was any man's game. He really imagined that, placed between Lord Peter and himself, a woman could possibly—well, why not? How was he to know? It wouldn't be the first time that a woman had made a foolish choice. If anything, he was paying her the compliment of supposing that she was not mercenary. Or, horrid thought, did he expect her to be completely promiscuous? That was it—he did! (232)

Throughout the scene, free indirect discourse and focalization through Harriet give the reader reliable access to her thoughts. At the moment when Weldon tries to force himself on her physically, though, the narration shifts to focalization from without: it portrays external events and prevents access to thoughts. This formal shift prompts the reader to reconsider Harriet's earlier thoughts in a new light. Her terror leads the reader not to blame her for the assault but to recall again that she is not really a detective. Her deliberate provocation of Weldon, which contravened both her politics and her nascent romance with Peter, is so dangerous as to make her search for clues seem not worth the risk. By contrast, scenes that depict Peter making mistakes prompt the authorial audience's sympathy rather than blame, because a single mistake by an expert tends not to undermine his authority. A mistake by an amateur, such as Harriet, tends to prompt regret for the amateur's ambition: why can't she just leave the job to the experts? Furthermore, by doing away with focalization, here, Sayers prompts the reader to make an ethical judgment. Her narrative form affects the ethical dimension of her rapport with the reader.

Harriet has reversed gender stereotypes by making Weldon wash the dishes after their picnic. "She ordered him about prettily and he obeyed with delighted willingness, tucking up his sleeves and getting down to the job." But when he feels he's humored her long enough, he drops the dishes and grabs her. The narrator informs us that "[i]t was then that Harriet became really frightened" (232), but otherwise describes her from the outside, refusing the reader access to what she thinks or sees. We assume she is frightened by his attempted assault, especially given the inequality between their physical strength, and that she has lost control of the situation she once ostensibly commanded. In fact, we are led to doubt retrospectively that she ever controlled the situation, and to regret her decision to use sex to try to obtain information.

When someone responds to her scream for help, Weldon lets her go, but instead of blaming him publicly for the assault, Harriet (to our surprise) explains that she has screamed because she saw a snake. Harriet's motivation is called into question; is she covering for her attacker, and if so, why? Without any access to her thoughts, we are prompted to use what cognitive theorists (including Zunshine) call our theory of mind: to deduce Harriet's state of mind from her actions. Her sudden apparent inability to control the situation suggests that she needs more rescuing, as she did in the previous novel when Peter's detecting saved her life. Sayers ends the scene with no corrective to this suggestion. Harriet returns from the picnic visibly shaken, and goes straight to Peter, evidently seeking his reassurance (though still, we can only guess at her motivations, as she is externally focalized). Such a scare could plausibly drive a young woman into the welcoming arms of a besotted nobleman. We are given reason to hope that, in a moment of weakness, Harriet will at last show a softer side to Peter. Again, romance affects the fundamentals of the mystery.

And yet, in the pages that follow, Sayers offers the reveal: Harriet screamed not because she feared Weldon would assault her but because, unbeknownst to the reader, she saw the tattoo of a snake on his forearm (he had rolled up his sleeves to do the dishes). The tattoo is the clue that ruins his alibi for the time of the murder, and leads both Peter and Harriet to solve the mystery. By manipulating focalization at the right moment, by blocking access for just a few lines to what Harriet sees, Sayers tempts her audience to assume Harriet's vulnerability *as a woman* before reversing that assumption with a surprise. She also solidifies Harriet's credentials as an investigator (if not detective), hinting all the while at the potential for romantic détente between Harriet and Peter. Harriet's risk seems in retrospect to have been more than worth it. The scene comes to signify Harriet's competence rather than her vulnerability, and it solidifies the reader's conviction that her competence, like her vulnerability, is linked to her gender. Moreover, she has uncovered a vital clue by methods unavailable to Peter. In this scene, Harriet and Sayers have performed parallel sleights of hand, both of which validate a feminist ethics. Just as Harriet's risk seems in retrospect to have been worth it, so has Sayers's trajectory of readerly judgments, moving from condescension to admiration. In each case, we thought a woman was doing one thing when in fact she was doing another—and the other was a sign of her considerable skill.

Sayers is often quoted as saying that in order to bring Harriet and Peter together, she had to humanize Peter—she had to transform him from an improbable, two-dimensional superman into a man with foibles and insecurities. But she also needed to let Harriet's sense of grateful obligation diminish. Inequity between the two characters seems fundamental at the end of *Strong Poison*. But one by one, each of Harriet's accomplishments rectifies both characters' sense of the power imbalance between them. Thus, every time Sayers draws the reader's attention to the feminist politics of the novel, she furthers the progression of the romance plot without doing damage to the mystery plot. Even scenes such as the ones I have examined in this novel, which are explicitly devoted to the mystery plot and do not contain any overtly romantic elements, build the reader's confidence that Peter and Harriet's romance will eventually succeed.

GAUDY NIGHT begins with a nod to E. C. Bentley's *Trent's Last Case*, the 1913 Golden Age detective novel Sayers admired for its characterization, intelligent plot, and coordination of courtship with detection.[42] A conversation early in *Gaudy Night* makes reference to a "liver-fluke," alluding to a momentous conversation (in which the liver-fluke is mentioned incidentally) in the last few pages of Bentley's novel. Shortly after this passing reference, Sayers makes clear that the question posed in the first line of *Trent's Last Case* will be of central importance in her own novel. "Between what matters and what seems to matter, how should the world we know judge wisely?"

In Bentley's novel, the question operates on several registers. First, the level of character: while living, the murder victim had seemed indispensable to Wall Street's daily function; but after he died, "the world" realized that he had only seemed to matter in the grand scheme of global financial health. No one, in fact, much regretted his death, which turns out to be an important factor in the case. Second, the question pertains to the act of detection: up to the end of his career, Trent's professional expertise permits him to distinguish what matters from what masquerades as mattering, and thus to solve mysteries most of the rest of "the world" cannot. Third, it underscores the difficulty of judgment in matters of the heart: Trent decides at a crucial moment that his love for Mrs. Manderson matters more than resolving the mystery (which had initially seemed to him to matter most). Although his decision does not preclude his correct interpretation of clues, it prevents him from acting on that interpretation. Mrs. Manderson herself later reveals that what Trent had thought mattered most (protecting her from "the world"'s criticism) had seemed to matter more than it in fact did, due to a misconception she then corrected for him. Combining romance with detection in Bentley's novel means that what matters and what seems to matter are reversed and then reversed again; it is reasonable to speculate that without the romantic element, the novel might have been much more straightforward—but also impoverished. Finally, as Frank Kermode observes of *Trent*'s opening sentence, "the words refer equally to the difficulty of distinguishing what, hermeneutically, matters and does not matter in the pages that follow."[43] In both novels, protagonist and reader alike make deliberate ethical judgments that contravene the conservative status quo represented by "the world." In both novels, the romance plot is integral to those ethical judgments.

Bentley's question is echoed in *Gaudy Night*. "'But one has to make some sort of choice,' said Harriet. 'And between one desire and another, how is one to know which things are really of overmastering importance?'" (37). The question in *Gaudy Night* operates in all the same ways it does in *Trent*: it pertains to certain characters' behavior, to the act of detection, to the complications of courtship, and to the act of reading the novel. However, Sayers's authorial purposes, which are unlike Bentley's in having a feminist dimension, suggest that the act of comparing what matters with what seems to matter also involves both character and reader in ethical judgments about gender. Sayers's novel captures a historical moment that offers more options than ever for women, particularly educated women. Given that context, the authorial audience is asked to appreciate the difficulty each woman faces of deciding for herself what really matters. *Gaudy Night* is set in Shrewsbury, a fictional women's college at Oxford University, six years after universal suffrage was achieved in Great Britain and fourteen years after Oxford began granting degrees to women. If "the world" expects women to behave in certain ways according to conservative convention—one of the novel's prominent examples is marrying and putting one's family before one's career—what seems to matter may easily be mistaken for what truly matters. For some individuals, Sayers observes, what matters most is one's family. For others, career matters most, and a society that pressures women to subsume career to family can help cause those individuals tremendous unhappiness if not personal ruin. Naturally, the problem cannot be reduced to a simple binary of family and career; Harriet's ruminations in the course of the novel acknowledge a wide spectrum of potential desires, ambitions, and priorities for women in her historical moment. Moreover, the question Bentley originally posed, and that Sayers adopted, was not simply about things that either do or do not matter; the priorities that merely "seem to matter" nonetheless consume a considerable part of a person's energies.

Gaudy Night progresses through two instabilities, but unlike in most detective novels, the global instability is internal rather than external. Harriet's struggles to balance love with work, to reconcile feminist principles with the wide variety of women's actual experiences, and to examine fragments of entrenched misogyny even within herself, dominate the novel's progression. The secondary instability, that between detective and criminal, is launched early in the novel but progresses very little until Peter appears on the scene three hundred pages later to solve the mystery. The global instability is Harriet's gradual process of deciding what—in both love and the mystery at hand—is "really of overmastering importance." Part of the reason the global instability is internal is that Harriet is, once again, not a sleuth. Hers is the intelligence pitted against that of the poison pen for most of the novel, and she is explicitly appointed the task of investigating the crimes by the College Warden, but she is not a detective. Because she is a writer by trade, she records data about the case, compiles that data into a book, and studies her own text in an effort to identify the criminal. She does, of course, take steps to deduce the poison pen's identity, but she openly "disclaim[s] all pretense to detective ability in real life" and accepts the task of investigating the poison pen solely out of loyalty to the college (78). The College Warden enlists her help because she is at once a Senior Member of the college (having earned her M.A. there nine years before) and a detective novelist with some real-world experience (the mystery in *Have His Carcase*). Because she is an alumna she recognizes how catastrophic public scandal could be to a women's college. "The world" in the early twentieth century is all too ready to believe that a group of unmarried intellectual women are prone to "unnatural" and immoderate thoughts and behavior.[44] Hiring a detective to ferret out a deranged member of the otherwise integrated community would mean exposing the college's problems to an outsider and thus putting the college's credibility at risk.

The other reason the novel's global instability is internal is a consequence of Sayers's concerted effort to coordinate courtship with detection. In her essay "Gaudy Night," Sayers identifies the "theme" of both plots as being "intellectual integrity as the one great permanent value in an emotionally unstable world" (82). According to her schema, the criminal would personify "emotion revenging itself upon the intellect for some injury wrought by the intellect upon the emotions," and the startling fierceness of this conflict would be mirrored by Harriet's increasingly desperate struggle to decide whether her heart or head should prevail in her relationship with Peter. This theme, Sayers claims, is what allowed her to blend two incompatible genres successfully: "The new and exciting thing was to bring the love-problem into line with the detective-problem, so that the same key should unlock both at once. I had Harriet, feeling herself for the first time on equal ground with Peter [who is also an Oxford M.A.], seeing in the attractions of the intellectual life a means of freeing herself from the emotional obsession he produced in her, and yet seeing (as she supposed) that the celibate intellectual life rendered one liable to insanity in its ugliest form" (85). But although Sayers's choreography of the twin themes of emotion and intellect figures prominently and consistently in the novel, a close study of that binary can't satisfactorily account for the powerful ethical dimension of feminism in the novel. The novel's thematic architecture, as described by Sayers's essay, is impressive. But Sayers's more significant accomplishment is evinced by Harriet's focalized judgments as well as the ethical judgments made by the authorial audience.

Harriet's investigation of her own heart and the poison-pen mystery consists primarily of scrutinizing all members of the Shrewsbury community: students, faculty, and staff. Her observations and deductions, rendered through internal focalization, pertain as much to the mystery as to the romance. Because the poison pen exclusively targets female scholars who compete with or criticize men, Harriet is persuaded from the outset that gender relations in academia are at the mystery's core. Her college reunion offers a sterling opportunity to ponder both mystery and romance. "As regards marriage—well, here one certainly had a chance to find out whether it worked or not. Was it worse to be a Mary Attwood (née Stokes) or a Miss Schuster-Slatt? Was it better to be a Phoebe Bancroft (née Tucker) or a Miss Lydgate?" (46). The women Harriet meets at the gaudy embody a dazzling variety of possible configurations of vocation and marriage for women in that historical moment. Some have sacrificed their original vocations and made marriage their job; some have forfeited the prestige of their Oxford degrees by becoming manual laborers alongside their husbands; some have intentionally or unintentionally let childrearing supersede their prior interests; and, in a felicitous but rare case, one woman (Phoebe Bancroft) has successfully coordinated her expertise in history with her husband's in archaeology. Pursuing their complementary vocations simultaneously has required "dumping" their children "casually upon delighted grandparents before hastening back to the bones and stones" (14).

Sayers also examines relationships between vocation and marriage in unmarried women's lives: some, such as the Shrewsbury faculty, have voluntarily foregone marriage in pursuit of scholarly careers; others have formed lesbian partnerships; while still others have remained single involuntarily, finding that their Oxford degrees intimidated and eventually discouraged potential suitors. Sayers expects the reader to evaluate each of these scenarios and to be dissatisfied with the ones that waste women's potential for fulfillment. Some cases, like those of Phoebe Bancroft and the unmarried English tutor Miss Lydgate, represent positive outcomes for women: their careers thrive while their emotional lives are either moderated (Bancroft) or voluntarily subordinated (Lydgate). Other scenarios are far less pleasant: Mary Attwood's and Catherine Freemantle's formerly "brilliant" minds have atrophied as a result of deception and disuse; they are both married to men who find intelligence threatening. The history tutor, Miss Hillyard, is intellectually successful but bitterly anti-man. For hundreds of pages the reader is asked to entertain Harriet's assumption that Miss Hillyard is bitter toward men because she has not been so fortunate as to marry. Toward the novel's end Sayers reveals that Miss Hillyard has in fact chosen not to marry, thereby correcting Harriet's and the reader's sexist assumption. As she surveys the small and rarefied slice of the British population who are female Oxford scholars, Harriet remarks (as do we) on the diverse range of experience, and on the substantial likelihood of disappointment for ambitious, smart women.

Harriet plans her own future with an eye to forgetting her mortifying past experiences, welcoming the idea that academia offers women intellectual fulfillment and a community of mutual respect outside of the bonds of marriage. "To be true to one's calling, whatever follies one might commit in one's emotional life, that was the way to spiritual peace. How could one feel fettered, being the freeman of so great a city, or humiliated, where all enjoyed equal citizenship?" (29). She relishes "that scrupulous and impersonal respect for a person's mission in life which the scholarly tradition imposes" (136). She is profoundly tempted by the idea of definitively rejecting Peter's proposal and committing her life to scholarship. She is attracted to the idea of pursuing one calling to the exclusion of all others. But she is also attracted to the fantasy that a feminist marriage, should it prove to be possible, would afford both vocational calling and emotional outlet—whereas scholarship, she concludes, lacks the emotional component.

Clearly, Harriet's observations and deductions about the extended catalogue of potential options for women, married or unmarried, contribute to her soul-searching about marrying Peter, and they pertain to the mystery, insofar as the poison pen's motives consistently reference gender relations in academia. But Harriet's thoughts do more than underscore the thematic importance of gender in the novel, since she repeatedly entertains the Victorian notion that extended celibacy, particularly in intellectual women, is what has triggered the villain's demented violence. As we have seen, she accepts the job of investigating the poison pen because she wants to protect the women of Shrewsbury from potentially damaging attacks from within and from outside the college. But frequently, Harriet's desire to protect the community of women is overwhelmed by her desire to be protected from it. "'Soured virginity'—'unnatural life'—'semi-demented spinsters'—'starved appetites and suppressed impulses'—'unwholesome atmosphere'—she could think of whole sets of epithets, read-minted for circulation. Was this what lived in the tower set on the hill? . . . Must one, after all, seek a compromise [leavening vocation with marriage], merely to preserve one's sanity?" (77–78). The authorial audience is asked to adopt, at least provisionally, her inculcated fear of demented female scholars. Although the fear is never endorsed by the implied author, the novel renders it just plausible enough to warrant the authorial audience's consideration. Even the eminently sensible College Warden corroborates the possibility that female celibacy has caused the threat: "I suppose it might even be one of ourselves. That's what's so horrible. Yes, I know—elderly virgins, and all that" (79).

Harriet's desire to protect the Shrewsbury women heightens the suspense of Sayers's courtship plot, since it drives Harriet toward embracing the life of the mind and casts doubt on the romance's comic ending. By the same token, her desire to be protected from the women heightens the suspense of the mystery plot, since it underscores how, over time, mere pranks have grown frightening and dangerous—not just to Oxford but to Harriet's mental well-being, to the extent that she and other feminist women internalize such misogynist assumptions. "The situation was becoming a nightmare. Faces had grown sly and distorted overnight; eyes fearful; the most innocent words charged with suspicion. At any moment some new terror might break bounds and carry all before it. . . . She was suddenly afraid of all these women: *horti conclusi, fontis signati*, they were walled in, sealed down, by walls and seals that shut her out" (286).[45] Harriet's fear also helps precipitate the romance plot, as it induces her to seek refuge in Peter, the rational outsider with the skill and detachment needed to deduce Shrewsbury's irrational secret (365). Her decision to seek his help comes very late in the novel. In fact, Harriet knows from the novel's outset that Peter has sufficient skill to solve the mystery. And yet, after her initial effort to consult him fails due to the accident of his being out of town, Harriet intentionally neglects to request his advice for most of the novel, believing that consulting him would be a betrayal of the community's shameful secret (80, 364).

Harriet's irrational attitude toward celibate female intellectuals pervades her reasoning and leads her to mistake "what seems to matter" for "what matters." Oversimplifying women's psychology leads Harriet to make a methodological mistake in her investigation. Moreover, Sayers's fair-play mechanism depends on our following Harriet's lead, first in her mistake and then in her enlightenment. After being compelled to accept, however warily, Harriet's oversimplification, the authorial audience finds it vehemently (and persuasively) denounced by Peter, then soundly invalidated by late revelations in the mystery. The reversal of Harriet's and the authorial audience's false assumption provides at once a useful ethical corrective—that asserts the dignity of the unfairly villainized spinsters—and a clarification that makes the real villain much easier to recognize.

Sayers goes to considerable lengths to make her generic blend in the first two novels heighten her reader's attention to the romance as part of her feminist agenda, and to give the reader hope that the romance will succeed. In *Gaudy Night*, however, she offers credible reasons why the romance may not succeed. Peter has been proposing, unsuccessfully, for five years. Harriet spends the entirety of this novel preparing at last to give him a definitive answer. She knows that she values, above all else, respect from others and freedom to do her work. She also recognizes a strong need to identify herself as either married or single: living out of wedlock with Philip Boyes before the events of *Strong Poison* resulted in her feeling, even five years later, "like Aesop's bat between the birds and the beasts": a creature accepted in neither camp (290). Her discomfort with this extended indeterminacy suggests that, by the end of the novel, she will either accept Peter's proposal or reject him for good. Visiting Shrewsbury reminds her of the value of intellectual integrity, of the pleasures and compensations of heeding a single calling, and of the fresh, unlimited potential she felt nine years before, as an undergraduate student. Although Sayers gives the reader no reason to doubt that Peter will solve the mystery, the outcome of the courtship plot is not a foregone conclusion.

Harriet's fear that feminist marriage is not practicable, with Peter or anyone else, is plausible (given her past experiences), reasonable (given the historical context), and designed to be shared by the authorial audience. The reader may like Peter enormously but still cannot know whether marriage with him would be what Harriet wants. Sayers prompts her audience to share Harriet's difficulty of envisioning feminist marriage and to be pleasantly surprised by its reality at novel's end. The authorial audience cannot be ahead of Harriet in this matter; if the outcome of the courtship plot is predictable, the novel loses much of its pleasure as well as its ethical impact. Whereas *Have His Carcase* prompted our attention to the romance's progression and the novel's middle, *Gaudy Night* employs suspense to heighten our investment in the romance's closure and the novel's end.

One element contributing to the romance's suspense is Harriet's preoccupation with the notion of compromise. In a conversation with the eminently admirable Miss de Vine, a character who epitomizes intellectual integrity and the conviction of answering her calling in life, Harriet asks a question that, as we have seen, resonates powerfully throughout the novel: "'But one has to make some sort of choice,' said Harriet. 'And between one desire and another, how is one to know which things are really of overmastering importance?' 'We can only know that,' said Miss de Vine, 'when they have overmastered us.'" (37). "If you are once sure what you do want," Miss de Vine opines later, "you find that everything else goes down before it like grass under a roller—all other interests, your own and other people's" (191). Harriet, who cherishes Miss de Vine's austere commitment to a single calling, finds this an appealing and persuasive worldview. She spends the novel trying earnestly to recognize which one of her desires—work or love—is paramount. "I don't think the compromise works," she tells Peter, peevishly (68). She worries repeatedly, silently and aloud, about how to narrow her myriad interests to one. Mere pages from the end Harriet still wonders, tormentedly: "Could there ever be any alliance between the intellect and the flesh? . . . [O]ne kept the bitter, tormenting brain on one side of the wall and the languorous sweet body on the other, and never let them meet. . . . [T]o seek to force incompatibles into a compromise was madness; one should neither do it nor be a party to it. If Peter wanted to make the experiment, he must do it without Harriet's connivance" (458).

In her essay "Gaudy Night" Sayers leans too heavily, as I noted above, on the overly simple binary of emotion and intellect. Harriet would seem to follow suit, distilling complex concepts into two-sided conflicts: work versus love, body versus mind, mad versus sane, married versus unmarried, Peter versus Oxford. Whereas the power of ethical choice (and the pleasure of suspense) in the mystery plot depends on the authorial audience's temporary adoption and later recognition/rejection of Harriet's mistakes, feminist ethics and suspense in the courtship plot both function as a result of maintaining our distance from this particular mistake of hers. We must recognize that her aversion to compromise, represented by her overly simple binaries, is an ethical misjudgment and rational miscalculation. It is conceivable that the flesh-and-blood Sayers endorsed such oversimplification of the global instability in her novel. But we can be certain that the implied author of *Gaudy Night* does not.

Harriet's admiration for Miss de Vine's integrity is understandable, but it leads her to dread compromise instead of appreciating balance. The authorial audience reads around Harriet's limited understanding to recognize that the implied author champions balance throughout the novel, emphasizing how difficult it can be but how worthy of the effort. A wide variety of characters are depicted making errors of single-mindedness that must be solved through counterbalance: a student who attempts suicide is rescued and rehabilitated, reckless behavior is curbed by a hospital stay, romantic infatuation is tempered with experience, Peter stops pursuing Harriet and lets her come to him. "If she wanted an answer to her questions about Peter, there it was, quite appallingly plain. He did not want to forget, or to be quiet, or to be spared things, or to stay put. All he wanted was some kind of central stability, and he was apparently ready to take anything that came along, so long as it stimulated him to keep that precarious balance" (396). Although this passage is internally focalized through Harriet, it does not represent the moment at which she comes to understand that she and Peter want essentially the same thing, and that feminist marriage with him is not only possible but also what would make her happiest. It is the moment at which Sayers most clearly shows her own hand in critiquing the limitations of Harriet's understanding. She represents balance as akin to health for most characters in the novel, particularly her principals. In this, Miss de Vine is an exception, and perhaps less realistically rendered because of it. Harriet's difficulty in understanding the value of balancing competing claims for one's time and attention sets her at a distance from the implied author and authorial audience for the majority of the novel. The patience required of the authorial audience as we keep company with Harriet heightens our appreciation of her eventual anagnorisis and acceptance of Peter's proposal.

The ethics of fair play in Sayers's Harriet Vane novels largely accounts for her success in blending detection with romance, because she applies fair play to both genres. But this formal achievement, impressive as it is, may be considered a means to a more significant, ethical end. Sayers crafts several opportunities throughout the series for the authorial audience to establish, test, correct, and maintain ethical judgments about gender relations in the context of a politically fraught historical moment. This popular detective fiction series asks its readers to extrapolate feminist beliefs from those ethical judgments and to recognize its happy ending as feminist as well.

CHAPTER 3

The Ethics of Persuasion

"'Heard through a door,' said Sara, pouring out the coffee,
'talk sounds very odd.'"

—Virginia Woolf[1]

VIRGINIA WOOLF's 1937 novel *The Years* presents a real puzzle with its many anomalies. In it, her only bestselling novel and the last published in her lifetime, she chose not to employ what she called the "beautiful writing" characteristic of her other fiction, selecting instead stark and blunt economy of phrasing. She saturated this novel with bland verbs such as "is" and "said," electing to use few adverbs and even fewer adjectives. She peopled it with characters whose verbal self-expression (whether silent or audible) is continually interrupted. She initiated progression through conventional instabilities but then ended them abruptly and prematurely, through anticlimax or redirection. She created an ensemble cast of characters, refusing to give primary importance or appeal to any individual. Unlike her previous novels, which made famous her ability to articulate poetic vision through prose, in this one she privileged fact over vision.[2] Novels from Woolf's middle period, such as *Jacob's Room, Mrs Dalloway, To the Lighthouse,* and *The Waves,* ask us to recognize, in the words of Lily Briscoe, "that's a chair, that's a table, and yet at the same time, it's a miracle, it's an ecstasy." But in *The Years,* it seems, we find mostly just chairs and tables.

More subtly, Woolf diverges from her previous novels in establishing a new approach to narrative ethics. At first glance, the interruptions, repetitions, and seemingly purposeless divagations, particularly on weighty ethical and political subjects, make *The Years* appear to resemble her middle-period novels, which Molly Hite has recently described as "tonal labyrinths, conveying varying degrees of authoritativeness, rather than monologic statements of position." Hite argues that "exploring and even getting lost in these labyrinths allows us to experience the complexity along with the urgency of ethical and political questions," but that we cannot definitively identify the implied author's answer to any such questions.[3] It is certainly true that the implied author—and, by all accounts, the flesh-and-blood author—of *The Years* forcefully repudiates monologic proclamations in this novel. Writing in the early to mid-1930s, an increasingly hostile historical period in which the threat of fascism encroached upon daily life, Woolf abhorred rhetorical positions amplified by the "loudspeaker," endorsing instead the "human voice at its natural speaking level."[4] This novel goes well beyond its predecessors in deploring authoritarian forms of power and control, including—especially—coercive language. It is, as Melba Cuddy-Keane has asserted, a "non-coercive ethical text."[5] But although *The Years* proves unwilling to replicate the tactics of authoritarians, its non-coerciveness should not be mistaken for an unwillingness to deploy rhetoric on behalf of appropriate causes, including, in particular, feminism and anti-fascism. I contend that, unlike its predecessors in Woolf's oeuvre, this novel both raises and answers ethical questions about power and control, and that the source of such answers is demonstrably the authorial figure responsible for shaping the text.

One of the difficulties in apprehending these answers, I believe, consists in the difficulty this novel presents in identifying the authorial figure in *The Years* as an implied author. Her authority in making ethical claims through both the telling and the told is dispersed beyond the bounds of the text itself, which makes her hard to recognize as an implied author, and makes her more properly understood as what I call a *project author*. The usual techniques for recognizing authorial purpose that are employed in a rhetorical approach to narrative are largely thwarted by this novel's particular kind of difficulty. The conspicuously unsettling formal characteristics described above—false starts to inconclusive instabilities, bland diction—are surface-level indications of an authorial figure not only unfamiliar (for readers acquainted with the career author) but also dispersed (regardless of readers' previous reading experience).

Taken together, Woolf's subtle ethical shift and her adoption of unusual narrative techniques call attention to an authorial figure startlingly anomalous in her oeuvre. Once our attention turns from the implied author and career author to the project author, the subtler effects of her urgent ethical paradigm in the project are revealed, and an intense, persuasive argument takes shape.

The Years is less a tonal labyrinth than a long hallway of closed and partially open doors, through which snatches of conversation can be overheard. Its narrative ethics is best understood when readers recognize and acknowledge the murmurs or echoes of the novel's drafts in manuscript, despite Woolf's figuratively closing the doors to them. Although the final, printed novel has a coherent ethics that rewards interpretation, the novel in relation to its drafts has a different and paradoxically more determinate ethical significance. Woolf developed the ethics of this novel over time as she wrote, rewrote, and revised her manuscript. What many call her "intentions" in the narrative changed radically in that time, and the reasons both for her intentions and her changes have received much scholarly speculation, though there exists no definitive evidence for those explanations. Indeed, speculation about why Woolf revised *The Years* as she did fueled a brand-new critical focus on textual studies by feminist scholars. Textual criticism as feminist practice gave rise to more than a decade of productive scholarship, a body of work I will engage with later in this chapter.

All who approach the question of how and why Woolf revised these drafts as she did can agree that the published edition of *The Years* is more enigmatic, both ethically and aesthetically, than its drafts, and that her intentions seem clearer in the drafts because her narrative voice is more "didactic" and "authoritative." This enigmatic quality stems in large part from the peculiar way in which Woolf compresses, distorts, or altogether silences exhortations in her manuscripts to render them non-coercive. Most readers can also agree that one of the factors that made revision hardest was Woolf's serious investment from the outset in blending two distinct genres, novel and essay, into a text that manages to coordinate indirection with argumentation. For many readers, though, the published novel is not just challenging and enigmatic; it's also not as appealing as Woolf's other novels. It is aesthetically inferior—it has lower narrativity, less beauty, less formal coherence—and is much more equivocal ideologically. Interpretations that focus only on the final, printed novel yield an implied author who seems significantly less impressive than the career author Woolf had established up to that point. Attending instead to the project author, who produces a series of unpublished and finally published drafts, yields a Woolf with not only comparable powers but also an admirable dedication to ethical argument through art unprecedented in her other works.

In this chapter I restrict my attention to three documents: the transcription of the first two volumes of holograph manuscript, published by Mitchell Leaska as *The Pargiters;* the remainder of the holograph, made available to me at the Berg Collection at the New York Public Library; and the first U.S. edition of the novel, published in 1937 and reprinted in 2008.[6] If we compare the narrative ethics of the drafts with that of the novel, we find the best evidence for understanding, if not her intentions (as that word implies the flesh-and-blood author's private thoughts) then her rhetorical purpose in revision, especially her evolving answer to the question of how one may persuade without coercion. Whereas previous scholarship has worked to establish why the flesh-and-blood author revised as she did, drawing fulsomely on diary entries and personal letters as evidence, for my purposes the more important question is *how* she revised and what that tells us about the project author's ethics. I read the novel by examining the authorial figure responsible for creating and refining it over a series of drafts: a figure whose purposive craft extends beyond the bounds of the "particular text," the "completed artistic whole" ordinarily seen as the domain of the implied author. In order to make this argument I amend the implied author concept as posited by Wayne C. Booth (1983) and revised by James Phelan (2005), arguing that the concept of project author is crucial to narrative ethics in *The Years.*

Interpreting the ethics of the telling in *The Years* as a standalone artifact, as the creation of an implied author, yields fairly good results, but reading it in relation to its drafts, as the creation of a project author, yields much better results. Although the rhetorical purposes of repetition can be traced to the published novel's implied author, on silence and compression as techniques the model of the implied author is of limited use. One cannot prove a negative, or at any rate, one cannot empirically examine absence without comparing it to plausible presence. Nor can one usually definitively establish that a silence or absence is deliberate choice, design, rather than oversight or omission. Moreover, Gerald Prince's concept of unnarration produces much better results for understanding narrators than it does implied authors. Considering the project author of *The Pargiters* and *The Years* permits a more thorough understanding of the ethics of persuasion, dispersed as it is over a series of drafts that feature a variety of persuasive strategies.

Furthermore, there is real utility in separating the implied from the flesh-and-blood author. In ascribing intentionality to an implied author we accept, by definition of the term, that rhetorical design can be attributed to a figure who created the text, someone who assumed that narrative meaning is both communicable to audiences and shareable among them. The vast majority of a writer's experience is tangential if not irrelevant to her creation of a single work; the notion of an implied author "streamlines" a much more complex human being. The rhetoric and ethics of *The Years* was created by that streamlined figure. On the other hand, practitioners of textual criticism, genetic criticism, fluid text editing, and, to a large extent, feminist criticism would all agree that the physical marks on the pages of manuscript and typescript were created by the human being.

In many instances, records of manuscript revisions substantially enhance interpretation, both of the work itself and of the progress a flesh-and-blood person made in honing the implied author of the eventually printed text. But in special cases, when revisions pare down a manuscript's significance, the project author's accomplishment is richer than the implied author's is. In these cases, authorial diaries and letters, being artifacts of the flesh-and-blood author, cannot offer definitive explanations for why a text was revised as it was. Rhetorical theory seeks to explain what is realized in the textual construction itself. In some cases, a rhetorical approach could be best accomplished by giving close attention to each of several drafts, including but not especially the published one. I do not suggest that all texts for which we have records of manuscript revision are productive opportunities for analysis of the project author. I believe, though, that in such special cases as I have just described, reading in terms of the project author can offer a substantial interpretive and theoretical advantage.

Conceiving of the authorial persona as a project author rather than implied author allows me to dislodge the printed novel from its privileged position in that project. It also allows me to demonstrate how this particular novel succeeds rhetorically in making a persuasive feminist argument through certain formal strategies, in its context in an oeuvre whose previous works obscure authoritative directions, and with its project author's enigmatic but urgent ethical vision. Further, it creates some productive connections between historically grounded textual criticism, feminism, and narrative theory.

MUCH SCHOLARSHIP on the novel tells the same story about its genesis. As World War II approached, so the story goes, Woolf wrote an anti-fascist novel. She wanted to create a persuasive, feminist, pacifist argument through art, but at same time to avoid "preaching," "propaganda," "being too didactic." This original intention was consistent with her goals in *A Room of One's Own,* to which this new work was a sequel. Late in 1931 she composed two volumes of manuscript—over 60,000 words—in a flurry of enthusiasm. She alternated feminist essays with narrative segments, calling it a novel-essay. Unfortunately, for obscure reasons about which Woolf scholarship provides virtually endless speculation, her generic hybrid didn't work.[7] She ultimately dismantled the hybrid, radically changed her technique in the narrative, and, after six years of writing, cutting, and rewriting, published a novel vastly different from the project she had begun. The creator of this work appears to be worlds apart from the witty and self-possessed creator of *A Room of One's Own.* Despite her early enthusiasm, her later diary entries show her calling the project a "failure," "impossible," "incredibly dreary," "that interminable book," "my vomit." Woolf's reasons for rejecting the hybrid and fundamentally rewriting the manuscript were not documented nor are they readily apparent through textual analysis. The authorial persona responsible for those radical and, in some cases, infelicitous changes is the project author: the figure who emerges when we take a rhetorical approach to interpreting the relationship between manuscript and published novel.

Woolf's manuscript has been interpreted most often by scholars who locate intentionality in the flesh-and-blood author, often through personal documents rather than in attentive rhetorical interpretations of the texts themselves.[8] Grace Radin, in her book-length study of the "evolution of a novel," poses the question I want answered: "The holograph, which is many times the length of *The Years,* is replete with details that have been expunged from the final text. What, we may ask, is its relationship to the novel that finally emerged?" But Radin's immediate answer to her own question—"Some clues may be found in Woolf's journal entries"[9]—is telling in its reliance on biographical documents. I admire the way Radin "projects" certain episodes deleted from the manuscript and galleys "back into the novel" as she gives a feminist reading of the project as a whole, but all of her larger claims about Woolf's purposes for revising as she did depend directly on the personal correspondence and diary, as well as on speculation.[10]

From the late 1970s through the early 1990s, feminist textual critics interpreted Woolf's novels as palimpsests, looking for "submerged" voices in the published texts. These critics, as Brenda Silver has noted, "shattered the idea of the stable text itself. Once we are aware of the manuscript versions and their alternate readings, it becomes impossible, except by a willed act of commitment to a particular interpretative stance, not to be conscious of their presence within the 'final' text."[11] Their approaches to this work were similar to the one I'm pursuing, but with two major differences: they typically adopted a poststructuralist framework, highlighting textual indeterminacy and the purported role of Woolf's unconscious mind; and they put a higher priority on questions and answers about the flesh-and-blood author than I want to. Such an approach highlights the external pressures that might coerce a flesh-and-blood author to curtail or efface her original intent to conform to more normative expectations. My conception of the project author, however, focuses exclusively on purposive manuscript changes. While such changes may be influenced in part by external forces, I regard all decisions of the project author to be determinate through empirical comparison of draft and published textual variants.

Radin and Leaska, in their critical editions of selections from drafts of *The Years*, both assert that Woolf altered her "original intention" as she revised by "pargeting," or whitewashing, over her explicit feminist statements with more evasive and oblique language.[12] Their claims formed part of the contemporary debate over whether Woolf had concealed her authorial voice against her better judgment, through self-censorship, or *because* of her better judgment, through a carefully orchestrated strategy. But subsequent critics, spurred by Jerome McGann's influential critique of authorial intention,[13] superseded this debate by questioning one of its premises: that drafts and publications have a teleological relationship.[14] These critics recognized draft sequences instead as "social texts," acknowledging the wide variety of factors beyond their own individual agency that influence flesh-and-blood authors' revision practices, such as editorial interventions, publishing standards, social norms, political climates, and economic forces. The social text is multiple; its component parts all command equal scholarly attention and can be placed in a variety of sequences. "Rather than searching for the 'authentic' version," Susan Stanford Friedman advocated regarding "all versions as part of a larger composite, palimpsestic text whose parts or imperfectly erased layers interact according to a psycho-political dimension."[15]

The palimpsest model of feminist narrative accounts extremely well for the many travails facing a woman writer hoping to surmount patriarchal obstacles to publication, whether they be male control of printing presses, misogynist attitudes toward women's intelligence, internalized masculinist prejudices, etc. The process by which Woolf chose to silence some aspects of her original manuscript in order to produce *The Years* doubtless involved influences of which she may not herself have been fully aware. But surely some of those choices belonged to her peculiar intelligence alone, and I have no wish to emphasize the obstacles to her genius rather than her genius. My concept of the project author is a study of the rhetoric of the tactical differences between manuscript and published text, rather than an attempt to excavate authorial intentions that were never explicitly recorded. The palimpsest model posits an ineradicable trace of the myriad influences that combined to enable a social text, no matter how tenacious the patriarchal adversity ranged against its completion. The project author concept lets me study an author's rhetorical tactics as she adjudicates between the potential and the possible. Neither model can produce a stable text or a definitive case for authorial intention. But both give needed attention and respect to intermediate drafts, and both can help recuperate the full range of accomplishments that authors—many of them women—accomplish as they negotiate a sometimes difficult path to publication.

The conventions of narratology dictate that the most convincing rhetorical analyses of *The Years,* while they acknowledge important differences between manuscript and novel, give cursory attention to the former, since their main objective is to interpret the latter. Rachel Blau DuPlessis notes that, "[i]n keeping with [a] dialogic stance, the [published] text does not privilege its own ideological positions. This explains why *The Years* looks a little unconstructed in its nonforceful resistance of unitary focus, and can also explain Woolf's very wrenching rejection of a brilliant mixed-genre design for the novel."[16] Susan Lanser likewise claims that "the most visible and assertive authorial voice in all of Woolf's fiction was . . . a voice she eventually sacrificed, in this case when she revised her unfinished essay-novel . . . into *The Years*" (112).[17] Both regret the loss of that voice, but they construct a sensible rationale whereby cutting the essays was rhetorically strategic rather than self-censoring. They reason that although Woolf's essays seem to be admirable, feminist denunciations of authoritarian oppression, quite possibly Woolf decided they were specimens of the very "patriarchal voice" she had set out to censure. While neither Lanser nor DuPlessis relies on the implied author concept, both want to account for rhetorical design, and both see the value of positing a coherent self orchestrating that design. The manuscript is perceived as interesting primarily for its deletions rather than its overall rhetorical design, and those deletions help them ascribe intentionality to the novel's implied author.

The foundation for conceiving any implied author is the final, published text,[18] or what Booth called the "completed artistic whole." But I find some wiggle room between Booth's original definition and Phelan's new one. Booth insists that the implied author is superior to the real writer because the implied author is by definition the end product of a series of felicitous revisions, of increasingly effective literary masking. In Booth's 2005 example, Saul Bellow claims that the act of revising a novel means "wiping out the parts of myself I don't like," and Booth declares himself grateful for Bellow's effort: "Through my years of knowing him personally I encountered other versions that nobody would like—Bellow-versions that, if allowed to dominate his novels, would have totally destroyed them. What's more, those who have studied his manuscripts (as I have not) find confirmation for that claim: he chose, from thousands of pages, a few hundreds that presented IAs he really liked, and that I love."[19] Phelan's redefinition includes no stipulation that revision makes the implied author superior to the real writer. He writes, "The implied author is a streamlined version of the real author, an actual or purported subset of the real author's capacities, traits, attitudes, beliefs, values, and other properties that play an active role in the construction of the particular text."[20] Although "particular text" doubtless refers to the "completed artistic whole," the particular *published* version, in many cases revisions to the holograph, galleys, and page proofs play an active role in the construction of a particular text. Especially as Phelan's definition locates the implied author outside of the text, I see no reason to exclude those factors in an implied author's construction of a particular text. Indeed, Phelan's definition leaves room for acknowledgment of drafts, but to my mind his methodology is not as supple an instrument for engaging fully with the rhetoric and ethics of drafts. As Booth well knew, not all textual variants are deleted because they are inferior; authors revise based on a wide range of calculations. Some texts—some implied authors—are richer when we acknowledge the echoes of previous versions, of deleted variants, in the particular text. As it stands now, rhetorical theory is not listening to those echoes.

I see no need to fix what isn't broken—the redefined implied author concept works beautifully—but I would like to posit the value of studying that concept's counterpart in manuscript revision, while keeping that figure theoretically separate from the flesh-and-blood writer. The creative figure responsible for a series of revisions, from manuscript through printed book, is a protean entity whose construction of a text has rhetorical importance and deserves closer attention by rhetorical theorists.

The difficulty is, of course, that she is protean at best, and incoherent at worst. The value of the implied author of a finished text is that she is just coherent enough to start conversations among readers who, for all their differences, can join a single audience and share interpretations. It seems unwise to posit that an evolving manuscript has a single implied author. I do not claim that every mark in a series of manuscripts reflects cohesive intentionality. Nor does it seem especially fruitful to posit one implied author per manuscript stage, so that we'd be giving the galleys and the page proofs their own respective implied authors. And it means, of course, that I'm positing a reading not available to the strictly constructed authorial audience of *The Years*. Instead, the audience I'm positing has read the unpublished drafts along with *The Years*. But this isn't so strange—after all, readings of the career author depend on how much a given author's work one has encountered, and we regularly reconstruct authorial audiences (not flesh-and-blood readers) as counterparts to career authors. We tend to mine holograph manuscripts and revisions for bits and pieces; we don't tend to construct readings of them as whole entities, nor do we create rhetorical readings that lay manuscript next to published book. In what follows I will outline three techniques Woolf uses consistently to adjust the ethical ramifications of her drafts. I will then offer rhetorical readings of the manuscript in comparison to their counterparts in the published novel, making a case for the utility of the project author concept as it pertains to narrative ethics.

MANY of Woolf's formal choices in the novel follow from her preoccupation with a question: How does one make a strong ethical argument without being didactic? How does one assert an ethical vision without imposing it? Cuddy-Keane notes that Woolf's aversion to didacticism "was not a matter of prejudice, nor of taste, but of ethics. Excising didacticism was one of Woolf's fervent aims in her revision of *The Years*—and it was perhaps her successful accomplishment of her goal that makes this such an intense and cryptic novel to read."[21] Elsewhere, Cuddy-Keane argues that one of Woolf's most effective rhetorical strategies, dialogism, depends for both effectiveness and ethicality on granting the audience freedom to see for themselves.[22] In her exegesis of the rhetoric and ethics of three feminist essays by Woolf, including *A Room of One's Own* and *Three Guineas,* she claims that, "with her faith in the reader's active engagement, Woolf rejects monologic peroration because she also believes it fails to be rhetorically persuasive. Our ideas, she asserts, tend to develop through resistance and reaction. . . . Preaching locks the reader into either a passive or an oppositional role; the alternative is a discourse that defines a space for exchange and negotiation" (144).[23] *A Room of One's Own* and *Three Guineas,* it is often acknowledged, are above all else in Woolf's oeuvre most intimately related to *The Years* in their feminist conviction, their ethical stances, and their rhetorical designs. Although she does not explicitly acknowledge *The Years* in this essay, Cuddy-Keane's rhetorical analysis applies equally well to it. She goes on to observe that

> a less obviously mediated dialogue creates a greater challenge for the reader. No longer situated as a spectator witnessing a debate, the reader undergoes repeated repositionings; it is as if the reader had just got comfortably settled in one easy chair only to be told to shift to another on the opposite side of the window. . . . [N]ot only is a new point of view introduced, but the new perspective also exposes the first one from a new angle. Furthermore, repeated shifts foreground the process of shifting; that is, repeated redefinition prompts the reader to consider the significance of interpretive structures in the creation of meaning, in the assigning of value. (139)

What one critic has called *The Years's* "monotonous repetitiveness" and "purposeless, self-duplicating actions"[24] Cuddy-Keane would recognize as "repositionings" that expose prior iterations "from a new angle." Accordingly, a number of critics have claimed that *The Years* provides its readers with more to do than its drafts; they describe the novel as having more gaps to fill, more puzzles to solve, more patterns to recognize. They frequently quote a journal entry from 1933, written during Woolf's concentrated period of *Years* revision, in which she admires Turgenev's "idea that the writer states the essential and lets the reader do the rest."[25] Negotiation of patterns in this novel is one overt manifestation of ethical reading practices.

In the published version of *The Years, repetition* is one of Woolf's three most prevalent formal strategies for rendering an ethics of the telling and the told, and the one that has received the most critical attention.[26] On the level of the told, characters encounter parallel iterations of similar situations; their utilitarian routines play out over and over again on a daily basis over the decades, as a long sequence of snapshots reveals; they repeat phrases, concepts, and even whole conversations with only minor differences. On the level of the telling, Woolf employs consistent, often mundane diction to depict characters and events. She repeats phrases, images, and ideas—sometimes with interesting differences and sometimes not, but always with the effect of repositioning the reader's vantage. For instance, she provides aesthetic continuity throughout the novel by repeatedly punctuating intradiegetic focalization of personal interactions with strikingly extradiegetic perspectives on the weather and changing seasons, drawing as much attention to the repeated act of telling about the weather as to the weather itself.

By repositioning the reader in relation to both telling and told, Woolf prompts an ethical reading of her repetitions. By repeating a motif or situation multiple times with small differences, and thus by foregrounding the process of telling, she compels the reader to consider her reasons for telling in this way. As Cuddy-Keane puts it, "[R]epeated redefinition prompts the reader to consider the significance of interpretative structures in the creation of meaning, in the assigning of value."[27]

Silence is a second prevalent formal strategy in the published novel, again deployed in both the telling and the told. This strategy has received much less critical attention than repetition, and none as it pertains to narrative ethics. Instances of silence on the level of characters and events abound. Young Maggie says nothing when presented with an unwelcome birthday gift, prompting her mother to "suppl[y] the words she should have spoken" (114); nearly all the characters, from time to time, let their sentences trail off into silence, even in the midst of conversation; Martin spends his lunch with Sara angry that "it was impossible to talk . . . conversation was impossible" (219, 221); and North thinks to himself that "there's something true—in the silence perhaps" (324). In many instances, a character's silence signifies his or her integrity, usually consisting in an unwillingness to impose one's views upon others. Strategic silence can be a means of avoiding dominating others, of counterbalancing in private discourse the excesses of the "loudspeaker" of propaganda and persuasion in public discourse.[28] It also allows Woolf to reposition the reader's vantage more fluently than using the loudspeaker would have done.

On the level of the telling, silence results from two dominant techniques: the narrator's avoidance of commentary and her use of summary. These techniques may seem at first not to count as silences. When one compares the novel to others in Woolf's oeuvre, it is unsurprising that the narrative voice does not feature evaluative commentary, and that it frequently summarizes complex events rather than dramatizing them. *The Years* is a fine example of what many have called "impersonal narration" and what Lanser terms "covert authoriality: the illusion of 'effacement' that is constructed from a suppression of narrative self-consciousness, of contact between narrator and narratee, and of explicit markers of narrative stance."[29] The absence of any particular narrative technique, particularly in a context of multiple narratives lacking that same technique, can scarcely be called a *silence*. But whereas this feature of the novel is consistent with her previous publications, it is strikingly, famously inconsistent with its draft versions, which feature overt authorial commentary. Only when one knows such commentary was deleted can one perceive its absence as a silence. Hermione Lee observes that Woolf's revisions were calculated in particular to mute her political voice:

> This voice [in her diary]—enraged, appalled at its own helplessness—emerges only in fragments in the published novel. There is certainly a political diagnosis in *The Years*, which sees the fabric of society as a constructed pattern. So it draws analogies between the exploitation of servants, the struggle for education by the working man and the middle-class daughter, anti-Semitism, the social uses of religion, and sexual oppression and hypocrisy. According to this analysis, the family home operates in exactly the same way as public institutions, and both are products of capitalist imperialism. But this point of view is only mutedly and evasively expressed. It is telling that the writers who might voice it are silenced in the move from *The Pargiters* to *The Years*. Sara and North are both authors in the first version, but they are made voiceless.[30]

Woolf's replacement of dramatized scenes with summaries also works as a form of silence. In the holograph manuscript, Bobby's letter to Eleanor describing his harrowing adventures in the Indian jungle is quoted at much greater length than it is in the published novel. In manuscript, Eleanor focalizes the passage, reading the letter while riding in a hansom cab.

> 'I took my rifle in case I saw any deer. Also there was said to be a tank in the jungle where the peacocks came . . ." Eleanor looked out of the window. They were trotting down Oxford Street, past [illegible]. "The jungle at this point forms a triangle so"—here was a diagram—"with the rest home at the apex, by the cross well I walked for perhaps half an hour, north, and then it struck me that . . . I could I thought I would try to strike across to the place where I took the tank to be. I found myself in the middle of a thick jungle. Imagine me in a thicket of brambles, with thorns about three inches long closing over my head. It got thicker & thicker."[31]

Eleanor's perspective coexists with Bobby's; his voice is interrupted by narration of her perspective, but the letter is quoted verbatim over three densely written manuscript pages. In the published novel, Bobby's (renamed as Martin) voice dwindles in relation to Eleanor's summary.

> She read again: "I found myself alone in the middle of the jungle. . . ."
> But what were you doing? she asked.
> She saw her brother; his red hair, his round face; and the rather pugnacious expression which always made her afraid that he would get himself into trouble one of these days. And so he had, apparently.
> "I had lost my way, and the sun was sinking," she read.
> "The sun was sinking. . . ." Eleanor repeated, glancing ahead of her down Oxford Street. . . . Martin was in the jungle alone, and the sun was sinking. What happened next? "I thought it better to stay where I was." So he stood in the midst of little trees alone, in the jungle; and the sun was sinking. (101)

Not only is Martin's voice controlled through editing; his extended, dramatic rendering in the manuscript of his vulnerability, resourcefulness, and, ultimately, his sense of foreignness in the Indian jungle supplies a vivid critique of imperialism silenced by the summary. Eleanor's silent questions—What were you doing? What happened next?—imply some impatience with the pace of Martin's storytelling, underscoring the low narrativity of his account and drawing attention away from its muted political dimensions.

Finally, Woolf's decision to compress the fulsome detail of her manuscript into the novel's sparse depictions is a third rhetorical strategy with particular ethical significance. Of the three strategies, *compression* contributes most to the intensity of the narrative's ethics, because so much meaning hangs on so few words, and the reader's active negotiation of that meaning can lead to ethical responsiveness in turn. Compression resembles summary in that it diminishes prolix manuscript into spare revision, but it is distinct from summary in that it freights the remaining details with extra significance. In Eleanor's summary of Bobby's letter, the imperialist critique is simply silenced. We can access that critique by recourse to the manuscript, but it appears nowhere in the novel. By contrast, an instance of compression leaves a remnant of significance intact in the final version. Recourse to the manuscript allows fuller appreciation of that significance, but if one reads the novel on its own, some hint of meaning remains perceptible.

Compression, more so than silence or repetition, distributes the full ethical effect of the scene across its several versions in the project. For example, the manuscript's rendering of a conversation in 1910 between

Rose and her first cousins Maggie and Elvira records every step of a repetitive, meandering argument about feminist politics. Although they are related, Rose has not met her cousins for many years, as the sisters have been living abroad. As outsiders, they find British politics confusing and frustrating; the well-informed political activist Rose finds herself in a position to answer their questions about poverty, suffragism, and abortion. When the conversation lingers over the issue of women's right to go outside unchaperoned, Rose blushes and says that if she had a daughter, she would not give her that freedom. Rose's blush and remark explicitly refer to an earlier scene, which I will explicate later in this chapter, in which, as a ten-year-old child, she walked alone unsupervised and suffered violent consequences. The manuscript's dinner scene both records political arguments and demonstrates their force with examples from earlier scenes.

In the manuscript, Rose's, Maggie's, and Elvira's respective political views are articulated and clarified at considerable length. But in the novel, the political has become exclusively personal. Woolf compresses a wide-ranging political discussion of civic opportunities for women into a conversation about circumscribed opportunities for certain members of the Pargiter family. As the cousins catch up on each other's news, Woolf compresses thirty years of social and civic progress (or, sometimes, the lack thereof) into personal histories. Rose thinks to herself, "They talked as if they were speaking of people who were real, but not real in the way in which she felt herself to be real. It puzzled her; it made her feel that she was two different people at the same time; that she was living at two different times at the same moment. She was a little girl wearing a pink frock; and here she was in this room, now" (158–59). The significance in the novel of Rose's being "two different people at the same time" deftly communicates the character's conscious synthesis of Victorian and Edwardian societies, and Woolf locates that synthesis in her extended metaphor about the family as British society. But as the conversation in manuscript takes a diachronic view not just of societal norms but also of political upheaval, alluding to specific types of violence and injustice against women, Woolf compresses her larger argument that patriarchal violence manifests both at home and in society at large.[32]

WOOLF'S ethics of persuasion operates on the level of sentence, paragraph, and scene through techniques such as repetition, silence, and compression. Larger narrative units, such as chapters and major components of narrative progression, employ those techniques as well. But these alterations on a larger scale create some anomalies, even mysteries, in both the telling and the told. For the remainder of the chapter, I will offer a reading of the manuscript's narrative progression in comparison to that of the novel, hoping both to illuminate the ethical consequences of her revisions and to interpret some dissonant moments in *The Years* that previous scholarship has not accounted for. In the manuscript's first chapter, an overtly authorial voice addresses a specifically characterized narratee: young professional women, members of the London and National Society for Women's Service, who are purportedly attending a lecture given by Woolf herself.[33] "Believe that I am trying to speak the truth," she asks them. "Acquit me of the desire simply to seduce and to flatter and to bring you round to my own way of thinking by means of flattery and seduction. The phrase that I have just used, for example—that I am grateful to you for earning your livings, that I respect you, that if I could help you, I would—is not flattery; it is strictly true. No other audience would have overcome my belief that speech making is an effervescence of foam—intoxicating of vanity, obstructive of truth" (1.6 [*P* 5]). Woolf here collapses the distance between author and speaker. She emphasizes a desire to be perceived as sincere. She presents herself as deliberately employing a medium she distrusts, at the request of a particular audience, because it is the mode she believes will best support and educate that group. She explicitly states the goals of her argument—"I wish to discuss professions in general and to justify my statement that, in trying to earn your living professionally, you are doing work of enormous importance"—as well as the primary warrant underlying that argument: "We cannot understand the present if we isolate it from the past" (1.12 [*P* 8]). Furthermore, she defends her decision to mix her genres: "If you object that fiction is not history, I reply that though it would be far easier to write history—'In the year 1842 Lord John Russell brought in the Second Reform Bill' and so on—that method of telling the truth seems to me so elementary, and so clumsy, that I prefer, where truth is important, to write fiction" (1.13 [*P* 9]). Actual readers, encountering these rhetorical moves not in a speech but in a novel-essay hybrid, pretend to inhabit the position of Woolf's narratee, thereby joining what Peter Rabinowitz has named the narrative audience.[34] But they simultaneously inhabit her authorial audience, which in this case is substantially different from the narrative audience. In fact, we find here a much greater distance between authorial and narrative audiences than any that exists in Woolf's published fiction. The authorial audience of this manuscript is not necessarily young, female, or professional. It is older than the narrative audience, of indeterminate gender, and capable of recognizing a vast array of literary and historical allusions the narrative audience can't understand. It observes the speaker's educational act from the outside; it is not the ostensible target of education.

The authorial audience recognizes that Woolf's argument is textual rather than spoken aloud and that it is penned by a flesh-and-blood celebrity who is, at least technically, distinct from the speaker. Further, it understands that the generically hybrid text, whose claim and reasons are nonfictional but whose evidence is fictional, is likely to be the origin of its own evidence. In other words, the authorial audience suspects that "The Pargiters" has been written for the occasion of serving as evidence, and is therefore a flexible rhetorical tool at the project author's disposal; the narrative audience believes it is a manuscript previously penned by the speaker. The narrative audience thus assumes the speaker to have constraints on her argumentation that the authorial audience suspects she does not have.

"We must forget that we are, for the moment, ourselves," Woolf tells her narratee (dispensing advice the narrative audience takes and the authorial audience does not[35]). "We must become the people that we were two or three generations ago. Let us be our great grandmothers. But as this being somebody else is not part of your profession—it would be a very serious drawback in some of them, I imagine . . . I am going to take the liberty of effecting this transformation for you. I am going to read you chapters from an unpublished novel which I am in the process of writing, called "The Pargiters." . . . [I]f I select the Chapter which deals with the Pargiters in 1880, I ought to be able to show you what you were like fifty years ago: to provide that perspective which is so important for the understanding of the present" (1.12–13 [P 8–9]). Older than the narrative audience, the authorial audience recognizes its counterpart will have difficulty imagining life in the 1880s. This is the foundation of Woolf's instructional move: she asks her actual reader to be both a person trying actively, with difficulty, to imagine something as well as a person who has little reason to find that imaginative act difficult. The world being imagined is specifically one in which women have far fewer opportunities than they do in the 1930s. But as the narrative audience enacts that difficulty, the authorial audience recognizes that the imaginative act has ideological value.

Authoritative direct address characterizes the manuscript's first chapter, which takes the form of an essay. The next chapter, purportedly an extract from somewhere in the middle of a multivolume novel titled "The Pargiters," employs impersonal narration, predominantly external focalization, and very few signals of any conventional narrative progression. Eleven characters are named in rapid succession. Their thoughts and behavior are mostly externally focalized rather than explained. The young female characters, in particular, seem restless, bored, and inhibited. Instabilities among characters are alluded to but not developed. The speaker from chapter 1 interrupts twice—"I skip the next few pages which describe how at last the kettle boiled" and, later on, "this has been described in volume three" (1.17, 1.18 [P 12, 13]). These interruptions call still further attention to the chapter's low narrativity.

The narrative audience of the first essay, pretending to be twenty-something young women of the 1930s tasked with becoming their own great-grandmothers, must in the first fictional chapter pretend to imagine themselves as twenty-something young women in 1880. The narrative audience is expected to find fulsome detail in this novel of fact inherently interesting, since such detail aids them in their double pretense. The authorial audience is under no such obligation, and may find—as do many readers of the published *Years*—that extremely protracted description of material conditions only exacerbates the manuscript's low narrativity. The unadorned chairs and tables alluded to at the beginning of my chapter confront the authorial audience starkly, without apparent figurative meaning at the novel's outset. "She then went to the window & drew the curtains. They swung with a familiar click along the brass & soon the windows were obscured by sculptured folds of claret coloured plush. The two lamps made yellow pools of light upon the two drawing room tables" (1.24–25 [P 19]).

As these details accumulate, however, it becomes clear that the chairs and tables, representative of the family's material circumstances, help explain the young Pargiter women's restlessness. With the exception of Eleanor, whose charity work outside the home draws her family's indulgent condescension, the girls are confined to the house, discouraged even from peeking out the window, let alone physically escaping (as Rose does, to her later regret). Material reminders of their terminally ill mother, who is now confined to an upstairs bed, fill the house: her idealized portrait as a young girl, her writing desk and stationery, her tea set and invalid's tray. Physical artifacts mutely signal an ideological distance between the confined domain of the Victorian mother, lingering on the verge of extinction, and the girls' suppressed potential. Actively identifying with the Pargiter girls means acknowledging the suffocating closeness of confinement.[36] Although both authorial and narrative audiences are capable of recognizing the seriousness of the girls' suppressed potential, the authorial audience alone knows that Woolf has customized these fictional details to suit her purposes. This audience comes to recognize that physical details have a motivated, self-conscious rhetorical and ethical significance; that they serve a political purpose. Narrative progression in the manuscript develops from a tension between the narrator's and implied author's expectations for, respectively, the narrative and authorial audiences.

The first fictional chapter appears designed to raise questions for two separate audiences that the subsequent chapter, essay 2, will answer. Essay 2 begins with another direct address of the narratee. "Those young women, Milly, Delia, and Eleanor rouse pity and contempt in you. I have only been able to give an outline of them. . . . Why, you may ask, did they not go to College? But if you think for a moment, you will remember that the women's colleges were only just in existence; there was a great prejudice moreover against them" (1.34 [*P* 28]). The narrative audience needs this reminder because it consists of women who have already made a success of an independent profession, and who are too young to have much institutional or political memory. The second essay ascribes to the narrative audience inadequate ethical judgments at odds with the ones the authorial audience makes. The authorial audience certainly doesn't have contempt or pity for the characters, and they have no intention of blindly mapping the gender politics of the 1930s onto the 1880s. But the real readers trying to inhabit the authorial audience may not be women or sympathetic to feminism. Even if we posit that the narrator is underestimating her narrative audience, talking down to them, we must recognize that the mental effort required to play three readerly positions at once—authorial audience, narrative audience, and narrative audience's pretense—promotes the novel's progression through tension, and that the tension centers on the project author's investment in a feminist argument. Ethical repositioning is accomplished not through shifts in focalization but through prompting the reader's simultaneous enactment of different attitudes. The ethics of the telling in the manuscript depends on the project author's feminist premises and the authorial audience's enactment of an increasingly feminist awareness in response.

Among all of Woolf's revisions to this project, the one most often regretted is her excision of authoritative, overt feminist statements, or what Julia Briggs has called the "less inhibited and more fully articulated impatience with social prejudices" found in the manuscript.[37] Woolf's third essay in the holograph manuscript provides the most apt example of that narrative voice. It is also pivotal in the evolution of her formal strategies of feminist argumentation. Most scholarship on this passage concentrates exclusively on her treatment of the threat posed to a little girl by a sinister man on the street. I believe other aspects of gender inequality and violence in this passage merit closer attention than they have received: the ethics of both telling and told in the novel are richer even than previous scholarship has acknowledged. A close look at the way voice operates in this section of the holograph as compared with that of the novel suggests the ethical significance of the project as a whole.

Woolf's innovations in essay 3 are clearest when considered in the context of the chapters that precede it. In essay 2, the speaker analyzes different types of love, and ends by elaborating on the pressures that "street love, common love, love in general" exert on the Pargiter family, especially the women (1.45 [P 36]). "Street love" is the speaker's euphemism for crass objectification of women, the double standard of propriety that ostensibly protects women and girls in 1880 against public predation but in fact alienates them from any "natural" attitude toward sex or love. "The influence of this street or common love was felt at every turn—it affected their liberty; it affected their purses. . . . [T]hey wanted to look at the young man; they knew it was wrong to look; they did look; they were caught looking; they disliked being caught; they were ashamed, indignant, confused—all in one—and the feeling, since it was never exposed, save by a blush, or a giggle, wriggled deep down into their minds, and sometimes woke them in the middle of the night with curious sensations, unpleasant dreams" (1.47 [P 38]). Throughout the essay, the speaker melds historical facts with fictional examples, underscoring how realistic and representative the Pargiter family is of their class in that era. She makes very few conspicuously evaluative comments, confining herself to description that, when paired with fictional examples, becomes didactic. "[S]o complex and important an emotion [as the girls' reaction to street love] can scarcely be analysed effectively," she concludes. "Perhaps a quotation from the novel may help to bring the scene into a better perspective" (1.48 [P 38]).

The second fictional chapter is located between essays 2 and 3. This chapter is internally focalized through the Pargiters' ten-year-old child, Rose, who has set her heart on buying a toy at the store down the street. Her sister forbids her from venturing outside alone, even in daylight, and recommends she ask her brother Bobby to chaperone her. As night approaches, Rose interrupts her brother's schoolwork to make the request, but he interrupts her, cursing, and orders her out of the room. "She had known that it was hopeless to ask him when he was doing his prep. because now that he was what she called 'a proper schoolboy' he was apt to sneer at her & treat her as if she were a baby especially when she interrupted his work" (1.50 [P 40]). The majority of the chapter dramatizes Rose's daring adventure in going to the store alone. She deceives her nurse; slips out of the house; encounters a man on the street who gazes lecherously at her; reaches the store and buys her toy; in her return home passes the man again, who reaches toward her, fondling and exposing himself; races home terrified; re-enters the house undetected; and suffers nightmares later that night. When Eleanor asks what has frightened her, Rose refuses to tell the truth.[38]

The chapter is dominated by the instability between Rose's inexperience and vulnerability as a young girl and the sinister lechery of the man on the street. Woolf's second essay, which precedes this chapter, equips both authorial and narrative audiences to identify the stultifying, terrifying threat to Rose as "street love," and to interpret both societal causes and personal ramifications of that threat. The persuasive, ideological work of the chapter is accomplished by the reader's application of the speaker's earlier comments, rather than by commentary in either the chapter or the subsequent essay. The case against such treatment of a child neither requires nor receives elaboration in the third essay. What is striking about the third essay, however, is the rapidity with which Woolf in just three paragraphs turns her attention from Rose's vulnerability to a seemingly tangential subject, Rose's relationship with Bobby. Woolf repositions the reader's vantage on street love not by explicating the scene of violence, which looms so large as the primary instability in the previous chapter, but by elaborating part of the fictional situation scarcely treated at all: the degree to which Bobby's peremptory refusal has both inadvertently exposed his sister and precipitated years of estrangement in their future. His contact with boys at school, the speaker explains, has "initiate[d] Bobby into what Bobby dimly felt was a great fellowship—the fellowship of men together—a fellowship which, he began to feel, yielded a great many rights and privileges, and required even of himself, at the age of twelve, certain loyalties and assertions; for example, it was essential to make it plain that the school room was his room; especially when his school friends came back to tea. It was essential that Rose should be kept out of it" (1.64–65 [P 54]).

Although scholars are accurate in calling the holograph essays didactic, her persuasive strategies in the essays are subtler than that word connotes. The third essay does much more than deliver pronouncements and interpret the fiction of the second chapter; it supplements what comes before it with new fictional information, considerably extending and elaborating the narrative. Not only does the second fictional chapter have much higher narrativity than the first—filled as it is with adventure, conflict, and suspense—but its companion piece, the third essay, retroactively heightens the second chapter's instabilities by filling in both causes and consequences of Rose and Bobby's interaction. The essay lends new significance to the fictional scene's past, present, and future, heightening the chapter's narrativity even further. But the essay also takes on narrativity of its own. The manuscript's first two fictional chapters are marked by effaced authoriality, as they contain almost no commentary whatsoever. But essay 3 enacts a blend of authorial commentary and fictional rendering.[39]

Essay 3 marks the point in the manuscript at which Woolf began to commit greater care and attention to generic hybridization. Instead of simply alternating essays with narrative segments, as she had done at the manuscript's outset, she began to infuse the essays with narrativity and the narratives with authorial commentary. From this point on—from the end of the first holograph notebook through the eighth and final notebook—she melded what she called "fact" with "vision." Accordingly, for example, the fifth essay supplies fictional details about Kitty Malone's first kiss (at age sixteen, by George Carter, behind a haystack) in order to illustrate her complex inhibitions and attractions years later in chapter 4; as well as about her mother's youth in Yorkshire and her father's courtship in 1848. Diegetic summary and the narrator's commentary exist, in this essay, alongside extensive sequences of fictional dialogue, marking yet further progress toward generic blending. The speaker introduces free indirect discourse for the first time when, in essay 5, she notes Kitty's feeling that "George Eliot was, after all, only a novelist" (2.43 [P 125]). And she ends the essay with a long fictional segment in which Kitty is externally focalized as she prepares for the events that take place immediately afterwards, in chapter 5.

Citing Woolf's diary, scholars have noted the precise day (February 2, 1933) when the flesh-and-blood author decisively abandoned her project of interleaving essays with chapters. "Today I finished—rather more completely than usual—revising the first chapter. I am leaving out the interchapters—compacting them in the text: and project an appendix of dates." But I am not persuaded, as most are, that February 2 or any other date marked a sea change in the project author's rhetorical strategy.[40] Her perception of the ethical dilemma—how to render a non-coercive ethical argument—did not falter, let alone fundamentally change, when she "compacted" her essays into narrative. Her formal choices, in both the manuscript and the published novel, followed from ethical concerns that required generic blending.

In the published novel, both the telling and the told of Rose's "street love" episode are dispersed across several passages. When Rose indicates she wants to go to Lamley's, Eleanor instructs her to ask Martin to chaperone. Following a section break in the text, Rose walks upstairs, reluctant to ask Martin since they have recently quarreled

> first about Erridge and the microscope and then about shooting Miss Pym's cats next door. But Eleanor had told her to ask him. She opened the door.
>
> "Hullo, Martin—" she began. He was sitting at a table with a book propped in front of him, muttering to himself—perhaps it was Greek, perhaps it was Latin.
>
> "Eleanor told me—" she began, noting how flushed he looked, and how his hand closed on a bit of paper as if he were going to screw it into a ball. "To ask you . . ." she began, and braced herself and stood with her back against the door. (17, Woolf's ellipses)

The scene ends here, abruptly. This passage differs from its counterpart in the manuscript in several telling ways. It has been drastically compressed, set off on either end by a section break, and separated from Rose's subsequent trip to the store by eight full pages of focalization through Eleanor on entirely unrelated subjects. Physical placement on the page isolates Rose and Martin's interaction for consideration in its own right. The novel's narrator has substantiated the conflict between the children by naming the subjects of their quarrel. Martin's exclusively male privilege of education is alluded to solely through references to his schoolfellow Erridge and to the microscope. These details are juxtaposed with a prank involving the neighbor's cat in which Rose and Martin's gender difference is less clearly pertinent. Neither of these examples is explained until much later in the novel, so, for now, readers can only infer their importance, or lack thereof. Furthermore, while the manuscript mixes external and internal focalization unsystematically, the novel focalizes this passage through Rose. The manuscript's narrator establishes authoritatively that "[in] fact he was learning some lines in Greek by heart," but in the novel, "perhaps it was Greek, perhaps it was Latin" further underscores the fact that, because she is a girl, Rose has no formal education in either language. In the manuscript Bobby warns Rose to "Cut along, or I'll shy something at you," whereas his threat is reduced to a scant trace in the novel, in his act of closing his hand on a piece of paper "*as if he were going to* screw it into a ball" (my emphasis).

To recall my metaphor of following the project author down a long corridor, Woolf has shut several doors in the novel that stood open in the manuscript. Behind one closed door, in the manuscript, Bobby threatens to hurl a paper wad at his sister for invading a space of male prerogative, a space "nominally still a common sitting room for them all" but one which he is "secretly determined to claim for his own room" (1.49 [P 40]) as his formal education instills in him a sense of entitlement. In the metaphorical corridor itself (the published novel), Bobby has no relationship of any kind to the schoolroom. Behind another closed door, Rose thinks to herself that, despite their occasional quarrels, "sometimes she & Bobby were the best of friends,—he had given her a sea-urchins egg two nights ago as a reward for not making a fuss when he broke the blade of her pen knife" (1.50 [P 40]). In the novel, however, Rose "braced herself and stood with her back against the door" with no such consolation (17). Standing in the corridor, the reader who listens for them can hear the muffled voices of the manuscript in spite of the closed doors. The project author's silence on Bobby's appropriation of the schoolroom, her replacement of the broken penknife with Mrs. Pym's cat, the uncertainty she renders through Rose's focalization over whether Bobby studies Greek or Latin all have greater ethical significance when understood in the context of the manuscript.

Several pages later in the novel, Rose's sister Delia happens to overhear the conclusion to the above scene. "Then on the floor above she heard children's voices—Martin and Rose quarreling. 'Don't then!' she heard Rose say. A door slammed" (20). Delia's eavesdropping permits Woolf to convey the facts of Martin's refusal as well as of Rose's resentment, but these facts are deprived of any of the importance they had in manuscript. In the earlier version, Rose pauses in the doorway instead of slamming the door, "looking around her, as if to assert that though Bobby claimed the school room for himself, she was not going to give up her claim without a fight for it—she was not a baby any longer to be kept with nurse in the nursery—" (1.50 [P 41]). The novel's door slam conveys Rose's defiance, but it leaves ambiguous whether the defiance is well considered, as in the manuscript, or merely impetuous pique.

In the manuscript, Rose immediately steels herself for her adventure by imagining it as a game she has played with Bobby, drawing for support on the positive dimensions of their relationship, even in the wake of their squabble. This playful dimension of the sibling's relationship, again, is not mentioned in the novel and so is not depicted as something that gives Rose courage when she needs it. In the manuscript, "[h]er mind was made up.

She would go to Lamleys alone. As she crept very stealthily upstairs again to the night nursery where her clothes were kept a sense of adventure filled her. She began instinctively to make this into one of those games that she & Bobby used to play, about Red Indians" (1.50 [P 41]). In the novel, Rose's stealthy preparations before going outside are laced with fantasy: "Now she had her pistol and her shot, she thought, taking her own purse from her own drawer, and enough provisions, she thought, as she hung her hat and coat over her arm, to last a fortnight" (25). But because her fantasy appears to be her original creation, the novel mutes Rose's simultaneous resentment of and reliance on her brother.

"After the adventure in the street," the manuscript's narrator explains in essay 3, in a characteristic blend of summary and explication, "Rose changed slightly but decidedly in her feeling for Bobby. Again it is difficult to say how far this change was the result of the shock; how far she felt some fear or dislike for her brother because of his sex; or how far she felt and resented the change that was making him, as she put it, into 'a proper schoolboy.' . . . Only, as she could not possibly tell Bobby about the man, and Bobby could not possibly tell her about [his experiences at school], there was nothing for it but an enmity which lasted until a very queer scene after their father's death, in the school room, fifteen years later" (1.65, 1.67 [P 54, 56]). Although the novel contains no such scene, it does include an encounter dated 1908 in which Rose, Martin, and Eleanor revisit the topic of Erridge and the microscope. Supplying details Woolf omitted over one hundred pages earlier, Rose recalls "that horrid, ferret-faced boy—Erridge . . . pretended that it was I who broke the microscope and it was he who broke it. . . . D'you remember that row?" (149). Martin acknowledges it as "one of the worst" rows between them, and then further recalls an image of Rose, furious, "wearing a pink frock, with a knife in your hand" (149). Rose reveals what had happened next, showing Eleanor a scar on her wrist. "When did she do that? Eleanor thought. She could not remember. Rose had locked herself into the bathroom with a knife and cut her wrist. She had known nothing about it. She looked at the white mark. It must have bled" (150).

Such simple diction belies an intense and disturbing undercurrent in this scene. It is a strikingly successful example of compression as an ethical strategy. The ethics of the told—Woolf's rendering of Rose's pain and frustration over what she perceived as betrayal by her brother—resonates even after the span of so many pages in the novel. Even independent of the manuscript, this latter scene is shocking, though it is characteristic of the novel that such shock would be conveyed through minimal reference to a "white mark." But the complexity of ten-year-old Rose's affection for and resentment of her brother, made much clearer in the manuscript, endows the novel's scene with a fuller, richer, and more persuasive ethical impact.

THE MANUSCRIPT'S third essay is special in at least one additional way: it marks Woolf's abandonment of the global tension between narrative and authorial audiences. As long as she maintained an imbalance between narrative audience and authorial audience, the novel-essay's main persuasive technique—as well as its fundamental mechanism for narrative progression—functioned through the imbalance. But in essay 3 the two audiences become conflated as the narratee is de-emphasized. The speaker maintains her pretense of lecturing at the outset, repeating the colloquial "of course" that has been directed at the narrative audience in earlier essays. But direct address of the narratee does not reoccur in the rest of the manuscript.

When Woolf excised her essays from the novel-essay hybrid, she silenced her own explanations of prospective and retrospective significance, letting the fictional scenes speak for themselves. It is easy to understand why so many scholars have identified self-silencing as the most prominent difference between manuscript and publication. But assertive narrative voice isn't the only distinctive aspect of these early draft chapters. When she converted her novel-essay hybrid into a novel, Woolf sacrificed something beyond the qualities of her narrator's overt feminist conviction; she erased the distinction between authorial and narrative audience that was essential to her original mode of persuasion. She eliminated the narrative audience, leaving the authorial audience with no lesson to overhear and only one role to inhabit. Details about material circumstances became testaments to historical accuracy, rather than interesting in their own right as catalysts for imaginative reconstruction.

Moreover, although progression in the manuscript depended on tension, when she erased the tension she did not replace it with a global instability. Instead she built on the instabilities she had established in the first few manuscript chapters—not to develop them, but rather to chain them together as local disruptions punctuated by the passage of time. No single instability attached to any character dominates or persists throughout the novel.

The published novel's low narrativity and its refusal of both closure and completeness can be partially explained by the echoes of the original global tension—that is, by our lingering association with the original narrative and authorial audiences. Near novel's end, two characters share a key conversation. Eleanor, one of the characters we know best in all drafts of the work, who was in her early twenties in the first chapter, is in the final chapter over seventy and full of hope for women's political and civic future. Her niece, Peggy, is a thirty-something medical doctor, rather misanthropic and irritable, who came of age at the time women gained suffrage. Their conversation reveals Peggy's frustration at the sacrifices she has had to make to be a success in her profession and her difficulty appreciating sacrifices made by other women long before her. This is the first time Peggy has appeared in the novel in any detail, so her juxtaposition to Eleanor resonates in many different ways at once. Woolf's close attention this late in the novel reads differently if we have at one point inhabited the position of the young professional woman chastised for lack of historical insight. When Peggy criticizes Eleanor silently we feel the slight all the more for having ourselves tried to become our great-grandmothers. We also recognize more keenly how much understanding of women's past and future Peggy stands to lose if she ignores the insights Eleanor has to offer. Our experience of the fact that Peggy suppresses her frustration and that it goes unrebuked by character and narrator alike suggests that knowledge of the manuscript enriches this scene. Whereas the implied author of this scene deserves credit for a nuanced and painful ending to a deliberately difficult novel, the project author's curtailment of her original progression through tension may help explain many flesh-and-blood readers' resistance to that difficulty.

CHAPTER 4

The Ethics of Attention

> " . . . that particular psychological mood of sympathetic nervous hilarity which can be so quickly changed by a crafty orator into passionate receptivity . . . a dream-heavy trance of curious felicity."
>
> —John Cowper Powys[1]

A T THE *Ulysses* censorship trial in 1921, the first witness for the defense was John Cowper Powys.[2] In testifying that *Ulysses* was "a beautiful piece of work in no way capable of corrupting the minds of young girls," Powys articulated the fundamental concern at hand: widespread fears about the vulnerability of young female readers. His testimony was valued, less because he was a judicious reader of James Joyce than because of his extensive engagement with historical and contemporary anxieties about female receptivity to mental influence and suggestion. Like the *Ulysses* trial, Powys's career contributed to the end of the centuries-long friction between the anxieties of moralists and the desires of supposedly vulnerable female readers.

Documented suspicions of the danger reading materials posed to all young and impressionable readers date from the first century, but the novel's rise in eighteenth-century England inspired fervent warnings and interdictions. The overriding concern was that girls and women were entirely passive readers: that their weak minds and limited experience rendered them incompetent to distinguish between fiction and reality. Novels could implant false, immoral, and/or overly exciting ideas directly in a susceptible reader's mind. These ideas could induce in the reader an inappropriate yearning for more stimulation. Accordingly, they could introduce or exacerbate a woman's dissatisfaction with her circumscribed opportunities, they could disrupt family harmony, and they could lead a young woman to condone sexual feelings in herself. For more than two centuries, efforts to protect young female readers from such corruption followed two basic strategies: to control or suppress the dangerous elements of novels (such as sex, love, and other rousing themes), and to control or suppress the readers themselves. In the late eighteenth and early nineteenth centuries, proponents of the latter strategy (including medical doctors and moralists) marshaled a formidable array of biological, medical, and social arguments to discourage the young female reader.[3]

Arguments about passive reading practices generated intense controversy as the nineteenth century progressed. Publishers, booksellers, librarians, teachers, and concerned parents, among others, contested various legal, pedagogic, and economic extensions of the issue. Novelists influenced the course of the debate as well. As Kate Flint has remarked, "By the mid-nineteenth century, the trope of fiction as a fast route to corruption was so familiar that it could be used not just in its own right, for didactic purposes, but as a way of encouraging readers to think critically about their own practices when consuming novels."[4] Flint claims that "[l]ike much Victorian fiction, . . . both sensation and 'New Woman' fiction mock within themselves the belief that women read uncritically, unthoughtfully: the very characteristics which their authors were themselves accused of engendering."[5]

At the start of the twentieth century, then, both conservative and progressive attitudes towards female readers remained in healthy circulation. From the late nineteenth century, Mrs. Grundy had been slowly passing into obsolescence. Yet legal battles over literary censorship persisted late into the century, including but not limited to famous cases such as those concerning *The Rainbow* (in 1915), *Ulysses* (in 1921 and 1933), *The Well of Loneliness* (in 1928), and *Lady Chatterley's Lover* (in 1960). At stake in every one of these trials was the supposed potential for literature to corrupt young and female readers.

Such attitudes were not unrelated, of course, to the debates over women's mental capacities that figured prominently in the suffragist movement. Recognition of women's intellectual capabilities was inherent in England's political decisions of 1918 and 1928, when women's suffrage was granted, first in part and then in full. But in Powys's work, feminist narrative ethics is not responsive to the political progress of the women's movement.

Instead, it is deployed as a means of transforming gender constructs. Specifically, Powys construes women's, and young girls', receptivity as an admirable strength and powerful asset.

Powys was no feminist. Nothing in his biography, personal papers, or novels suggests any investment in women's civic advancement; quite the contrary. In both fiction and nonfiction he represented derogatory, even humiliating attitudes toward women, consistently representing women as physically weak, narcissistic, highly sexed, and aligned with nature and revelation as opposed to the supposedly male faculties of reason and science. Of the four writers considered in this study, he endorsed by far the most retrogressive gender politics. However, like Woolf, Sayers, and Forster, he deliberately used formal innovation and feminist narrative ethics in his fiction to compel his audience to inhabit a specific, even progressive, ethical stance on a contemporary feminist issue.

While the entire history of the novel entails an adjacent discourse of female vulnerability, the immediate literary context of Powys's concept of receptivity signals a new interest in probing the limits and cultural constructedness of that vulnerability. Much fin-de-siècle fiction features, for example, themes of mesmerism, hypnotism, spiritualism, and other modes of mental influence that were fashionable at the time. These forms of influence, of course, were saturated with gender roles and expectations. Hypnotic control was a form of virility, whereas young girls were considered to be at the highest risk for moral and spiritual corruption by various contemporary dangers, among which the occult figured prominently. As I have argued elsewhere, Powys appropriated some occultist practices in his thirty-two-year career as a public lecturer, figuratively but also literally mesmerizing crowds and performing his own mediumship on stage.[6] In his lectures and, later, his novels, Powys's experimental collapse of boundaries—those between women and men, medium and subject, agent and recipient, audience and speaker, to name a few—violated many of his contemporaries' comfortable assumptions about power dynamics and gender roles. But about a decade before Powys's writing career began, authors such as Oscar Wilde, Robert Louis Stevenson, Bram Stoker, and George du Maurier had tested those very boundaries both thematically, in the plots of their novels, as well as dynamically, in the way they compelled certain readerly responses.

In Stoker's novel, for example, the cadre of men trying desperately to protect Mina Harker from Dracula's hypnotic control realize at last that her thrall makes her a potentially useful extension of the vampire. When Van Helsing himself hypnotizes Mina, she reports on Dracula's whereabouts because she identifies so fully with the vampire. One way of reading this scene is as Van Helsing's counterattack: Mina has mentally penetrated into enemy territory. A more compelling (Powysian) alternative, however, is to read Mina's susceptibility as receptive mediumship in which she performs Dracula's identity by becoming part of him. The success of the endeavor depends in part on Van Helsing's men suppressing their doubts that hypnotism works in the first place, on squelching their fears that Mina's mental proximity to Dracula will corrupt her irremediably, and on learning to consider her passivity as productive.

Even as some late-century Victorians worked to dispel centuries-old misconceptions about women's vulnerability to reading fiction, the act of reading was newly figured as transgressive for both genders. Garrett Stewart has argued persuasively that "the violation of [a character's] 'privacy' constituted by reading . . . exposes reading as transmitting not only the feminized receptivity (we might call it masochism) of anxious participation but also a quasi-erotic 'sadism' . . . of penetrating access."[7] Certain fictions prompt readers to oscillate between enjoying privileged access to a character's thoughts, on the one hand, and feeling guiltily voyeuristic, but Stewart claims that fin-de-siècle texts such as *Trilby, The Picture of Dorian Gray, The Strange Case of Dr. Jekyll and Mr. Hyde,* and *Dracula* demand this uncomfortable oscillation with particular force. Just as Mina is both reading Dracula and being read by Van Helsing, fin-de-siècle novels prompt a double reading experience. In other words, the novels both read and are read by their readers, in the sense that they prompt a reflexive activity on the reader's part.

Stewart supplies other examples. Wilde depicts Dorian's visceral response to reading the unnamed, profoundly influential book given him by Lord Henry, while simultaneously suggesting an analogous response to *The Picture of Dorian Gray.* Even after Svengali's death, Trilby is mesmerized by his photographic portrait; she reads the photo until she falls into a trance. Novels such as these command readerly engagement in part by depicting that engagement. Powys's novels, likewise, are calculated to absorb his audiences in part through their portrayal of absorption. However, whereas Stewart notes that the novels under consideration remind readers of their own physical presence as onlookers, holding books, Powys's novels are designed to draw their audiences into receptive rapture. Far from rewarding the reader's "penetrating access," his narrative dynamics thwart it. As I will demonstrate—and then complicate—later in this chapter, Powys despises the very idea of penetration. He consistently figures it as a violation that, though perhaps titillating for some, is invariably trumped by an ethically superior receptivity. At first glance, the blatant gender coding of conflict in Powys's novels seems hardly a subtle instrument of meaningful rhetorical or ethical value. However, when recognized as a counteraction to the literary context of fin-de-siècle narrative dynamics, as a progressive comment on the history of women's reading practices, as an integral dimension of his feminist narrative ethics, and as the basis for an inventive new form of narrative progression, Powys's privileging of receptivity may be recognized for the first time as significant indeed.

Powys revolutionized plot dynamics for ethical ends in his most important novel, *A Glastonbury Romance.* He replaced conventional hermeneutic plotting (the gradual resolution of narrative instabilities) with what I call an *erotics of progression,* in which instabilities circulate freely and readerly attention is receptive rather than goal-directed. The novel's sexist representation of female characters makes it difficult to hypothesize feminist motives for the implied author's construction of this unusual narrative progression. But, like the nineteenth-century fiction Flint examines, Powys's major novels—foremost among them *Glastonbury*—reveal through both story and discourse a self-conscious, critical stance toward the long history of assumptions about female readers. Although he is not a feminist implied author, his rhetorical strategies demonstrate a progressive attitude toward the subject of gendered reading practices. Unlike his predecessors, Powys defines female receptivity as a form of active, assertive attention, an intentional, intermental connection,[8] something quite different from passivity. He perceived credulity and ingenuousness as assets, rather than liabilities, of the attentive reader, and he crafted novels that reward what he called "young-girl-like receptivity." As I will demonstrate, receptive attention to a Powys novel is an adaptive skill a reader develops through experience, rather than a default position resulting from naiveté.

Powys's formal experiments prompt attentive reading practices, explicitly coded as female, that require critical thought about gender roles. Moreover, his long novels of the 1920s and 1930s, which he called his romances, meld outmoded generic conventions established centuries earlier with late Victorian and modernist narrative techniques. Powys's striking generic blend of romance with novel suggests his sophisticated engagement with a long literary historical tradition. It suggests a degree of literary self-awareness rarely recognized in him by scholars. Those who do admire his work tend to account for his sprawling, meandering plots as being the direct result of his generic experimentation. But I contend that his model of young-girl-like receptivity is even more influential, pervasive, and radical than his work with genre in these novels. His literal romanticization of both obsolete social norms and antimodernist narrative techniques starkly contrasts with his stance on contemporary political struggles over women's relationship to fiction as it is borne out through his rhetorical strategies. *A Glastonbury Romance*, in spite of—or in fact because of—its contradictions, cultivates in its reader ethical attentiveness and judgment and celebrates the capacity of reading like a girl.

IN THE COURSE OF arguing "Against Interpretation," Susan Sontag claims that "[i]n place of a hermeneutics we need an erotics of art" (14). This challenge appears for the first time, without gloss or elaboration, as the last line of her essay. It is a compelling but vague call for literary scholars—and good readers in general—to do something outside their ken: take a work on its own terms without constructing a paratext in which all the symbols are unpacked, all the meanings laid bare. Sontag identifies "interpretation" as "presuppos[ing] a discrepancy between the clear meaning of the text and the demands of (later) readers. . . . The modern style of interpretation excavates, and as it excavates, destroys; it digs 'behind' the text, to find a subtext which is the true one" (6). She also notes that "interpretation of this type indicates a dissatisfaction (conscious or unconscious) with the work, a wish to replace it by something else" (10).

Many authors whom Powys particularly admired, such as James Joyce and Henry James, wrote novels that invite and reward careful hermeneutic explication. Sontag names Joyce and James in her short list of authors "around whom thick encrustations of interpretation have taken hold" (8). Their novels operate on several levels of significance simultaneously, developing intricate, intellectual relations between implied author and authorial audience, prompting the latter's interpretation largely through their progressive exploitation and resolution of various tensions and instabilities. But in response to the influence of his contemporaries, Powys composed several digressive, improbable, ecstatic fictions that employ a conspicuously unfamiliar system of narrative progression, baffling his reader's efforts at interpretation. The neglect shown to Powys's work by most scholars and teachers alike may be seen as a symptom of this bafflement.

Moreover, Powys constructed this effect on readers intentionally. With growing intensity, as Jerome McGann has noted, Powys's novels from *A Glastonbury Romance* forward self-consciously "break the spell"

of their own fictionality by "evacuating" the primary conventions of novelistic realism (such as probability, verisimilitude, organic integrity) and
"metamorphosing" them with the conventions of the romance.[9] McGann
claims that "Powys's historic importance in the history of fiction lies
in this: that he worked to incorporate the novel back into its romance
origins" (178). He argues that *Glastonbury* is like Gertrude Stein's *The
Making of Americans,* Joyce's *Finnegans Wake,* and Dorothy Richardson's *Pilgrimage* in having "been written not so much to be read as to
explore and expose the scene of reading itself" (175), but his essay makes
a historical, rather than narratological, argument. If we combine historical and narratological approaches, the "scene of reading" is revealed to
have major implications for understanding the novel's gender politics.
While McGann is content describing the reader's experience of *Glastonbury* simply as "catastrophic" (181), I want to examine that experience,
specifically that of the authorial audience, in more detail. Powys's gender
politics of reading in this novel gives it greater "importance in the history
of fiction" than has been previously recognized.

Powys's rather perverse narrative progression in *Glastonbury* discourages many highly competent flesh-and-blood readers from joining the
authorial audience and, often, from finishing the book. McGann cites
the response of one such reader, Powys's editor, as representative. Refer-
ring to Powys's later novel *Porius* (which shares many of *Glastonbury*'s
eccentricities), the editor complains, "[Y]ou seem to be resolved to slow
up and obscure and entangle the progress and movement of your story
in every conceivable way—by homilies, dissertations, diversions of all
kinds ? [*sic*] by loading it up with non-essentials, inconsequent details,
trivialities, sheer perversities by which I mean, for one thing, the constant
playing with Celtic and Brythonic words, which you frequently drag in
by the heels for your own pleasure and not for that of the reader, who
cannot be expected to share your philological interests" (177).[10] The difficulty of joining Powys's authorial audience has largely obscured his value
to narrative theorists.

How does a narrative with no hermeneutic puzzle to decipher and no
story-level problem to solve compel readers to keep reading to the end,
particularly if it is over a thousand pages long? What are the consequences
when a novelist manipulates tensions and instabilities in deliberately
unsatisfying ways? How does the narrative progression of Powys's novel
direct the reader's experience, and in what ways can a scholarly appraisal
of his unusual form of narrative progression contribute to contemporary
narrative theory? And what does this unique form of progression have

to do with gender? In addressing these questions, I join several literary theorists who have connected an erotics of art with models of narrative progression.[11] I suggest that Powys offers us a fresh theoretical opportunity to reconsider narrative progression, first by demonstrating some productive and compelling ways in which his narrative strategies diverge from our dominant narratological models, then by offering a rhetorical reading of the erotics of progression in *Glastonbury,* and finally by submitting a rejoinder to Robert Caserio's work on this novel. In this novel Powys accomplishes something narrative theorists have not anticipated, namely, that he separates the erotics of progression from the hermeneutics of progression, and does so without sacrificing narrativity.

SONTAG notes that an erotics of art should be developed through attention to form and structure. Concerned that the "arrogance of interpretation" arises from overemphasis on content, she suggests readers develop a "descriptive, rather than prescriptive, vocabulary—for forms" (12). Her suggestion found early influential responses in the work of Peter Brooks and Robert Scholes. Both scholars posit sexual arousal as the dominant model for narrative form. In "The Orgastic Pattern of Fiction," Scholes claims, "What connects fiction . . . with sex is the fundamental orgastic rhythm of tumescence and detumescence, of tension and resolution, of intensification to the point of climax and consummation. . . . [M]uch of the art consists of delaying climax within the framework of desire in order to prolong the pleasurable ·act itself" (26). He adds that "the abstractable content is not the meaning of a work of fiction. The meaning is in our experience of it" (28). Not only the structure of the book, but the reading experience itself, has an analogue in sexual intercourse, according to this argument.[12] Scholes notes that both reading and writing can be types of narcissistic self-gratification, but that superior literary experiences involve both reader and writer respecting each other's "dignity" by "assuming a sensitivity 'out there' that will match" that of their own (27). In other words, the pleasures of literary activity are maximized by imaginative, reciprocal contact between reader and writer.

Brooks's *Reading for the Plot* extends and complicates Scholes's premise, while explicitly acknowledging his initial influence: "Beyond formalism, Susan Sontag argued some years ago, we need an erotics of art. What follows may be conceived as a contribution to that erotics" (36). Starting with Roland Barthes's claim that readerly engagement is based on a "passion of (for) meaning," Brooks asserts that readers follow narratives with interest because they are fueled by a desire for meaning and significance, which they can only attain by accumulation and synthesis of information in the plot (37). All narratives, he claims, are hermeneutic (34). Brooks's sense of the term *erotics* departs significantly from Sontag's, as his denotes interdependence between hermeneutics and desire, whereas hers repudiates interpretation in favor of ludic immersion. But the tension between these two definitions turns out to be productive, as I will argue, in a close examination of Powys's novel.

Drawing on Roman Jakobson's theory of metaphor and metonymy as paradigmatic and syntagmatic poles of language, Brooks claims that any given narrative begins with a "blinded metaphor of transmission" that must then be unpacked and explicated as metonymy in the course of the book, so that it may be reassembled as an "enlightened metaphor of transmission" by narrative's end (27). In other words, in Brooks's view, a narrative begins with a hermeneutic puzzle that must be worked out by the reader through time, culminating in the reader's recognition of significance. Or, according to his two thematic models (based on physics and male sexual arousal), it begins with potential energy ("initial arousal") that is exploited as kinetic energy ("expectancy") in the unfolding plot, culminating in a climax ("significant discharge") followed by quiescence (101).

Of course, examples abound of novels that do not follow Brooks's pattern, and readers' experiences stray widely from his model. James Phelan has demonstrated that because in Brooks's model "the dynamics of the plot itself merge with the dynamics of reading that plot, . . . Brooks is working with a model of a single-layered text" that fails to account for the "accompanying sequence of *attitudes* that the authorial audience is asked to take toward that pattern."[13] Phelan's double-layered, rhetorical model of narrative progression is one I regularly emulate in this chapter, but unlike Phelan I want to consider the erotics of that progression. Susan Winnett's critique of Brooks adopts that erotics as its central concern, rejecting his overreliance on male tropes that assume a male experience. While she accepts Brooks's basic premise that plots tend to be built and resolved on a tumescence-detumescence model, Winnett, like Phelan, suggests that Brooks's conflation of textual dynamics and readerly response is inadequate. Suggestive as Brooks's erotic model is, it precludes patterns of sexual arousal other than tumescence and detumescence, most conspicuously, female pleasure.[14] Winnett's salty rebuke to Brooks and Scholes notes that "[e]verything that the last two decades have taught us about human sexual response suggests that the female partner in intercourse has accesses to pleasure not open to her male partner. . . . [S]he can begin and end her pleasure according to a logic of fantasy and arousal that is totally unrelated to the functioning and representation of the 'conventional' heterosexual sex act. Moreover, she can do so again. Immediately. And, we are told, again after that" (507).

Winnett criticizes Brooks for his insistence (we may note, against Sontag's particular recommendation) on prescription, rather than description, of male sexual arousal as *the* model for readerly investment in general. Brooks prescribes a single model into which he fits several examples, whereas a descriptive taxonomy would necessarily derive one or more models from a range of examples. But Winnett's primary objection is to Brooks's inflexible model of linear trajectory, in which textual significance and readerly investment build progressively from the story's very first incident and find a single, primary climax near the story's end. Winnett argues that not all sense-making must be retrospective, and points to beginnings and endings that take place in the middles of narratives, suggesting them as vital sources of pleasure and sense-making that may have nothing to do with a final climax. Brooks and Winnett are preoccupied by essentially the same thing: how narrative progression is related to the pleasure a reader takes in recognizing textual significance. But they are divided on the question of what happens in the middles of narratives to foster that recognition.

Brooks's discussion of textual dynamics depends upon the notion that each narrative is "a system of energy which the reader activates" (112). He accordingly thematizes this transaction, citing the nineteenth-century preoccupation with motors as emblematic of plot structures common to Victorian narratives: "I think we do well to recognize the existence of textual force, and that we can use such a concept to move beyond the static models of much formalism, toward a dynamics of reading and writing. In the motors and engines I have glanced at, including Eros as motor and motor as erotic, we find representations of the dynamics of the narrative text, connecting beginning and end across the middle and making of that middle—what we read *through*—a field of force" (47). Metonymy, and the reader's response to it, together constitute the field of force in Brooks's formulation. Metonymy is a syntagmatic code that functions through contiguity. Metonyms may be linked together sequentially to reveal, or suspend, cumulative information in a narrative over the course of several pages. They are thus apprehended by the reader over time, and in that period of time they may be used to various authorial advantages, chief among which (for Brooks) is the whetting of the reader's appetite, or desire, for resolution.

His choice of the word "force" also intentionally suggests a plane of resistance: as the reader's desire increases, the temptation of a short cut becomes increasingly appealing—one wishes to skip to the last page—but a strategic interplay of revelations and deferrals in the middle of a narrative counteracts this urge. "As Sartre and Benjamin compellingly argued, the narrative must tend toward its end, seek illumination in its own death. Yet this must be the right death, the correct end" (Brooks 103). The right death, then, is the one that rewards close attention to each twist and turn all the way through: the optimal experience of the middle defers the final release of energy and promises a satisfying conclusion.

Winnett (uninterested in the physics metaphor) offers two alternatives to sex as a model for narrative trajectory: breastfeeding and giving birth. Both models are "*pro*spective, full of the incipience that the male model will see resolved in its images of detumescence and discharge. Their ends (in both senses of the word) are, quite literally, beginning itself" (509). Mary Shelley's plot structure in *Frankenstein* serves as Winnett's central example of this point. Noting the difficulty critics have shown in using "a traditional narratology" to account for the novel's innovative narrative progression, Winnett claims that the disruptive effects of that progression are dramatized on the level of character, in Shelley's depiction of Frankenstein himself. "That creation would demand anything of him *beyond* the moment when scientific genius culminates the trajectory of its intellectual self-stimulation seems never to have occurred to him" (510). She proposes that Frankenstein is reading his life for the plot exactly as Brooks would have him do—but for the fact that he's reading the "wrong story," with disastrous consequences (510). Frankenstein's anticipation of retrospective self-satisfaction blinds him to the fact that the conclusion of his labors will be not an end but the beginning of new responsibilities. Winnett argues that the reader's apprehension of significance through textual dynamics, as well as the pleasure she takes in that process, are both diminished by male bias. "Once we recognize how a psychoanalytic dynamics of reading assumes the universality of the male response," she argues, we can read Frankenstein's unpleasant surprise as a rebuke for his incompetent reading (511). The Creature's birth is an example of textual dynamics that "force us to think forward rather than backward," which Winnett sees as a first step in accounting for female readerly pleasure in relation to narrative dynamics (509).

POWYS'S *Glastonbury Romance* begins with a surplus of energy—an embarrassment of riches for the Brooks model. As an ordinary man, John Crow, steps innocuously off a train, he is immersed in a world of titanic force. The sun is endowed with a "conscious personality," full of inexplicable malice personally directed against the little man: "Roaring, cresting, heaving, gathering, mounting, advancing, receding, the enormous fire-thoughts of this huge luminary surged resistlessly to and fro, evoking a turbulent aura of psychic activity, corresponding to the physical energy of its colossal chemical body, but affecting this microscopic biped's nerves less than the wind that blew against his face" (21). Unbeknownst to Crow, the earth also possesses a consciousness, which likewise singles him out with deep, obsessive hostility. The novel's plot is thus apparently launched through an instability between supernatural consciousness and a thoroughly unexceptional man. But as Crow finds his way across the countryside to his grandfather's funeral, he meets ordinary people and conducts realistic conversations. Ironically undercutting the bombastic energies present in the novel's first few pages, these mundane events establish several local instabilities and carry the plot forward, while the potency of the sun and earth recedes in importance. The reader recognizes in retrospect that the initial conflict between Crow and the elements has very little to do with the novel's progression. Rather than signaling a conflict within the story world, the keen supernatural attention trained on Crow comes to represent Crow's worthiness of close attention, even fascination. When the sun, earth, and other superhuman centers of consciousness turn their rapt attention to other characters as well, their intense curiosity suggests that the details of everyday life in Glastonbury possess profound cosmic significance. Powys makes this move several times.[15] He converts conflicts with potential hermeneutic value into bald assertions that the characters and events of *Glastonbury* are intensely interesting in themselves, rather than in their relationship to plot.

Glastonbury progresses through a network of many tenuous narrative strands. A deceased patriarch's estate bypasses his expectant relatives and is given instead to a fanatical preacher. A father and son pursue the same married woman. A capitalist and a communist compete for control of Glastonbury. A sadist struggles to subdue his impulses. Queer and straight relationships begin, change, and end. All of these strands, Powys's narrator suggests, are extensions of Glastonbury itself. The narrator asserts early in the novel that "[t]he strongest of all psychic forces in this world is unsatisfied desire," and promises that Glastonbury, as a magnetic nexus of particularly powerful psychic energies, will be shown in the course of the novel to be a crucible of desire (125–26). It seems that the erotic saturation of *Glastonbury*'s story-world would invite application of Brooks's or Winnett's models. As the characters' lives change and intertwine with one another, as the various narrative strands develop, adding interpretive depth to the novel, one might expect Glastonbury's psychic energy to grow and interest the reader, fostering readerly investment in the resolution of the plot.

The reader is advised that "[n]one approach these three Glastonbury hills without an intensification of whatever erotic excitement they are capable of and whatever deepening of the grooves of their sublimated desire falls within the scope of their fate" (784). But the flesh-and-blood reader may very well find her or his own response falling short of the narrator's standards. This is likely because, for Powys's narrator, "the most desirable of all electric vibrations is just this very sort of erotic desire, neither altogether gratified nor altogether denied" (623). We may safely treat this statement as a norm of the implied author, and see that the difficulty of joining the authorial audience is epitomized here. As the local narratives on which *Glastonbury*'s forward movement depends develop and change, they meander rather than seek resolution. Although desire in this novel is most powerful when it is "unsatisfied," it is also most "desirable" (in both senses of the word) when it is neither fully gratified nor fully denied. While this kind of desire can fuel plots, it is not the sort that seeks "the right end." In fact, the right end is impossible under these circumstances. Glastonbury's erotic charge may be read as the engine for the novel's narrative energy, but because that desire demands no resolution, it does not accumulate intensity in the ways Brooks prescribes.

A Glastonbury Romance fundamentally departs from Brooks's model of narrative plotting. Its plot is more "a measured piece of land" than a "plan or main story." The narrator describes Glastonbury as both a palimpsest of human emotions and a personality.[16] In other words, it is both paradigmatic and syntagmatic, located in a single space from which all its narrative energy radiates. Although a large number of local instabilities develop and intertwine in ways that prompt readerly interest, the narrative as a whole appears to progress very slowly, if at all. The novel offers no mystery or suspense at its outset, nor does it develop through metonymy. Instead it relies upon synecdoche. As a personality, Glastonbury embodies the personalities of all its inhabitants and visitors, past and present. "'I sometimes think,' said Mr. Dekker, 'that we don't realise half enough the influence we all have upon the personality of our town. Don't you feel, Elizabeth, that Glastonbury has a most definite personality of its own?'" (519). The narrator helpfully corroborates: "Mat Dekker was right when he said that a town which has had so long an historic continuity as Glastonbury acquires a personality of its own" (540). The novel hosts over fifty characters, each with his or her own narrative trajectory. Any changes experienced by the characters in their own lives register in the encompassing personality of the town. The characters, then, may be read as synecdoches for Glastonbury: "Everyone who came to this spot seemed to draw something from it, attracted by a magnetism too powerful for anyone to resist, but as different people approached it they changed its chemistry, though not its essence, by their own identity, so that upon none of them it had the same psychic effect. This influence was personal and yet impersonal, it was a material centre of force and yet an immaterial fountain of life" (125).

If this passage describes the "field of force" at the text's center, it also appropriately notes the unpredictable and inconsistent character of that force, which is altered by even incidental behavior of individuals in a large, disorganized group. Whereas Brooks's metonymy has a linear trajectory, synecdoche is centrifugal. While Brooks's linear model assumes an endpoint that fosters retrospective sense-making, Powys's circular model emphasizes the significance of each point along the path, orbiting but not connecting with a central, totalizing meaning.

Moreover, the passage comments on the superficial nature of changes to Glastonbury's chemistry. The narrator claims that the denizens of Glastonbury embody and enact their town's "psychic energy" (125), and by extension, the characters may be said likewise to manifest and promote the novel's narrative energy. But this is a superficial energy, enacted on the novel's surface; the essence—or personality, words Powys uses interchangeably—of Glastonbury remains unchanged. The narrator's choice of words suggests a larger purpose here: the superficiality of changes in Glastonbury represents the implied author's refusal to allow the reader to draw large hermeneutic circles of coherence. The characters do not represent larger concepts, and their individual trajectories do not dovetail into sweeping patterns of significance. Instead, the narrator presents tiny and insignificant events with dramatic flourish, suggesting their greater meaning, but invariably undermining such events before the reader may construct a full interpretation. Whereas narrative dynamics in other novels typically prompt productive, interpretive readerly participation, *Glastonbury*'s implied author circumscribes the reader's hermeneutic connections by restricting them to the surface of the text.

Because Glastonbury's personality (the composite of its various narrative strands) appears to be static, and because the authorial audience's ability to make hermeneutic connections is particularly limited, the novel's narrativity may appear compromised. If Brooks is correct that all narratives are hermeneutic, and if the reader's anticipation of closure is a particularly privileged condition of narrativity, then *Glastonbury* has a very low degree of narrativity.[17] Assessed as such, the novel might appear to be an indiscriminate collection of characters and events that could accrue indefinitely. But this is not how the authorial audience is asked to experience the text. *Glastonbury*, read properly by the authorial audience, feels unmistakably like a narrative, even in the absence of any possibility of retrospective sense-making. Its forward movement, and consequent pleasures for the reader, function according to an erotics of progression, something that operates independent of hermeneutics. The novel's textual dynamics prompt the reader's attentive curiosity to the tales being told, even while preventing interpretive anticipation of narrative closure. Narrativity here is measured not by the optimal revelation of enlightened metaphor through metonymy, but by the reader's intense investment in the narrative's continuation. For the novel's characters, curiosity is often a sensual, even erotic sensation, and paying close attention generally entails a state of abandon, of receptivity, to a person or object. Powys's authorial audience is expected to emulate this state of attention, reading in a state of thrall to the implied author.

Powys thematizes this possibility by employing heterodiegetic authorities other than the narrator who observe events of the story-world with scrupulous attention. As a purported substitution for the reader's hermeneutic interaction with the text, the novel possesses a separate diegetic level that models patient contemplation, while denying analysis, through figures who suggest the story-world's worthiness of continual attention. In the second half of the book the narrator sporadically refers to "the Watchers of human life in Glastonbury" (557), figures whose role it is simply to be interested and imaginatively invested in observing the characters and events of the book. In one representative instance they heighten the reader's suspense by dramatizing their own: "This moment was a moment of such a fatal parting of the ways, that the Invisible Watchers who were standing at the brink of the deep Glastonbury Aquarium . . . had never crowded more eagerly around their microscope to learn what the issue would be" (1029).

The narrator also uses the Watchers to assess narrative events. For instance, as some characters decide on a site to build their new commune, the narrator remarks, "And yet to the invisible naturalists of Glastonbury, commenting curiously upon the strange history of the place, it must have been apparent that [the communists] were led to select this spot for the inauguration of their wild scheme by some kind of instinct" (721). Here the narrator attributes to the Watchers an assessment he easily could have made on his own. In their role as observers, though, the Watchers give voice to judgments readers might make if they were intimate with Glastonbury life. These are not complex interpretations; they are judgments based on observation. In this case, the discourse has provided too little contextual information for the reader to infer anything about the communists' instincts. Here, as earlier in the narrative, the Watchers see and know things the reader cannot, which suggests that the story-world brims with important information that overflows the narration, and that the reader should emulate the Watchers in their careful collection from all sources of information.

Although *Glastonbury* does not respond to Brooks's theory of narrative progression on a large scale, before discarding them it is worth trying to apply the models of Brooks and Winnett to this novel on a smaller scale, that of characters' particular stories. Even if the notion of Glastonbury as a totalizing personality, as a seemingly static composite narrative, is an accurate model of the text, it may not be the determining factor in the novel's progression, since the reader may choose to ignore the composite Glastonbury in favor of its individual parts. Is the source of *Glastonbury*'s forward movement its individual characters' trajectories, as Winnett demonstrated to be true of *Frankenstein*? Both Brooks and Winnett name ambition, for instance, as a characteristic theme of the novel genre and demonstrate the manifestations of character ambition in plot structure. Several of *Glastonbury*'s characters may be described as ambitious, and their ambition is surely mirrored by the structure of the plot. But these characters' accomplishments often appear in the narrative suddenly, without buildup, and are then unsystematically undermined by external circumstances or, in some cases, by the characters' own incompetence. Their trajectories meet with obstacles, as in both theoretical models, but Powys either deflates these conflicts with anticlimax, or uses the obstacle to deflect the character's progress onto a new trajectory altogether, thereby again preventing Brooks's "right end" to the original trajectory, and frustrating the authorial audience's investment in that progress.[18] Regardless of whether a conflict meets with anticlimax or a deflection of trajectory, however, the narrator invariably turns his attention away from a character immediately after the conflict, declining to explore the consequences or significance of that conflict, and attends instead to another character's situation.

John Geard's rise in Glastonbury, for example, is a logical consequence of his surprise bequest of Canon Crow's substantial inheritance at the novel's outset. Geard (the aforementioned fanatical preacher) is arguably the most prominent character in the book, the most likely agent of change in the town, the one character all the other characters know, and the character most closely associated with the spiritual energy of Glastonbury itself. His upward mobility would be, in a conventional plot, the novel's central strand. But Geard's ambition to be mayor of Glastonbury, the manifestation of his social climb, is not narrated as an experience for the character. The reader first learns of Geard's ambition in the midst of a teatime chat between Mat Dekker and Elizabeth Crow (202). Elizabeth's nephew Philip also is given narrative time to muse on his resentment of Geard's ambitions (230), but the reader has no access to what Geard himself thinks. While the narrator attends to Sam Dekker's lust for Nell, Geard becomes mayor-elect in an unspecified, unnarrated event. Even Geard's ascension to mayor is marked by ellipsis and then anticlimax: instead of polishing his acceptance speech, Geard dozes off in a cave and sleeps through the entire event. The townspeople of Glastonbury gather, expecting to hear his address, but are regaled only by the opportunistic Philip, taking advantage of the audience to rail against Geard. Although at the moment of the speech the crowd cheers for Philip, the narrator describes the town's ultimate disappointment in Geard: "As the night fell on the roofs of Glastonbury it was as if She Herself, the historic matrix of all these happenings, had been thwarted and fooled at the critical moment of her mystic response. The generative nerve of Her body had descended into Her womb, but all to no purpose! Cold and hard and pragmatic, the words of the Norfolk iconoclast had cut off the consummation of Her desire" (343). Geard's wife and daughters presently return home to find him sitting in his armchair, phlegmatically drinking some gin. The narrative then turns promptly to Sam Dekker.

This sequence reveals Powys's resistance to conventional plot progression (with his use of ellipsis and anticlimax), as well as a sketch of the alternative he employs in this novel. Glastonbury is explicitly female, and her desire is profoundly receptive. She is not passive, for she is ready for Geard's speech with a "mystic response" of her own. Glastonbury thinks and acts with intermental accord:[19] "Every person," claims the narrator, "was conscious that something deep had been stirred up, ready to respond to Geard of Glastonbury's communication, and this Something had been suppressed" by Philip's speech (342). As in multiple crowd scenes throughout the novel, this audience epitomizes Glastonbury by becoming profoundly receptive. The narrator places special emphasis on the group's collective, eager readiness for experience, for communication, and particularly for communion with John Geard. Geard's magnetism is at once sexual, rhetorical, and spiritual, making him the appropriate center of Glastonbury's rapt, intermental attention. But Philip's usurpation, figured as tantamount to an opportunistic seduction, leaves Glastonbury with "a queer, vague, irritated sense of uncomfortable remorse"—not a feeling of violation, but rather of pique and dissatisfaction (342).

This response indicates that Powysian receptivity is a form of assertion: an intentional quest for experience. This could suggest that Winnett's model of reader response is an appropriate reference point. Like breastfeeding and birth, Powysian receptivity requires interaction of two figures or parties, while refusing the subjugation of one to another. By this point in the novel, the authorial audience is well trained in responding to anticlimax with equanimity rather than frustration. And Geard's inauguration is precisely the sort of beginning that Winnett wants to champion in novels: it should be a moment that launches new significance, new sources of investment for the reader. But even this event provokes no advance in the reader's interpretation of textual significance. Philip's speech tells the reader nothing new about his personality or his relationship with Geard, and the would-be turning point for Geard's forward momentum is carelessly squandered by Geard himself. Winnett's model of speculative, forward-thinking reading is inapplicable when the reader can only react to the story's twists. Here is more evidence suggesting that Powys does not, in general, exploit narrative events to encourage the reader's interpretation. Rather, he uses them to intensify the reader's attention to the surface details of the text. This scene encourages the reader to focus attention exclusively on Glastonbury's surface: that is, not to make inferences by connecting textual detail with meaning or significance. While Geard sleeps in a cave, literally underneath Glastonbury's plot, the action takes place on its surface.[20] Because he is below, he misses the entire point of the event. His effort to think hard at a deep level results in unconsciousness. "[E]very time he deserted his vague, rich, semi-erotic feelings and tried to condense his scheme into a rational statement," Geard's mind fails him, a condition only exacerbated by his trying mentally "to call up that audience of people and to imagine their response to what he said."[21]

The narrator foregrounds Geard's anticipation of his audience's reception because, in this story-world, receptivity is what matters most to all the primary characters.

THE NARRATIVE PROGRESSION of Powys's novel demands an erotics of reading that self-consciously denies the pleasures of hermeneutic involvement. Powys's alternative to Winnett's prospective and Brooks's retrospective models, I contend, is what he called young-girl-like receptivity.[22] Drawing on his own conceit of young girls as presexual, innocent, open, absorptive, yielding, and curious, Powys envisioned a connection between implied author and implied reader not dependent on the tumescence-detumescence model. He exploited this model both thematically and structurally in *Glastonbury*.

Instances of receptivity as a theme are easy to find in this novel. Geard's predecessor, Mayor Wollop, for instance, exists constantly in a state of receptivity.

> The Mayor was obsessed with a trance-like absorption of interest; by the appearance of our world *exactly as it appeared*. What worries some, disconcerts others . . . had no effect upon the duck's back of Mr. Wollop. . . . Below the *surfaces* of appearances he never went! . . . The appearance of things was the nature of things; and all things, as they presented themselves to his attention . . . fed his mind with slow, agreeable, unruffled ponderings. Bert [a young boy] and Mayor Wollop diffused the projection of their amorous propensities over the whole surface of their world; and their world was *what they saw*. (219–20)

Mr. Wollop, Bert Cole, Nancy Stickles, and Mr. Geard all share this capacity for entranced absorption of superficial information. It allows all of them to remain in exceptionally contented frames of mind for two reasons. First, because their "amorous propensities" are outwardly directed, Mr. Wollop and his ken do not suffer from the intense, Romantic self-scrutiny that comes with repressed or narcissistic desire, such as that of Mr. Evans or Crummie Geard. Second, those in trances of absorption are not troubled by other people's vagaries, with which Glastonbury is brimming. As a mayor and religious leader, Geard is depicted as more effectively altruistic for being able to concentrate his attention on a single task at a time, even if this makes him impervious to the needs of everyone else around him.

Receptivity in explicitly erotic encounters in *Glastonbury* is fueled by the sympathy of one person for another. Girls in a state of receptivity to their lovers may be seen as analogous to the properly attentive authorial audience. Girls read their lovers, both women and men, by sympathetically apprehending both the lovers' external details and their identities. For instance, when Nell and Sam consummate their love, the narrator remarks: "She has reached a level of emotion where everything about him is accepted and taken for granted; and not only so, but actually seen for what it is, without a flicker of idealism" (298). At the height of their passion, while "she for him had become absolutely impersonal—a woman's flesh in empty space—he remained for her the *actual, personal, conscious man she loved*" (310).[23] For girls in this novel, the personality or essence of anything—a person, a tree, family lineage—is of paramount importance. The apprehension of that essence is achieved through sympathetic identification with the other person, even to the extent of self-forgetting. But personality without superficial detail loses meaning in this novel. The narrator comments on Nell's attention to Sam's personality, but amply supplements this with description of Nell's sexual response to Sam's body. Likewise, Glastonbury is at its heart a historic, mystical convergence, but without its swarms of townspeople in the narrative present-day, it holds little but symbolic significance.

The authorial audience's responsibility, then, is to extrapolate Glastonbury's personality from its superficial details. The reader is actively discouraged by the text's teeming sprawl from making large hermeneutic connections. Instead, the implied author cultivates the reader's young-girl-like receptivity to the narrative. Evocation of sympathy is a common enough tactic in novels, but what makes this sympathy unusual is the paucity of justification for it. Powys's characters are not particularly compelling as objects of pity or compassion. They have bizarre peculiarities, they are not roundly or consistently characterized by the narrator, and it is often very hard to see the characters for themselves when the narrator's voice is so much more prominent and compelling. The novel is, in fact, rather crowded and impersonal, for all the narrator's efforts to emphasize individuality and minute detail. How, then, is young-girl-like receptivity an appropriate (or even remotely pleasurable) response to this novel?

The novel suggests answers to this question in Geard's Glastonbury Pageant, the novel's *mise en abyme* and a prime example of young-girl-like receptivity in a crowded, impersonal setting. Here the book's characters, both Pageant performers and members of the audience, gather and forget themselves in an orgy of attention to the semireligious, semimystical

Pageant. During the Passion Play segment of the program, Mr. Evans, dazed and enervated by his long stint as Christ on the cross, falls into a trance of receptivity. "The pain he endured turned his pedantic acquisitiveness into a living medium, acutely sensitive, quiveringly receptive, through which the whole history of Glastonbury began to pour" (615). Evans as medium absorbs the "revenants," or essence, of Glastonbury's history. He feels himself become Christ, even become Glastonbury itself. Evans hears a voice speaking to him, condemning his sadistic impulses, and he responds to it. While this conversation ensues between Evans's personality and that of Glastonbury/Christ, the narrator notes that Christ's voice "was like a wind stirring the horns of snails and touching the hairs in the throats of night jars, and moving the antennae of butterflies, and lifting the gold-dust from the cracks of puff-balls, and blowing the grey dust from the droppings of weasels" (617–18). Throughout the long passage, the narrator juxtaposes superficial details of the Pageant with the inner world of Evans, who, at the heart of the Pageant, is the figure most deeply receptive to the Pageant's essence.

The dazzle and confusion of the Pageant—fulsomely described by the narrator, excessively plotted and planned by Geard, overflowing with too many performers and too many audience members—may be seen as analogous to the novel's energetic but chaotic structure. The chapter's events make it clear that a proper, though risky, response to the Pageant is full receptivity to it. At the Pageant's outset, "a cumulative wave of crowd-hypnosis shivered through these assembled people, straightening their shoulders, lifting their heads, turning their faces toward the grassy terrace on the slope above them" (556).[24] As the day wears on, however, the crowd's attention divides and wanders, signifying an improper response (one that the novel's reader may find familiar).[25] Several production mistakes in the Pageant as well as many disruptions in its vicinity distract the large audience, whose attention—unlike that of Evans—is divided repeatedly and disastrously throughout the long event, suggesting a less-than-optimal reading experience. As a contrast, the steadfast young-girl-like receptivity enacted by a handful of girls—Morgan Nelly, Persephone, Angela, and Cordelia—highlights the redemptive value of credulous, close attention: "Perhaps in that whole vast assembly only Father Paleologue and one other realised the full poignancy of the acting of Judas. . . . Morgan Nelly's heart leapt up in sympathy as she followed the figure of Judas wandering among some small thorn bushes. . . . In the end he disappeared behind the western pavilion, and long before he had disappeared the main interest of the Pageant had shifted from him altogether; but the little girl's heart was still with him. She knew who it was" (599). Morgan Nelly's identification not only of the actor's name but of his personality, his self, is her reading of the Pageant. The event means more to her than to others because she is able to feel sympathy for the character simply by paying attention and being receptive to the actor on stage. No one more than a young girl has the privilege of such a connection in this story-world. Meanwhile, Persephone renders herself receptive to Evans's consciousness as she embraces the base of Evans's cross: she feels "vibrating through its dense oaken veins the wild triumph of his tense tormented nerves, the savage rapture of his self-immolation" (611). Persephone's sympathy for Evans's agony is so extreme that she becomes ill, infected by his torment. And obsessively watching Persephone's figure on stage is her lover, Angela, whose "face was white and her whole body was trembling with excitement. The soul within her yearned to that beautiful form that now with uplifted arms was embracing the feet of the suspended Figure" (601). These examples illustrate ardent, attentive readers of the Pageant in the throes of passionate absorption in their text. Their ardor and ecstasy allow the novel's reader no doubt of the Pageant's orgiastic quality. In this chapter the narrator highlights the corruptive potential of close reading, particularly for young girls, and he depicts the overtly chaste narrative of the Passion Play as a vehicle for seduction.

What makes receptivity appropriate as a readerly response, despite its risks, is the fullness of experience it offers.[26] Powys compels his authorial audience to decide between resisting the novel altogether or surrendering under pressure to absorbing the novel's myriad details. Its sheer length and scope discourage the reader who would skim the text, since the novel's rewards lie in extrapolating Glastonbury's personality from a full absorption of its surface. The immediacy of contact between the receptive reader and the implied author in a situation such as this has overtones of erotic proximity. In *Libidinal Currents,* Joseph Allen Boone considers the eroticism of "that delirious process of surrender into otherness" that some novels encourage in readers: "Truly close reading demands that we give ourselves over to the 'closeness' of the relationship that texts elicit in readers, acknowledging the affective dimensions of reading that are not caught up in a reading for mastery but that seek an understanding of what it means to occupy, however temporarily, the place of the other as part of oneself" (20, 25). Herein consists the pleasure of young-girl-like receptivity: the erotically charged stimulation of surrendering to another consciousness. For all of his uninterest in conventional narrative constructs,

Powys works hard to cultivate a story-world that demands this particular sort of attention from its readers.

MANY CHARACTERS spend a good portion of the book in various states of receptivity. Although this behavior is often coded as positive, since it engenders sympathy and communication between characters and suggests an optimal reading strategy for the novel itself, receptivity is also shown to be potentially crippling when it lacks an ethical purpose. For instance, Mayor Wollop is a curiosity for his absolute absorption in the inessential, but he also must be a shockingly incompetent mayor. Total absorption in one's own sensations is not just unethical; it is also selfish and antisocial. Likewise, after Sam has cruelly deserted the pregnant Nell and turned to a life of private asceticism, he wanders about town in a trance-like state of absorption, thoroughly relishing his freedom from domestic responsibilities as he concentrates on twigs and rodents in his path.[27]

But the antithesis to receptivity in this novel is not inattention; it is intermental penetration, invasive mind reading. As a means of interpersonal connection, and as the privileged site of assertive agency in the novel, young-girl-like receptivity trumps penetration. This marks an advanced stage in the flesh-and-blood Powys's decades-long, intense struggle with the dualism between penetration and receptivity. He enacted his struggle early in the twentieth century on the university extension lecture circuit and in his earliest novels. He analyzes this struggle in his *Autobiography*, written just two years after *Glastonbury*. Powys's radical philosophical experiments with gender and sexual identity attest to his deep-seated desire to supersede normative sexual tropes of activity and passivity. *Glastonbury*, unlike Powys's previous writing, offers young-girl-like receptivity as an efficacious alternative to phallic aggression. Penetration—physical, mental, spiritual—pervades the novel, but the narrator codes it in all but a few cases as an unwelcome intrusion, if not a hostile violation, and figures it, rather than a human character, as the primary villain in the novel.

Phallic aggression, like young-girl-like receptivity, is an imaginative power. Its force and direction are generated by a character's mind. In its more intense form it is an obsession with physical assault, held by both men and women who harbor antisocial impulses such as bloodlust or sadism: Owen Evans, Mad Bet, Red Robinson.[28] Its nonviolent form motivates characters' efforts to influence each other through suggestion or even hypnotism. The narrator characterizes both Geard's and Philip's powers of oratory as phallic, and Paul Trent's ineffectual efforts to convert the townspeople to communism are described as failures of his phallic energy.[29]

Several critics have focused on phallic aggression in Powys's novel without accounting for the implied author's ubiquitous valorization of receptivity.[30] Philip's aforementioned oratory, for instance, which the narrator dubs a "Dolorous Blow" to Geard's mayoral ascendancy, is important enough to give the chapter its title. But Philip's performance is focalized through Glastonbury, keeping the reader's attention on Glastonbury's reception of Philip rather than on Philip's experience of oration. At considerable length, the narrator describes the crowd's perception of Philip, and then grants just one paragraph to quoting the phallic rhetoric. In defiance of its title, the chapter concludes with an extended meditation on Glastonbury and her humbled hero, Geard.

One particularly compelling voice on this subject is Robert Caserio's, in his argument that the phallic aggression of *Glastonbury*'s villains fuels what little forward movement the plot offers. Further, he argues, the novel suggests a reader's response on the same model of phallic aggression. Whereas in my reading the reader is asked to enact young-girl-like receptivity in response to the novel, Caserio asserts that the novel's structure "stimulates the reader to penetrate the text's mass, to break into it or spear it, so that the spirit of analytic reading moves into alignment with the characters who are figures of aggression."[31]

In his close reading of the novel's politics, Caserio rightly connects the sadistic impulses of Owen Evans and Red Robinson with phallic symbols such as iron bars and lances; notes that Red's cohorts, a couple named Spear, complement his aggressive rhetorical attacks; and argues that phallic penetration thematizes sadistic aggression in the novel. He deduces the "reader's partisanship with sadism" from a characteristic of the novel I have analyzed above: "the reader's progress from one episode to another is an ever-thwarted attempt at movement in an ocean-like crowd of divaricating elements. The result for reading is a loss of analytic orientation: in the continuous crowd of elements one scarcely can discover in which direction analysis ought to go" (98). If the reader can cognitively penetrate the text, by this model, s/he can interpret it. Like Geard's miraculous healing of the cancer patient Tittie Petherton, in which he imaginatively plunged "that Bleeding Lance of his mind" into the tumor, textual interpretation can be "vital and curative" as a "break or disruption in the crowded banality of things" (Powys 709; Caserio 99).

Caserio's argument assumes that the novel offers the reader "the promise of buried truth to be discovered in the narrative's elisions," and that this stimulates the reader's intervention, but he offers no evidence for this claim (98). I cannot find any such promise in the novel's structure: the "divaricating elements," seemingly digressive or unnecessary subplots or narratorial asides, are not tumors to be eradicated, nor do they conceal a secretly healthy masterplot trajectory. To understand what these elements do, and to appreciate what the novel asks its reader to do, is to comprehend the dynamics of *Glastonbury*'s narrative progression. A refusal to penetrate the text analytically is precisely what Susan Sontag calls for.

Furthermore, the model of penetration as a model of readerly investment bears examination beyond Caserio's thoughtful analysis. Though he does not argue that all penetration in the novel is sadistic,[32] Caserio notes that even "vital and curative" penetration, such as Geard's healing powers or the reader's interpretation, qualifies as a "certain sadism" (99). He identifies Geard's daughter Cordelia's emergency seduction of her husband, the deeply troubled Owen Evans, as a form of sadism. But the novel offers evidence to the contrary. All examples of "vital and curative," or ethical, penetration involve large amounts of sympathy and intense attention to detail. As she faces her miserable husband, Cordelia can choose to be "cold, chaste, inert, irresponsible, absorbed in her own personal condition," or she can decide to be "warm, alluring, unchaste, and self-forgetful, thinking only of her love for the unhappy man before her!" (1029). Noting that "she wasn't the daughter of Geard of Glastonbury for nothing," the narrator describes Cordelia's "incontinent" flood of sympathy for and attention to Evans. She absorbs every detail of who Evans is at that moment. The "annihilating ray" Cordelia directs at Evans to eradicate his misery is indeed penetrative, but it is rooted in her sympathy and young-girl-like receptivity (1035).

As Geard of Glastonbury attempts to heal to Tittie Petherton's cancer, in one of the novel's most dramatic moments, "his face twisted in a spasm of physical pain," and he suffers acutely in his body the pain she feels in her own (290, 506). Like Cordelia's, Geard's phallic force is energized by compassion. Many townspeople distrust this extremity of sympathy. Mary Crow, a reliable commentator, remarks that "I believe he's got some weird nervous sympathy . . . mind you I don't like him. . . . [H]e has some nervous peculiarity which makes him *imitate* every infirmity he meets" (547). Geard and Cordelia's receptivity is threatening, of course, because it allows them to read, to inhabit other people's minds. Its dangers—as well as its powers—are akin to those of mesmeric or hypnotic control, or those of losing oneself in a novel. But this kind of receptivity is also fundamentally ethical, and its resemblance to the authorial audience's proper reading of *Glastonbury*'s indicates that for Powys, receptive reading is an ethical enterprise.

Powys's *Glastonbury* offers scholars of novel history and structure a new form of narrative progression to consider. In this extremely long and digressive novel, the "plane of resistance" Brooks identifies in a traditional plot is distended almost beyond recognition, with no clear trajectory of revelations and deferrals to keep the reader's attention focused on a particular resolution. But *Glastonbury* does function according to a double-layered progression traceable through both narrative dynamics and the implied reader's response. This progression depends upon the authorial audience's sustained surrender to the implied author's rules of engagement, which, though unconventional, nonetheless operate consistently and reliably throughout the novel. Powys's novel not only offers an opportunity to refuse, utterly, the temptation to "excavate" and "destroy" through interpretation. Its structure and discourse work together to cultivate an erotics of art as the only appropriate response.

✑ CONCLUSION

THIS BOOK offers close readings and a concomitant theory of feminist novels that make few, if any, overt claims to be feminist. Most of them do not contain any feminist characters, their narrators do not make feminist remarks or judgments, and their authors (with the exception of Woolf) are not known for being feminists in real life. Nevertheless, these novels covertly persuade their readers to think differently, if only for a short while, about the urgency of social change through feminism. I have defined *feminism* as the conviction that gender roles are constructed; that such roles place systematic, inequitable constraints on women and men, to women's especial disadvantage; and that gender relations can and must be revised to eliminate that disadvantage.

The tacit persuasion I identify in these novels consists largely in the ethics of the telling, operating independently of the ethics of the told and the ethics of rhetorical purpose. I isolate vital passages, even individual words, for special consideration, contending that certain dimensions of the telling, however brief, contribute to a pervasive undercurrent of persuasive feminist conviction. That conviction, I argue, can and must be attributed to the implied author of each work.

I have limited my attention to feminist novels produced during the modernist period—novels written before and just after full suffrage was gained for women in England, in 1928. But the novels in this study stand apart from other forms of modernist experimentation, as well as from most examples of feminist propaganda, because they depend in part on narrative ethics, as determined by feminist politics, for their effects. The goal of this book is to bring into conversation rhetorical narrative ethics, feminist theory, literary interpretation, and cultural history. It is to propose a new theory of feminist narrative ethics.

Most of the novels I am considering postdate 1928, when a major backlash against feminism was in full force. These authors' use of relatively oblique argumentation through narrative technique does not suggest diminished aspiration or capitulation to antifeminism. On the contrary, it corresponds to a sea change in the feminist movement. I see narrative ethics as a powerful next stage of feminist argumentation in 1930s Britain: one of many tactics adopted after the vote was won for gaining wider public participation in comprehensive gender equity. Certain novels of this period encouraged readers to replace feminism-as-political-tactics with feminism-as-ethical-worldview, and to replace adversarial impatience with the lived experience of feminist beliefs.

To shed light on the intersections I am proposing between theory, interpretation, and history, I have established four paradigms of feminist narrative ethics: the ethics of distance (Forster), the ethics of fair play (Sayers), the ethics of persuasion (Woolf), and the ethics of attention (Powys). While these paradigms are relevant to the British modernist fiction I examine here, they could easily be applied to prose fiction from other periods and cultures as well. The ethics of distance, for example, operates prominently in Frances Burney's *Evelina*. First-person narrator Evelina's thoroughly feminized passivity pervades the ethics of the told: her gentleness on the level of story stands in vivid contrast to most of the other characters' violent outbursts. Evelina must evade assaults, navigate courtships, and even prevent a friend from committing suicide, all by way of her resolute passivity.[1] But the ethics of the telling has a subtler, more compelling rhetorical significance. In *Desire and Truth*, Patricia Meyer Spacks observes that, "[f]rom the point of view of the modern reader, the characters directly engaged in power games indeed generate the best stories. But Evelina, and presumably her creator, dimly apprehend another principle of narrative, one related to but extending the mode of the sentimental novel. . . . Evelina believes the vulgar [characters] provide no narrative material of value."[2] Spacks makes only a passing reference to

Evelina's creator, but I believe the implied author of *Evelina* crafts a thoroughly passive narrator to explore the ethics of distance. Burney's highly calculated deference to male privilege in the ethics of the told (as well as in the novel's dedication and preface) stands in curious tension to the ethics of the telling, in which masculine power struggles are deemed unnarratable because they are uninteresting. The paradigms I have proposed can shed valuable light on certain novels by each of the authors I have considered in this study. But they can also, more broadly, help define a new dimension of rhetorical narrative ethics, one which is, in this case, turned to feminist ends.

Each of my ethical paradigms, as I have remarked, relies on the highly contested concept of the implied author. In this study I validate the implied author, showing not only its usefulness as a concept but also its real necessity in recognizing tacit persuasion in narrative form. I engage with a wide variety of arguments to the contrary, acknowledging and responding to each in turn, through both theory and practice. My close readings of a very broad spectrum of implied authors help illustrate my examination of the concept as an indispensable part of rhetorical ethics and of narrative theory more broadly.

To my mind, a full appreciation of an ethical rapport between author and audience must be informed not only by evidence of the flesh-and-blood writer's decisions (that in some cases includes archival evidence of manuscript revisions), but also by the implied author's rhetorical strategies, which are subtly but powerfully influenced by historical and cultural context. I am convinced that practicing historically sensitive narratology is the best means of gaining insight into the ethical ramifications of prose fiction. In some cases, though, our awareness of historicity must make the physical history of the text itself relevant to the discussion. Therefore I propose one new way of coordinating narratology with textual criticism, through the concept of the project author.

A number of theorists and scholars have observed the difficulty—some even say the impossibility—of doing justice in a single study to both history and form. But on the contrary, I believe that a historically aware narratology—a study of narrative form that respectfully engages not only theory and interpretation but also history and culture, in equal measure—is the hallmark and indeed the future of postclassical narratology. I am grateful for the examples set by Alison Case, Melba Cuddy-Keane, Harry Shaw, and Robyn Warhol, among others. Their work continues the enrichment of narrative theory through contact with other fields of literary study. I have written this book inspired by them. Although narratology began as a highly rarefied science for specialists, it has matured and continues to flourish whenever it intersects with other discourses. At this moment, the most promising intersections for postclassical narratology seem to be those with rhetoric and ethics, with feminism, and with cognitive science. Other innovative connections will doubtless emerge. The most productive and interesting of these connections will likely be those that coordinate in equal parts theory, interpretation, and cultural history.

I suspect that a hybrid approach to prose fiction that employs both narratology and critical bibliography may emerge soon. The history of the book as a physical object, the culture and politics of book publishing, and theories of narrative transmission all have much to gain from one another. James Phelan and Wayne C. Booth as well as Jerome McGann (in a different context) have some important connections among these fields, but the truly hybrid approach has not yet become well established. I hope I may contribute to its establishment. Chapter 2 and especially chapter 3 of this book offer rhetorical readings of holograph manuscripts in relation to publications, but I see much more good work to be done in this area. I look forward to enlivening the project author concept with more research and theory alike in the years ahead.

✎ NOTES

INTRODUCTION

1. Susan Lanser's *Fictions of Authority* includes a chapter on what she terms "covert authoriality" in modernist novels: "the illusion of 'effacement' that is constructed from a suppression of narrative self-consciousness, of contact between narrator and narratee, and of explicit markers of narrative stance" (104). She argues that "[t]he convention of 'effaced' authoriality seems to me to have carried particular double edges for modernist women novelists. On the one hand, overtly hegemonic forms of narration such as those appropriated by George Eliot and her successors were (in part perhaps for that reason) no longer desirable as literature; women writers would have to choose, as it were, between authoriality, with its fertile ground for figuring woman's relation to public culture, and canonicity. On the other hand, the deconstruction of realist authority—which had never been significantly feminized—opened spaces for antihegemonic representations and alternative constructions of female subjectivity. But so long as female subjectivity remained marginal, so too could the writings that represented it" (104–5). Lanser's chapter offers a number of persuasive insights, especially into Woolf's "pivotal and liminal" relations to both feminism and modernism. However, I take some exception to Lanser's analysis of Woolf's *Pargiters* and *The Years* in my chapter 3.

2. For a concise overview of several directions in which scholars are expanding the parameters of modernism, see "The New Modernist Studies" by Mao and Walkowitz.

3. This definition applies to first-wave feminism as it was understood and practiced by many in Great Britain in the early twentieth century. It accurately describes the basis for ethical argumentation about gender adopted by the four authors in this study. The definition is my own, however, marked by twenty-first-century retrospection and by more than two decades of productive intersection between feminist theory and queer theory. I

doubt any feminists of the early twentieth century would have used precisely these words to define their beliefs. It is worth noting that the word *feminism* was often used pejoratively in this period and that, like many of their contemporaries, all of the authors in this study—even the ones devoted to women's rights—distrusted it as a term. Moreover, feminist ideals at this historical moment were considered primarily in relation to middle- and upper-class white women; gender-based constraints felt by anyone else were far less frequently addressed. This latter point is one that motivates two of the four authors considered here.

4. Phelan, *Experiencing Fiction*, 10.

5. Two works for which I have special admiration and respect, and that have greatly helped shape my thinking in this book, are Case's *Plotting Women* and Shaw's *Narrating Reality.*

6. Several such questions come to mind. What makes a novel feminist? Is feminist authorial intention required? Can narrative techniques be intrinsically ethical or political? Is a novel feminist if its reader perceives feminism in it? Can tacit, conditional, or irresolute feminism still be ethically potent? How does a novel's production and reception history help shape its gender politics?

7. Winnett and Phelan have both offered attractive methods for de-emphasizing endings in order better to appreciate middles and beginnings. See especially Winnett's reading of *Frankenstein* in "Coming Unstrung" and Phelan's reading of *Great Expectations* in *Reading People, Reading Plots*. Both analyses demonstrate shortcomings in Peter Brooks's famous, and strikingly gendered, privileging of narrative endings in *Reading for the Plot.*

8. I borrow the term "tensions" from Phelan's model of narrative progression. "Tensions" here refers to discourse-level imbalances "of value, belief, opinion, knowledge, expectation" that create distance between the implied author and/or narrator and the reader. Phelan contrasts tensions with "instabilities," which are unstable relations among characters in the story (*Reading People*, 15). Phelan's definitions pertain not to any given reader but to one who is responsive to a narrative's rhetorical cues; a person who, consciously or not, joins what Rabinowitz has named the authorial audience. In "Truth in Fiction" (1977) Rabinowitz established this crucial term to represent the hypothetical ideal audience for whom a given implied author is writing. Recently, though, rhetorical narratologists invested in narrative ethics have recognized the value of examining the judgments that texts prompt real (not just hypothetical) audiences to make (again, see esp. Phelan, *Living to Tell about It* and "Rhetoric, Ethics, and Narrative Communication"). Accordingly, although I employ Rabinowitz's useful concepts of authorial and narrative audiences (particularly in my chapter 3), I work to establish, in all the novels under consideration, some ethical efficacy that goes beyond the hypothetical.

9. Of course, British novelists have been coordinating art and politics since the seventeenth century; the innovation at this moment was to coordinate specifically modernist techniques with politics.

10. For an excellent account of the broad spectrum of goals and objectives within the women's movement—the vast majority of which were subsumed by suffragist activism at a (relatively) politically opportune moment—see Kent, *Sex and Suffrage.*

11. They stand apart from most others as well in having turned these generic experiments to ethical ends. Most writers in the modernist era were less invested than these writers in narrative ethics, let alone feminist narrative ethics.

12. "Career author" is Wayne Booth's term for the composite figure that emerges

from similarities among implied authors in a single writer's oeuvre (*Critical Understanding*, 270–71).

13. This is not to say that feminist scholars have not done impressive work with the implied author concept. Few narrative theorists have thought more responsibly or cogently about the implied author than Susan Lanser. Likewise, Alison Booth, Alison Case, Melba Cuddy-Keane, Susan Fraiman, Molly Hite, Kathy Mezei, Ruth Page, Catherine Romagnolo, Robyn Warhol, and Jean Wyatt, to name a just a few distinguished feminist scholars, have all engaged with—if not invested significantly in—the concept. My hope is to contribute to the conversation they have begun, in part by offering a new way of coordinating rhetorical narratology with feminist theory.

14. Rabinowitz, "Absence," 104. See Booth's 1988 book *The Company We Keep: An Ethics of Fiction* for an extended consideration of the implied author as friend.

15. Genette, *Narrative Discourse Revisited,* chap. 19.

16. Nünning, "Deconstructing and Reconceptualizing the Implied Author," esp. 97–99; Kindt and Müller, *The Implied Author,* chap. 3.

17. Chatman, *Coming to Terms,* chap. 5; Rimmon-Kenan, *Narrative Fiction,* 89.

18. Abbott, *Cambridge Introduction to Narrative,* 85.

19. Hogan, "Multiplicity of Implied Authors," passim.

20. Herman, "Narrative Theory and the Intentional Stance," passim.

21. Serpell, discussion during NEH seminar "Narrative Ethics."

22. Rabinowitz, "'Absence of Her Voice from that Concord,'" 100, 101.

23. Richardson, "Implied Author," 7. Although I describe Richardson's summary as representative of consensus, and I agree with his assertion that the implied author cannot be located inside the text, I take exception to his claim that the implied author does not communicate. Throughout this chapter, and indeed this book, I hope to demonstrate that the implied author's fundamental purpose is communication.

24. Lanser, "The Implied Author," 156.

25. Schmid, "Implied Author," paragraph 28. Quoted by Lanser in "The Implied Author," 156.

26. It is commonplace to recognize that all writers, regardless of genre, elect to present themselves in certain ways. A student explaining in writing why she wants to drop a college course mid-semester will enact a different persona when she addresses her professor as opposed to her friends or her parents. The differences in those personae can be deduced by contrasting the reasons, evidence, and warrants she relies on in each separate written account. Contemporary fiction writers readily agreed, when I casually queried them, that the figure responsible for the creation of any written work is itself a construction, a fragment of the whole writing self, a representation of the writer at the time of writing. This common assumption takes various forms in narrative theory. For example, David Herman's CAPA model as well as the playful argument mounted by Luc Herman and Bart Vervaeck proudly denounce the implied author concept, but go on to acknowledge the vital importance of "distributed intention" and an author's "self-presentation" in any given text (see Herman, "Narrative Theory and the Intentional Stance" and Herman and Vervaeck, "Secular Excommunication").

27. Woolf, *Writer's Diary,* 20 January 1931 and 25 April 1933.

28. In chapter 3, I cite many of the best efforts of scholars to deduce arguments from both the telling and the told in versions of Woolf's novel as it was finally published in Britain and the United States. I do not suggest that it is impossible to find such arguments in the isolated, published artifact; but I am convinced that all such arguments are clearer and more meaningful in the context of Woolf's revisions.

29. Flint, *Woman Reader*, 15.

CHAPTER 1

1. Forster, *Commonplace Book*, 59.
2. Forster, *Feminine Note*, 21. Earlier in his speech, he observes that the couple that follows the rules of chivalry "are a fine and for the moment happy couple. He has strength, she charm. But the happiness leaves no tenderness behind it, and neither the strength nor the charm will ever be touched into beauty" (17).
3. Furbank, *E. M. Forster*, 1:180.
4. Forster, *Commonplace Book*, 59.
5. Furbank, *E. M. Forster*, 1:180.
6. Furbank, *E. M. Forster*, 2:56.
7. Very likely it was precisely because it was an uncomfortable topic, and he needed to figure out what he thought about it. I do not wish to pin a teleology of enlightenment on the sequence of his published novels—by which logic *Howards End* would have more progressive gender politics than, say, *Where Angels Fear to Tread,* and thus would prove Forster's growth. His last published novel, *A Passage to India,* is by no means his most progressive one in its treatment of women.
8. Trilling, *E M. Forster*, 16–17.
9. Forster muses in his *Commonplace Book,* circa 1930, that "[i]f women ever wanted to be by themselves all would be well. But I don't believe they ever want to be, except for reasons of advertisement, and their instinct is never to let men be by themselves. This, I begin to see, is sex-war" (60). In 1932 he added, "One can run away from women, turn them out, or give in to them. No fourth course. Men sometimes want to be without women. Ah why is the converse not equally true?" (92–93).
10. Langland, "Gesturing toward an Open Space," 253; Miller, *Novel and the Police,* 154–55.
11. Furbank, *E. M. Forster*, 1:217.
12. Leavis, "E. M. Forster" (1938), rpt. in Bradbury, *Forster,* 3.
13. Piggford, Introduction to Forster, *Feminine Note,* 9.
14. For more on the relationship between gender identity and queer politics in Forster, see especially Martin and Piggford, *Queer Forster;* and Moffat, *Unrecorded History.* For more on gender identity and feminist politics in *A Passage to India,* see especially Showalter, "Marriage Fiction" and Silver, "Periphrasis."
15. Goldman offers a useful overview of the scholarship in general on Forster and women in her 2007 *Cambridge Companion* chapter.
16. His scrutiny of conventional constraints on masculinity in *Maurice* is palpably self-confident, but of course, *Maurice* was shared in manuscript with a few select friends, and published only posthumously. Such self-assured, overt critique of gender roles simply does not appear in his other novels. A few have argued that Forster actually does offer radical critiques of gender in his heterosexual romances by constructing his female characters as mere stand-ins for men. They have claimed that Forster's first three novels feature a "homoerotic subtext." See, for example, Markley, "E. M. Forster's Reconfigured Gaze."
17. Langland, "Gesturing toward an Open Space," 256.
18. Martin is among several writers, including Forster's official biographer (Furbank) and friends (for example, Virginia Woolf), who have referred in passing to Forster's

misogyny. After careful scrutiny of primary and secondary sources, I can find no evidence of actual misogyny in Forster's speech or action, private or public. His sporadic exasperation with women hardly constitutes hatred. Moffat addresses this question directly in *Unrecorded History.*

19. Martin, "Umbrella," 267. Martin demonstrates that Howards End, a family home inherited through the generations by women, is a thematic extension of Forster's "political project that seeks to redefine a nonpatriarchal family" (270).

20. Although Markley stresses aesthetics more than politics in "Reconfigured Gaze," his argument in that essay comes closer to a political reading of *Room with a View* than most.

21. These high stakes are both interpretive (that is, crucial to the understanding of individual narratives) and theoretical. One of narratology's most important and enduring critical disagreements, the debate over Booth's implied author concept, appears to have been resolved through rigorous theorization of unreliable narration. In *Living to Tell about It*, Phelan asserts that the concept of unreliable narration necessarily entails the implied author concept. Because interpretation of certain narratives requires the concept of unreliable narration, the implied author concept is also necessary at least in those cases. See my summary of the debate in this book's introduction.

22. Graham, *Indirections*, 9.

23. Trilling, *E. M. Forster*, 16–17.

24. Graham, *Indirections*, 158.

25. Graham's chapter "The Forster Angle" is a masterful analysis of the rhetorical effects of Forster's double turn. He does not examine distance in any detail, though he mentions in passing the idea of distance between narrator and character. Of *Howards End*'s famous opening line, he remarks, "The narrator's 'One may as well' . . . is a gesture that creates a little leeway between him and these apparently uncontrollable and interesting events. And across that leeway, within that narrated field, characters and scenes can take on a certain independence, and can eventually be seen to cast their own shadow, while the narrator's shadow falls at a slightly different angle—the true Forster angle" (158).

26. Kettle, *Introduction to the English Novel*, 137.

27. Furbank's description of the flesh-and-blood author corresponds nicely to this description. "[P]eople [at Cambridge] found him hard to place and tended to think of him as someone else's friend. He went his own way. A little later Lytton Strachey coined the name 'the taupe' [i.e., mole] for him, and this was apt; he was drab-coloured and unobtrusive and came up in odd places and unexpected circles. There as something flitting and discontinuous about him; one minute you were talking with him intimately, the next he had withdrawn or simply disappeared. He was freakish and demure, yet at times could be earnestly direct, as if vast issues hung upon simple truth-telling. And all the time there was something hapless or silly-simple about him" (*E. M. Forster*, 1:66).

28. Rabinowitz observes: "Vladimir Nabokov appears to derive an almost sadistic satisfaction from knowing that his authorial audience is intellectually well above his actual readers—although it is possible that Nabokov in fact writes for an authorial audience quite close to his actual readers but writes in order to make that authorial audience feel intellectually inadequate" ("Truth in Fiction," 126).

29. Not only does Booth consider Forster's irony stable, he considers Forster as an exemplary practitioner. Forster along with Fielding, Sterne, Austen, George Eliot, Beerbohm, Twain, James, Emily Dickinson, and Auden "stand behind each ironic stroke as warrantors of the continuing validity of what we are about. Once we have read a few

pages by any of these authors we have experienced so many stable ironies that the appetite for more of them becomes essential to whatever effects the works intend" (*Rhetoric of Irony*, 176).

30. To my knowledge, only Graham, Langland, and Martin (quoted above) have made such deductions. A large number of critics have posited certain convictions based on Forster's biography or nonfiction and then demonstrated how formal qualities of his writing parallel those convictions: they have worked from the outside in to explain formal strategies based on supposed convictions. Rhetorical narrative ethics, by contrast, works from the inside out, deducing convictions from form. As Armstrong observes, "Asking questions about how formal textual strategies seek to engage a reader's assumptions and conventions is a specifically literary way to do the work of social, political criticism" (Preface to *Play and the Politics of Reading* x).

31. See my chapter 3, on the ethics of persuasion, for more on the application of rhetorical narrative ethics to nonfiction, particularly the essay genre.

32. Forster, "Me, Them and You," 26.

33. The casual comment quoted above from his *Commonplace Book,* in which he distances himself from about the suffrage-era feminist—"She shall have all she wants [politically]. I can still get away from her, I thought. I grudged her nothing except my company"—echoes felicitously here.

34. Booth, *Rhetoric of Irony,* 189.

35. Booth, *Rhetoric of Irony,* 176.

36. Booth deems Forster and Fielding to be two of the "great personal essayists" who "provide subtle mixtures that require us to shift gears constantly and skillfully. They do not invent a radically distinct mask and offer every word in his tone of voice; rather they develop a tone which becomes known as their true style and which includes frequent stable ironies" (*Rhetoric of Irony,* 185). Here Booth refers to Forster's nonfiction. I do not think it may be applied to his prose fiction, however. In the latter, Forster's narrators are not "radically distinct mask[s]." But I don't believe it follows that, in the absence of radical, systematic difference between narrator and implied author, we should accept that the narrator's style simply "becomes known" as the implied author's style.

37. Martin and Piggford, Introduction to *Queer Forster,* 4.

38. Forster, *Room with a View,* chapter 1, passim.

39. Goodlad argues that Forster is practicing Young's kind of ethics, enacting the "moral humility" of one who "starts with the assumption that one cannot see things from the other person's perspective and waits to learn" (Young, "Asymmetrical Reciprocity" 49). In the context of analyzing *Where Angels Fear to Tread,* Goodlad argues of all Forster's novels that, "Although the Forsterian narrator puts several viewpoints into play, subjecting each to varying modes of irony and assessment, such irreducibly different perspectives cannot, finally, be synthesized, balanced, or reconciled" ("Where Liberals Fear to Tread" 321). My idea of the parallax makes the opposite argument: Forster represents both positions in order to prompt the reader's engagement with both sides simultaneously, and the onus to make an ethical assessment is the rhetorical reader's.

40. Armstrong borrows Richard Rorty's notion of ironic liberalism to make his case. See Rorty, *Contingency, Irony, and Solidarity.*

41. Armstrong, *Play and the Politics of Reading,* 110, 125.

42. Armstrong, *Play and the Politics of Reading,* 127, 129n2.

43. See Kettle, *Introduction to the English Novel:* "[T]he tentativeness, the humility of Forster's attitude is not something to undervalue. The 'perhaps' that lie at the core of his novels, constantly pricking the facile generalization, hinting at the unpredictable

element in the most fully analyzed relationship, cannot be brushed aside as mere liberal pusillanimity. He seems to me a writer of scrupulous intelligence, of tough and abiding insights, who has never been afraid of the big issues or the difficult ones and has scorned to hide his doubts and weaknesses behind a façade of wordiness and self-protective conformity" (163).

44. Walsh, *Rhetoric of Fictionality,* chapter 4, esp. pages 70–78.

45. Walsh's approach is influenced by the work of Dan Sperber and Deirdre Wilson, especially "Rhetoric and Relevance" and *Relevance.*

46. Walsh would likely respond to me that Forster's narrator is simply the author narrating multiple, inconsistent perspectives. Of course, if we conflate implied author with narrator and posit one figure, we risk mistaking that figure's provocative and productive inconsistency for unreliability. This would be a serious mistake, since Forster's rhetorical purpose depends on the reliability of his narrator. But even if we were to conscientiously rule out such an interpretive mistake, agreeing to the reliability of the narrating figure, I believe Walsh's elimination of the narrator concept makes a distinction where there is no difference. Walsh's "narrating author" and my "narrator" are the same figure. What matters more than terminology is how this writer employs the resources at his disposal, and I contend that the figures who narrate Forster's fiction and nonfiction alike are his indispensable resource for communicating complex, sometimes contradictory ideas.

47. Whereas my reading of Forster through his narrator focuses on gender politics, Armstrong's focuses on sexual politics. He refers to both narrator and implied author as "closeted," treating Forster's real-life attraction to men as the linchpin. "Attuned to the closet's double game of conforming while rebelling . . . a reader can understand the contradictions in the narrator's performance as a provocation to reflect about the functions [of narrative realism] they disrupt rather than a failure to execute them" (*Play and the Politics of Reading,* 112). He notes, however, that "[w]ithout the biographical context of Forster's closeted homosexuality and the guidance of the theory of the closet, the pattern I am describing would be invisible" (112n2). Particularly in his reading of *A Passage to India,* Armstrong makes a persuasive case that Forster concealed certain queer dimensions of his writing. On the subject of feminism, however—a topic from which Forster evidently had more personal and philosophical, formal and ethical distance—I contend that Forster's patterns are both visible and meaningful independent of biographical context.

48. Emerson's position echoes that of Edward Carpenter's argument in his 1896 book *Love's Coming-of-Age.* Tony Brown summarizes Carpenter's argument: "[R]elations between the sexes will not improve until physical sexuality is seen as 'pure and beautiful' (*LCA,* 19), part of a tender relationship between two human individuals. This, however, will not be possible until woman is granted 'the freedom to face man on an equality; to find, self-balanced, her natural relation to him; and to dispose of herself and of her sex perfectly freely, and not as a thrall must do' (*LCA* 53)" ("Edward Carpenter," 282). Brown illustrates the influence of Carpenter's ideas on Forster's drastic revision of *Room with a View* in manuscript (see esp. 285).

49. Phelan, "Rhetoric," 65.

50. Shaw, "Loose Narrators," 101.

51. Shaw, "Loose Narrators," 100.

52. Shaw, "Loose Narrators," 101.

53. Forster, *What I Believe,* 8.

54. Rosecrance, *Forster's Narrative Vision,* 15.

55. Rosecrance, *Forster's Narrative Vision,* 134. Not surprisingly, Armstrong cites this very passage by Rosecrance in making his case for Forster's ironic liberalism. He applauds her recognition of the "narrator's duplicity" but believes she "does not understand the contradictions of his closeted position, attempting to pass for normal even while secretly rebelling against the normative" (*Play and the Politics of Reading,* 112). I find both Armstrong's conflation of narrator and implied author with the term *closeted* and his contention about sexual politics unpersuasive; see my note 47.

56. I am grateful to Steve Arata for helping me think through this extended passage. Along with his more serious insights, he observed that, under such counterfactual circumstances, Henry could conceivably inspire an equivalent dose of familial rage. If he were to bequeath Howards End to, say, a mistress or illegitimate child, to the National Trust, the Temperance Society, or a charity for fallen women, Henry's status as patriarch would not protect him from the ensuing vitriol. As appealing as this scenario is, though, the fact remains that Forster and his narrator both resent the Wilcoxes' normative denigration of their mother.

57. Booth, *Rhetoric of Irony,* 81.

58. Although that is pure speculation, I have not read any essay or book that mentions Leonard Bast, even in passing, without trying somehow to account for this passage.

59. Margaret thinks to herself: "How wide the gulf between Henry as he was and Henry as Helen thought he ought to be! And she herself—hovering as usual between the two, now accepting men as they are, now yearning with her sister for Truth. Love and Truth—their warfare seems eternal" (227).

60. Dorrit Cohn's felicitous phrase echoes here: "By leaving the relationship between words and thoughts latent, the narrated monologue [free indirect discourse] casts a peculiarly penumbral light on the figural consciousness, suspending it on the threshold of verbalization in a manner that cannot be achieved by direct quotation" (*Transparent Minds,* 103). Alan Palmer has sensibly observed that, in truth, narratology's speech category bias lends a misleading glamour to free indirect discourse; he makes a convincing case against anything "peculiarly penumbral" about representations of latent mental functioning (*Fictional Minds,* 72–73). Forster's free indirect discourse, however, articulates such a range of political positions that it deserves to be called both peculiar and penumbral.

61. "Kind" as a misnomer for "domineering" appears in the passage just quoted—"unweeded kindness"—as well as earlier in the novel, in a different context. Margaret's aunt Mrs. Munt meets Charles Wilcox at the train station and asks him to drive her to Howards End. Before they depart, he shouts rudely at a clerk, muttering to Mrs. Munt that, "if I had my way, the whole lot of 'em should get the sack." Then he asks, "May I help you in?" She accepts his offer. "She was more civil than she had intended, but really this young man was very kind. Moreover, she was a little afraid of him: his self-possession was extraordinary" (14).

62. Graham, *Indirections of the Novel,* 175.

CHAPTER 2

1. Sayers, Introduction to *Great Short Stories of Detection, Mystery and Horror,* 1:39–40.

2. An example of *unfair* play can illustrate how seriously this responsibility was taken. One very famous example is Agatha Christie's *The Murder of Roger Ackroyd* (1926), in which (spoiler alert) the character-narrator does not reveal to the reader that

he is the murderer until he is unmasked by the detective, Poirot, at the end of the novel. It is also, therefore, an equally famous example of unreliable narration. It is indicative of the strong feelings inspired by perceived unfair play that outrage is still felt over eighty-five years after its publication. Interestingly, and less well known, Christie was not deterred by the controversy and repeated the trick forty years later in *Endless Night* (1967).

3. The short story written in 1942 ("Talboys") was not published during her lifetime. In 1937 Sayers transitioned from writing detective fiction to her full-time concentration on theology. "The Haunted Policeman" was printed in 1938, and two more short stories appeared in the 1940 collection *In the Teeth of the Evidence*. During World War II she published a series of letters from Wimsey and members of his family to bolster public morale. For more on the end of the Wimsey series, see Reynolds, *Dorothy L. Sayers*, 340 and McGregor, *Conundrums for the Long Week-End*, 192–202.

4. Focalization takes a number of different forms. Internal focalization obtains when the act of narration is informed by—and restricted to—the private, inner thoughts of a focalizer. In external focalization, the point of view resides outside of the characters and events being narrated, and thus is restricted to what those characters and events look like on the outside. But many acts of focalization are not purely internal or external. To be psychologically realistic, for instance, a character-narrator should not be able to access a fellow character's inner thoughts. However, one can easily find examples of internal and external focalization breaking that rule, presenting other characters' inside views. Rimmon-Kenan proposes a useful distinction, applicable to both internal and external, between *focalization from within* and *focalization from without* (*Narrative Fiction*, 77–78, 82). Focalization from within benefits from the inside views of characters other than the focalizer; focalization from without is restricted exclusively to the external appearance of those characters. In the current chapter as well as chapter 4 of this book, I depend on Rimmon-Kenan's fine distinctions to explicate several complex acts of telling by Sayers and Powys.

5. A more detailed account of Sayers's use of focalization follows later in this chapter. In short: before 1932's *Have His Carcase*, the majority of scenes in Sayers's novels, including many entire chapters, feature external focalization by an extradiegetic narrator who selectively presents Peter's perceptual point of view (what he sees: external focalization from without) and occasionally his conceptual point of view (what he deduces: external focalization from within). I describe him as focalizer here, not to disregard the importance of the extradiegetic narrator, but because fair play in the novels depends on the external focalization of Peter's perceptions and deductions. Internal focalization by Peter or any other character is rare before *Have His Carcase*.

6. In his taxonomy of friendships between implied authors and implied readers in *The Company We Keep*, Booth observes, "Authors of murder mysteries often testify to immense labor designed to deceive us: weeks and months spent building a puzzle that we will never spend longer than a few hours on, as we follow, more or less energetically while the knots are tied and untied. It is as if they were our servants, hired to entertain us for an hour, with no expectation that we would ever invite them to come live with us and be our loves" (186). I contend that in the Harriet Vane novels Sayers resists and corrects the imbalance between servant and employer. Her implied author offers its authorial audience an extended opportunity for "living in friendship" based on a feminist ethos.

7. Sayers, *Gaudy Night*, 192.

8. "Are Women Human?" 130–31.

9. Zunshine, *Why We Read Fiction*, 143.

10. Zunshine, *Why We Read Fiction*, 150.

11. Sayers comments on the perceived pressure of real time in a 1931 essay: "A year or two ago, it was confidently predicted that the detective-story was going to slump heavily. It was pointed out that all the possible combinations and permutations would shortly be exhausted. . . . So far, however, publishers' sales do not support this rather depressing theory. In spite of unfavourable world-conditions, they show, in this country at any rate, a solid and satisfying steadiness, and this is a healthy sign. . . . [But] so hard have detective-writers worked in the last half-century, that there are now remarkably few tricks the reader does not know." Introduction to *Great Short Stories of Detection, Mystery and Horror*, 2: 12, 19.

12. Chesterton, "Errors about Detective Stories," 69. This essay was originally published in the *Illustrated London News* on 28 August 1920.

13. In a memorable but not especially flattering analogy, Sayers describes her ideal reader: "His co-operation is all-important. He must—and, to do him justice, he nearly always does—come to his reading with an alert and amiable mind. The reader we mystery-mongers really like to lead for our little walk up the garden comes out like an intelligent terrier, ears cocked and tail wagging, ready to run after what is thrown to him and to root cheerfully among the shrubbery till he finds it." Introduction to *Great Short Stories of Detection, Mystery and Horror*, 2:22.

14. Quoted in Irwin, "Mysteries We Reread," 28.

15. Her introduction to *Great Short Stories of Detection, Mystery and Horror* (1928) was published in the United States in 1929 as the introduction to *The Omnibus of Crime*.

16. Sayers, Introduction to *Great Short Stories of Detection, Mystery and Horror*, 1:39–40.

17. Van Dine, "Twenty Rules for Writing Detective Stories," 191–92.

18. Caillois, "The Detective Novel as Game," 10–11.

19. Sayers, Introduction to *Great Short Stories of Detection, Mystery and Horror*, 1:38, 1:25.

20. Sayers, Introduction to *Great Short Stories of Detection, Mystery and Horror*, 1:37.

21. Sayers, "Detectives in Fiction," 5.

22. Sayers, "The Detective Story," 10.

23. Chesterton, "How to Write a Detective Story," 20. This essay was originally published in *Hearst's International* in November 1921.

24. Collins, Preface to *The Moonstone*, 3.

25. Introduction to *Great Short Stories of Detection, Mystery and Horror*, 1:33.

26. For definitions and more examples of external and internal focalization, both of which may be from within or from without, see Rimmon-Kenan, *Narrative Fiction*, 75–78.

27. Haycraft, *Murder for Pleasure*, 131–32.

28. Conan Doyle, "The Musgrave Ritual," 634.

29. For more on Peter's employment of "superfluous" women, see Kenney, "Detecting a Novel Use for Spinsters"; and Reynolds, *Dorothy L. Sayers*, esp. 200–201.

30. If Peter's social class were the only determining factor in his methodology, critics such as Q. D. Leavis, Julian Symons, and Colin Watson, who descry Sayers as a "vulgar admirer of the aristocracy," might have more substance for their accusations. The genre convention that a detective's methodology is a window onto that of the implied author leads some readers to treat everything in the detective's mind as little more than an indi-

cator of his creator's thoughts. As Sayers's series develops, however, she transforms him from a fantastic superman into a character with certain habits of mind and characteristic reasoning skills.

31. Citing Sayers's disappointments in several personal relationships with men, critics have sometimes disparaged her by claiming that she created Wimsey merely to satisfy her own romantic fantasies. This seems to me a rather reductive, sexist application of biographical detail. Other critics, with an eye more on genre convention than biography, suggest that the real Sayers must have been in love with Wimsey because, as an implied author, she repeatedly prompts the reader's admiration and affection for him. Although such an inference about the flesh-and-blood author can never be definitively disproven, I find no evidence that the implied author of the Wimsey series is in love with the protagonist.

32. Previous scholarship on Harriet tends to divide into two camps. The first, larger camp consists of arguments that focus primarily on the emotional impact of her focalization. Such studies typically approach Harriet's viewpoint mainly as an opportunity for seeing Peter through new eyes: as a chance for Sayers to endow her protagonist with humane complexity, and an occasion for the reader's appreciation of a new, romantic side of Peter's ever-more-endearing character. This camp offers perceptions that are good as far as they go, but they don't go far enough; they overemphasize her role as love interest, to the detriment of her richness as a character-focalizer. The other camp stresses her role as detective, comparing her methodology with Peter's. These arguments tend to overlook all the evidence that Harriet is not, and does not want to be, a detective.

33. Sayers, "Gaudy Night," 79.

34. Many scholars take at face value Sayers's claim that although Peter was a source of "monstrous weariness" to her, her "puppets" had resisted her original "infanticidal" intention to end the series with *Strong Poison*. But biographer and scholar Barbara Reynolds sensibly points out that Sayers, "who rather enjoyed pulling the wool over her readers' eyes," might be embellishing a bit in this account of her creative process. She had just signed a contract with her publisher for a book per year; even if the contract did not mandate that she write Peter Wimsey books, presumably (as Reynolds observes) the publisher would have been dismayed to find the lucrative protagonist retired by year's end (*Dorothy L. Sayers*, 229–30).

35. Obviously, it is possible that earlier drafts of the manuscript once existed or have not yet been found. The extant manuscript, held at the Wade Center, is believed to be the first and only draft she composed, and Sayers typically wrote very clean first drafts, but it is always possible she made an exception in this case. Because she wrote in notebooks with detachable pages, it would have been easy for her to rewrite and replace individual pages that bore too many revisions, without leaving any trace of having done so. Sayers scholar Laura Simmons attests that, having read a large number of manuscripts of Sayers's theological nonfiction "in which we have a handwritten draft and a typed draft, . . . there's usually little difference between them. Her rewrites of handwritten documents might involve a few sentences or at most a paragraph, but I remember very little where there were wholesale changes of the sort Dr. Nash is exploring." E-mail communication, 16 June 2010.

36. Sayers, holograph MS of "Strong Poison," 175.

37. Sayers, holograph MS of "Strong Poison," 181.

38. Wald, "Strong Poison," 105, 100.

39. The murder weapon's meaning is obscured by Harriet's focalization: "Beyond a very slight crack on the ivory handle, it showed no very striking peculiarities" (51).

Similarly, evidence given by Farmer Newcombe, rendered in indirect discourse and focalized by Harriet, appears as follows: "No, he never mowed that meadow on account of the (agricultural and botanical detail of which Harriet did not grasp the significance). No, Mr. Newcombe wouldn't be about in that meadow much, no, nor yet the men, on account of its lying a long way from the rest of his land (interminable historical detail dealing with the distribution of tenancies and glebe round about that district, in which Harriet became completely lost), nor they wouldn't need to . . . " (212).

40. Miss Climpson and Miss Murchison are employed at Peter's Cattery, a typing bureau front for covert detective work (*Strong Poison*, 49–50; for more on the Cattery, see Kenney, "Detecting a Novel Use for Spinsters"). Marjorie, Sylvia, and Eiluned have inside information about Harriet because, as artists, they are professionally connected to the writers Philip Boyes and Harriet (*Strong Poison*, 80, 89, 92–95). Mrs. Pettican and Hannah Westlock are household employees of Boyes's cousin, Mr. Urquhart, and key witnesses to Boyes's last dinner (*Strong Poison*, 97–105).

41. Sayers's technique is an instance of Bakhtin's notion of heteroglossia (see "Discourse in the Novel," esp. 280–85 and 324–31).

42. See Sayers, Introduction to *Great Short Stories of Detection, Mystery and Horror*, 1:39. Reynolds writes of Harriet and Peter in *Gaudy Night*: "As readers we are involved in their problem and want it to be resolved, as we are involved in Philip Trent's love for Mrs Manderson in E. C. Bentley's *Trent's Last Case*. There had always been a number of similarities, especially in mannerisms, between Trent and Wimsey. Dorothy confessed to E. C. Bentley how ashamed she was to think how much her 'poor Peter' owed to his Trent" (Reynolds, *Dorothy L. Sayers*, 257).

43. Although Kermode irritably objects to the phrase "'the world we know,' which suggests that our reading is always going to be the one prescribed by the narrator," and exhorts us not to be the kind of "docile" reader who submits willingly to such conscription, I propose that neither Bentley nor Sayers is guilty of conflating the authorial audience with "the world" (Kermode, *Novel and Narrative*, 11).

44. See Havelock Ellis and John Addington Symonds's dire pronouncements about same-sex communities in *Sexual Inversion* (1897).

45. *Horti conclusi*: enclosed gardens; *fontis signati*: sealed wells. *The Pocket Oxford Latin Dictionary*, 3d ed, accessed 8 July 2013, http://www.oxfordreference.com/views/ENTRY.html?subview=Main&entry=t131a.e4000.

CHAPTER 3

1. Woolf, *The Years*, 162.

2. As many Woolf scholars have been quick to point out, her choice to privilege fact over vision is striking in an author who had famously criticized Arnold Bennett, H. G. Wells, and John Galsworthy for overemphasizing material details in their novels. See esp. Woolf's essays "Modern Novels" (1919) and "Character in Fiction" (1924) in *Essays*.

3. Hite, "Tonal Cues and Uncertain Values," 254.

4. Margaret Comstock remarks that "The way the novel is written discourages a reader's inclination to "march in step after a leader"—a phrase central to *The Years*. There is no character whose life is captivating; the author's voice is unusually unobtrusive; there is not even any "beautiful prose." The novel is made up largely of people talking to one another, and not very articulately at that. Out of these materials Woolf creates for her readers the opportunity available to some of her characters: the chance

to achieve meaning in a fragmentary world and join the attempt to fill "the present moment . . . fuller and fuller, with the past, the present, and the future, until it shown, whole, bright, deep with understanding" (*Years*, 406). . . . People who experience their own lives in this way are not the sort who will stand waiting to see the king" (Comstock, "Loudspeaker and the Human Voice," 254).

5. Cuddy-Keane, "Inside and Outside the Covers," 172.

6. Woolf's usual practice was to write longhand in the mornings and then type her morning's work in the afternoons. Between October 1932 and January 1936 she filled eight holograph notebooks and produced a concurrent typescript. It is impossible to compare holograph with typescript since only eight pages of her typescript are known still to exist (Radin, *Virginia Woolf's* The Years, 111). Her first galleys, set in March 1936, much more closely resemble the novel than the holograph (116), though the galleys number 600 pages and the first published British edition is only 472. For more on the typescripts, see Susan Squier, "A Track of Our Own." For more on the relationship between galleys and the first U.S. edition, see Radin, "Two Enormous Chunks" and *Virginia Woolf's* The Years, chapters 7–8.

7. The most reasonable among these explanations is that Woolf would have feared losing her audience, through an unfamiliar genre, through objectionable politics, or both.

8. The editor of the only published transcription, which includes just two of the eight holograph volumes, makes strong claims about Woolf's intentionality in the act of revision, but bases them on discredited psychoanalytic speculation (Leaska, Introduction to *The Pargiters*, esp. xiii–xx).

9. Radin, *Virginia Woolf's* The Years, xxi.

10. Radin speculates a good bit about Woolf's private intentions and beliefs, though she does not always supply firm textual evidence (from either novel or personal papers) to support her claims. For example: "It must have become increasingly obvious to her that [the essays] were a clumsy device that impeded the narrative flow of the novel," she states. "What their presence in the early chapters does indicate is the extent to which Woolf felt the creative and analytic functions of the brain to be essentially separate" (*Virginia Woolf's* The Years, 33–34). Later, she speculates about why, in revision, Woolf diminished the role of the character Elvira. "Perhaps Woolf feared that Elvira might take over the novel because she sensed that this character expressed something in herself that could get out of control. . . . Elvira acts as a mouthpiece for Woolf's attempts to deal with her material, a way of talking to herself as she goes along" (40, 46). "It was Woolf's deepest belief that . . . " (35) "It is possible to conjecture that . . . " (54) "It had been her intention to. . . " (55).

11. Silver, "Textual Criticism as Feminist Practice," 194.

12. For more on Leaska's argument about pargeting, see his introduction to *The Pargiters* as well as his more forceful essay "Virginia Woolf, the Pargeter."

13. See in particular McGann, *A Critique of Modern Textual Criticism*: "This training, or contamination, begins with the author's first revisions and editorial corrections, and it continues through the proof stage, the publication, and the subsequent reprintings both during and after the poet's lifetime. Many persons besides the author are engaged in these events, and the entire process constitutes the life of an important social institution at the center of which is the literary work itself (the 'work' being a series of specific 'texts,' a series of specific acts of production, and the entire process which both of these series constitute). For the textual critic, all phases and aspects of these matters are relevant" (52–53). See also McGann, *Textual Criticism and Literary Interpretation*: "[W]e shall not be able to understand the significance of these literary acts—the meaning of

their meanings—unless we are able to situate them in the larger sociohistorical field that sanctions their operations. 'Meaning,' in life as well as in its processes of reflection and self-reflection (including literature), is a social event, a complex engagement between various people and groups" (viii–ix).

14. This fallacy is what S. M. Parrish has called the "Whig interpretation of literature." He argues that overreliance on "authorial intention" leads textual critics to treat "discarded variants, abandoned versions" as "false starts, misjudgments, or lapses of taste on the part of the [author]" that are "happily rectified as the work, by obedience to some inner logic, reaches final form" ("Whig," 344–45). Parrish argues instead that "the language of early versions, especially when those versions are complete, [should] be valued not for what it contributed to the late versions, not as a step in an inevitably evolving design, but for its own sake, as an achievement separate from the later history of the text" (345).

15. Friedman, "Return of the Repressed in Women's Narrative," 146.

16. DuPlessis, *Writing Beyond the Ending*, 174.

17. Lanser's violent word "sacrificed" corresponds to other prominent Woolf critics on the same subject: Hermione Lee laments Woolf's "killing of the novel that lies buried underneath *The Years*," (Lee, "Introduction," xvi); Eleanor McNees puts it that Woolf "broke the structural backbone of the novel" through her "torturous" revision process ("Introduction," xli). In a comic twist of Woolf's own words, Mark Spilka describes his revulsion at reading this "murky and tedious" novel by asking how much "dank rice pudding we can ourselves stomach without ourselves exploding" ("New Life in the Works," 179, 183).

18. As textual scholars Julia Briggs, D. F. McKenzie, and Brenda Silver have observed, Woolf's published texts are not self-identical, either. Silver notes that Woolf often consciously introduced variants in her published texts "as she corrected two sets of identical page proofs, one for the Hogarth Press and one for her American publishers. . . . Woolf did not seem to care about 'final authorial intention' or a stable text. She knowingly set out different versions, different texts" ("Textual Criticism as Feminist Practice," 196). Briggs and McKenzie assert that "surprisingly little attention has been paid to her practice as a reviser of her own work" and that "despite ample evidence of Woolf's extensive revision of her work before publication, there has been a reluctance to admit that the process of revision also extended beyond initial publication. . . . Woolf created two distinct lines of textual transmission . . . so that, in effect, her British and American readers encounter different novels" ("Between the Texts," 144, 147, 152). They do note, however, that the American and British versions of *The Years* are more similar to one another than are most of the earlier novels (156).

19. Booth, "Resurrection of the Implied Author," 77–78.

20. Phelan, *Living to Tell about It*, 45.

21. Cuddy-Keane, "Inside and Outside the Covers," 177–78.

22. Cuddy-Keane notes that Woolf's theory and practice preceded by a number of years Mikhail Bakhtin's canonized establishment of the same concept in "Discourse Typology in Prose." For more on the relationship between Bakhtin's and Woolf's approaches to dialogism, see "The Rhetoric of Feminist Conversation," pp. 137–39.

23. This ethical conviction is consonant, of course, with historically specific generic conventions, as I explore further in this book's introduction. In particular, Woolf's approach matches the modernist proclivity for impersonal narration. It is worth noting, though, that her emphasis on decentered impersonality is more pronounced and experimental than most modernists.

24. Middleton, "*The Years*," 163.

25. Woolf, *A Writer's Diary*, 16 August 1933.

26. A number of critics have commented on the repetition of motifs in this novel, though none of them to my knowledge has examined the ethical dimension of repetition. Grace Radin observes that the novel's "reverberative structure" does not exist in the manuscript. She describes Woolf as superimposing it on her narrative only after reaching the galleys stage. Radin further claims that repetition lends the novel a "unity" that is missing in the manuscript ("'Two Enormous Chunks,'" xxii). See also Robert Caserio's work on "tychism" and the recurrent trope of missed opportunities (*Novel in England*, 68–79).

27. Cuddy-Keane, "Rhetoric of Feminist Conversation," 139.

28. See Comstock's consideration of the relationship between integrity and silence in "Loudspeaker and the Human Voice," 272–73.

29. Lanser, *Fictions of Authority*, 104.

30. Lee, "Introduction," xxiii.

31. This is my transcription from Woolf's holograph MS of [*The Years*], vol. 3, pp. 80–81 (cased M42, dated 11 October 1932–15 November 1934, held at the Berg Collection). All subsequent quotations employed in this chapter appear in the first two volumes of the manuscript, which was officially transcribed and published by Mitchell Leaska in *The Pargiters* in 1977. Page citations are provided first of the manuscript and then, in brackets, of Leaska's transcription.

32. This, of course, is the explicit and central claim of Woolf's next book, *Three Guineas*: that patriarchal violence worldwide may be traced to the way fathers treat their daughters and husbands treat their wives.

33. Like *A Room of One's Own*, this project began as a lecture. And like *Room*, its audience was young, upwardly mobile women. The lecture that was later revised and published as "Professions for Women" was delivered to the Junior Council of the London and National Society for Women's Service on 21 January 1931. The Junior Council was largely comprised of young, professional women (Doughan and Gordon, *Women, Clubs and Associations in Britain*, 58). In her diary entry on the previous day, Woolf noted, "I have this moment, while having my bath, conceived an entire new book—a sequel to *A Room of One's Own*—about the sexual life of women: to be called Professions for Women perhaps—Lord how exciting! This sprang out of my paper to be read on Wednesday to Pippa's society (*Writer's Diary*, 20 January 1931).

34. See Rabinowitz, "Truth in Fiction," 127. We find a comparable rhetorical relationship in both *A Room of One's Own and Three Guineas*. In both cases the narrative audience "overhears" a nonfictional address, in the former through lecture and in the latter as a series of letters. Our rhetorical models aren't very subtle for dealing with pretended "real" address.

35. By definition, authorial audiences read self-consciously. Unlike narrative audiences, which lose themselves in narration, believing that the narrator and story are real, authorial audiences know they are reading books.

36. Moreover, one must recognize that the death of the mother will not in itself end Victorian gender conventions. Their confinement isn't going to end when the mother dies; this isn't an instability between mother and daughters; it's a societal problem that is represented self-consciously by an artist highlighting the thematic functions of her characters.

37. Briggs, "Between the Texts," 149.

38. It has frequently been noted that Woolf granted her characters lengthy speeches

and internal monologues in manuscript, but revised by interrupting, abbreviating, or altogether silencing those characters' self-expression in the novel. But chapter 2 of the manuscript provides a good example of two characters, Rose and Bobby, whose speech is already interrupted and truncated. Focalized through Rose, only snippets of the nurse's conversation are overheard; Bobby prevents Rose from forming her question; his own speech breaks off with a dash; Rose's conversations with the shopkeeper, her nurse, and Eleanor all falter through her self-censorship. In this unusual case, silence operates in the *manuscript* as a resource for prompting ethical reading.

39. The ethics of the told, consisting in the drama of assault, depicts an obvious harm to women. But the subtler gender hierarchy that turns Bobby into a misogynist is the greater harm, and this is rendered largely through the ethics of the telling. Thus the "story" of Woolf's persuasion of her authorial audience is not itself a narrative and yet it does contribute to her narrative ethics as well as the narrativity of the draft.

40. Radin proposes that Woolf made two sea changes: "Woolf's new scheme [dated 25 April 1933 in the diary] is ambitious; she will try to combine fact and vision, to write a novel that is as objective as *Night and Day* and as introspective as *The Waves*. Thus the progress of the novel is a kind of dialectic; first she swings entirely to fact, excluding vision; then [after 2 February 1933] she is tempted to poetry or vision (they are nearly synonymous here) and finally to an idea for fusion, with both modes going on at once" (*Virginia Woolf's* The Years, 40). Radin claims that the first two volumes of holograph are "entirely" devoted to fact; that Woolf's development in the next volumes of her character Elvira represents experimentation with vision; and that, by the time Woolf revised Elvira into the novel's character Sara, she had established "fusion."

CHAPTER 4

1. Powys, *A Glastonbury Romance*, 888, 323.

2. Powys was one of only two defense witnesses in this trial. For a superb account and analysis of the *Ulysses* trials of 1921 and 1933, see Vanderham, *James Joyce and Censorship*.

3. For more on these strategies, see in particular Flint, *Woman Reader;* Golden, *Images of the Woman Reader;* and Phegley, *Educating the Proper Woman Reader.*

4. Flint, *Woman Reader,* 266.

5. Flint, *Woman Reader,* 15.

6. Nash, "John Cowper Powys's '*Great New Art*'," 38–66.

7. Stewart, *Dear Reader,* 344.

8. I borrow the term "intermental" from Alan Palmer, whose studies *Fictional Minds* and *Social Minds in the Novel* apply cognitive science to narratology in order to examine the effect fictional figures' minds have upon one another. See this chapter's note 19.

9. McGann, "Impossible Fiction," 186, 178.

10. McGann quotes from Ballin, "'A Certain Combination of Realism and Magic,'" 26.

11. In addition to the works by Susan Winnett and Peter Brooks discussed at length in this essay, see particularly Judith Roof, *Come As You Are;* Joseph Allen Boone, *Libidinal Currents;* and Ross Chambers, *Story and Situation.*

12. As Roof and Winnett, among others, have observed, this formulation betrays a powerful heterosexual bias.

13. Phelan, *Reading People,* 114–15.

14. "I would like to explore what would happen if, having recognized the Master-plot's reliance on male morphology and male experience, we retained the general narrative pattern of tension and resolution ('tumescence and detumescence,' 'arousal and significant discharge') and simply substituted for the male experience an analogously representable female one" (Winnett, "Coming Unstrung," 508).

15. Powys's reception history is so fraught with the regrettable conflation of the flesh-and-blood Powys with his narrators that a strong argument for his implied author may serve as a corrective to earlier scholarship. Such conflation, of course, underestimates differences of expression, perspective, and diegetic agenda that Powys's narrators contribute to the novels. Scholars who insist on finding Powys the man in his narratives tend also to assume that Powys lacked control over his craft as a novelist. This single error of conflation has exacerbated the critical undervaluation of Powys's oeuvre.

16. For Glastonbury as a palimpsest, see the description of Number Two's cluttered antiques shop as a miniature representation of the town's history: "Glastonbury here, layer by layer through the centuries, was revealed in certain significant petrifications, certain frozen gestures of the flowing spirit of life" (345). With its basement full of books, and its management under the alternating control of the hapless Bartholomew Jones and the sadistic bookworm Owen Evans, the shop serves as a *mise en abyme* of the town. Glastonbury's personality and vivacity are remarked upon at pages 694 ("They both felt as if Glastonbury, at least, in her sleep, were an actual, living Creature!"), 795 ("Where the guide books make their great mistake . . . is in treating Glastonbury as a fragment of history, instead of something that's *making* history"), 801–2 ("Glastonbury will be a living entity again"), and 998–99 ("Glastonbury a person? . . . These old, obstinate, irrational indigenes of the place understood this wayward and mysterious Personality better than any philosophical triumvirate could do, and had expressed their feeling through the mouth of this wide-eyed child!"). In the last passage, the wide-eyed child is, of course, a young girl—a fact whose significance will be evident later in my argument.

17. The insistence on narrative closure, so prominent in Brooks, is less conspicuous in Gerald Prince's definition of narrativity as "[t]he set of properties characterizing narrative and distinguishing it from nonnarrative. . . . The degree of narrativity of a given narrative depends partly on the extent to which that narrative fulfills a receiver's desire by representing oriented temporal wholes (prospectively from beginning to end and retrospectively from end to beginning), involving a conflict, consisting of discrete, specific, and positive situations of a human(ized) project and world" (*Dictionary of Narratology*, 65).

18. Although it is hard to imagine two authors more dissimilar than Virginia Woolf and John Cowper Powys, it is worth noting that *The Years*, like *Glastonbury*, refuses to focus on any one character and is characterized by anticlimax and dispersed (as opposed to totalizing) meaning.

19. In *Fictional Minds*, Palmer argues that groups of two or more people—real and fictional alike—can carry out mental functions such as assessment, problem-solving, emotion, response to social norms, and decision-making on an intermental plane (see esp. 208–9, 218–30). Drawing on the fields of cognitive science, psychology, and psycholinguistics, Palmer's study develops the notion of *socially extended cognition*, or *intersubjectivity*, in conjunction with what he terms *situated identity*. Intersubjectivity is defined as "the process in which mental activity—including conscious awareness, motives and intentions, cognitions, and emotions—is transferred between minds . . . [it] manifests itself as an immediate sympathetic awareness of feelings and conscious, purposeful intelligence in others" (Clark and Chalmers, "The Extended Mind," 415–16). Situated

identity is the notion that an individual's mind is constituted in part by other persons, settings, and circumstances. Intermental thinking in *Glastonbury* occurs with such frequency and suggestive significance that Powys's use of it warrants further study. For an excellent application of this concept, see Palmer's extended reading of the Middlemarch mind in *Social Minds in the Novel*.

20. I am grateful to Robert Caserio for suggesting this pun to me in conversation at the Narrative Conference.

21. Here is the full quotation: "Mr. Geard was not good at concentrated thinking. His deepest thoughts always came to him, as the author of *Faust* declared his did, crying, like happy children, 'Here we are!' and the result of this was that a brief half an hour spent in composing his speech for that night exhausted him far more than the most protracted physical exhaustion would have done. He found himself caught and, as it were, pilloried, in the repetition of certain particular phrases. This happened to him every time he deserted his vague, rich, semi-erotic feelings and tried to condense his scheme into a rational statement, and it became really troublesome when, with his eyes tightly closed, he set himself to call up that audience of people and to imagine their response to what he said" (332).

22. Powys, *Autobiography*, 457.

23. The reading of identities does not in any way suggest deep, profound, or lasting understanding. The connection between Nell and Sam is narrated with emphatic emphasis on how satisfying their union is for both of them. But this connection does not last long. Nell's "sublime realism" about Sam and their romantic union ends soon after they get out of bed (310).

24. The narrator remarks that even a casual, outside observer—a person conspicuously unlike the reader, who is unlikely to be casual or outside the story-world this far into the novel—would find this tableau of the rapt audience noteworthy: to such an outsider "it would have been of fascinating interest to note the varieties of human types gathered so close together" (557).

25. For more on wandering attention and the rhythms of reading, see Patricia Meyer Spacks, *Boredom*, and Jonathan Culler, *Structuralist Poetics* (262–64).

26. At a crucial moment just before the novel's crisis, the Watchers surface again in the discourse: "The invisible watchers—those scientific collectors of interesting human experiences in this ancient town—communicated to one another the conclusion that certain essences and revelations are caught and appropriated by an old maiden lady, like Miss Crow, which are never touched by turbulent, tormented lives like those of Mr. Evans and Codfin" (991). Here, at a crucial moment in the text, the Watchers do nothing more than espouse a central tenet of Powys's narrative: that girls and women (particularly unmarried ones) have a special capacity for receptivity. By this point not only is the reader well aware of this notion, but the implied reading experience has been largely determined by it. The Watchers, however, appear to be making the discovery for the first time, which calls attention to the fact that the reader has surpassed the Watchers in interpreting Glastonbury. The Watchers' exclusive interest in the appearances of things prevents their making profound inferences, and even a fairly simple deduction on the reader's part goes beyond the Watchers' understanding. Through the Watchers, Powys may be revealing an anxiety about how closely readers will attend to the overabundance of details at his novel's surface.

27. Here is Sam Dekker: "[W]ithout being in the least conscious of the importance for humanity of the psychic law he had blundered upon or of its rarity in the world, Sam had found out that when a person is liberated from possessiveness, from ambition, from

the exigencies of desire, from domestic claims, from every sort of authority over others, he can enjoy sideways and incidentally, as he follows any sort of labour or quest the most exquisite trances of absorption into the mysterious essence of any patch of earth-mould, or any fragment of gravel, or any slab of paving-stone, or any tangle of weeds, or any lump of turf that he may come upon as he goes along" (927). As a romance, of course, *A Glastonbury Romance* may be expected to be modeled on a quest plot. Sam's spiritual journey throughout the text bears resemblance to a quest, but notably it does not culminate in his dramatic vision of the Grail, which occurs midway through the novel, but rather in his anticlimactic homecoming toward novel's end, where he discovers that Nell, having finally given up on waiting for him, has left.

28. Mad Bet's snake-nerve is described on pp. 1047–49; Owen Evans's is described most vividly and directly on pp. 1004, 1012, 1020f, and 1054.

29. For Philip's oratory see pp. 233, 550, 665; for Geard's see pp. 457, 796, 707–10. Paul Trent's impotence is highlighted on p. 719.

30. See, for example, G. Wilson Knight, "Powys and the Kundalini Serpent"; and Brebner, *The Demon Within*.

31. Caserio, "Politics and Sex," 98.

32. The flesh-and-blood Powys had a horror of heterosexual coitus, and his early work makes clear the connection he saw between mental influence (particularly what I term as "intermental penetration") and physical violence. His stance on homoeroticism, however, is less well defined. In his collected *Letters to Henry Miller*, for example, Powys refers at one point to his "twice inverted lesbianism" (19) but later asserts that "I have not got the *faintest touch* of homo-sexuality in me" (96). Caserio gives a smart reading of the anal eroticism of Sam's Grail vision, arguing for the centrality of anal eroticism and homoeroticism in the novel, and asserting that the "penetrative counter-aggression of the Grail appears to release Sam from his sadism" ("Politics and Sex," 99). Caserio does not characterize this counter-aggression as sadistic. He asserts convincingly that Powys does not seek to redeem either anal eroticism or sadism in the novel, but we should note that the counter-penetration that redeems Sam would be conspicuously unlikely in a heterosexual union with his beloved Nell.

CONCLUSION

1. As Spacks has observed, Evelina manages to prevent Mr. Macartney's suicide attempt by collapsing four times: she saves his life, but as passively as possible (discussion, April 3, 2001).

2. Spacks, *Desire and Truth*, 143.

✍ BIBLIOGRAPHY

Abbott, H. Porter. *The Cambridge Introduction to Narrative.* 2d ed. Cambridge: Cambridge University Press, 2008.

Armstrong, Paul B. *Play and the Politics of Reading: The Social Uses of Modernist Form.* Ithaca, NY: Cornell University Press, 2005.

Bakhtin, Mikhail. "Discourse in the Novel." In *The Dialogic Imagination: Four Essays,* edited by Michael Holquist and translated by Caryl Emerson and Michael Holquist, 259–422. Austin: University of Texas Press, 1981.

———. "Discourse Typology in Prose." In *Readings in Russian Poetics: Formalist and Structuralist Views,* edited by Ladislav Matejka and Krystyna Pomorska, 176–96. Ann Arbor: Michigan Slavic Publications, 1978.

Ballin, Michael. "'A Certain Combination of Realism and Magic': Notes on the Publishing History of *Porius.*" *Powys Notes* (Fall and Winter 1992): 11–37.

Boone, Joseph Allen. *Libidinal Currents: Sexuality and the Shaping of Modernism.* Chicago: University of Chicago Press, 1998.

Booth, Wayne C. *The Company We Keep: An Ethics of Fiction.* Berkeley: University of California Press, 1988.

———. *Critical Understanding: The Powers and Limits of Pluralism.* Chicago: University of Chicago Press, 1979.

———. "Resurrection of the Implied Author: Why Bother?" In *A Companion to Narrative Theory,* edited by James Phelan and Peter J. Rabinowitz, 75–88. Malden, MA: Blackwell, 2005.

———. *The Rhetoric of Fiction.* 2d ed. Chicago: University of Chicago Press, 1983.

———. *A Rhetoric of Irony.* Chicago: University of Chicago Press, 1974.

Brebner, John A. *The Demon Within: A Study of John Cowper Powys's Novels.* London: Macdonald, 1973.

Briggs, Julia, and D. F. McKenzie. "Between the Texts: Virginia Woolf's Acts of Revision." *Text: Transactions of the Society for Textual Scholarship* 12 (1999): 143–65.

Brooks, Peter. *Reading for the Plot: Design and Intention in Narrative.* Cambridge, MA: Harvard University Press, 1984.

Brown, Tony. "Edward Carpenter, Forster, and the Evolution of *A Room with a View.*" *English Literature in Transition, 1880–1920* 30, no. 3 (1987): 279–301.

Caillois, Roger. "The Detective Novel as Game." In *The Poetics of Murder: Detective Fiction and Literary Theory,* edited by Glenn W. and William W. Stowe Most, 1–12. San Diego: Harcourt Brace, 1941.

Carpenter, Edward. *Love's Coming-of-Age.* Manchester: Labour Press, 1896.

Case, Alison. *Plotting Women: Gender and Narration in the Eighteenth- and Nineteenth-Century British Novel.* Charlottesville: University Press of Virginia, 1999.

Caserio, Robert. *The Novel in England, 1900–1950.* New York: Twayne, 1999.

———. "Politics and Sex in *A Glastonbury Romance.*" *Western Humanities Review* 57 (2003): 94–101.

Chambers, Ross. *Story and Situation: Narrative Seduction and the Power of Fiction.* Minneapolis: University of Minnesota Press, 1984.

Chatman, Seymour. *Coming to Terms: The Rhetoric of Narrative in Fiction and Film.* Ithaca, NY: Cornell University Press, 1990.

Chesterton, G. K. "Errors about Detective Stories." In *G. K. Chesterton's Sherlock Holmes: Original Illustrations,* edited by Steven Doyle, 67–69. New York: The Baker Street Irregulars, 2003.

———. "How to Write a Detective Story." In *The Spice of Life and Other Essays,* edited by Dorothy E. Collins, 15–21. Philadelphia: Dufour Editions, 1966.

Clark, Andy, and David J. Chalmers. "The Extended Mind." *Analysis* 58 (1998): 7–19.

Cohn, Dorrit. *Transparent Minds: Narrative Modes for Presenting Consciousness in Fiction.* Princeton, NJ: Princeton University Press, 1978.

Collins, Wilkie. *The Moonstone.* Edited by Sandra Kemp. New York: Penguin, 1998.

Comstock, Margaret. "The Loudspeaker and the Human Voice: Politics and the Form of *The Years.*" *Bulletin of the New York Public Library* 80, no. 2 (1977): 252–75.

Conan Doyle, Arthur. "The Musgrave Ritual." In *The Adventures of Sherlock Holmes,* 619–37. 1893. Reprint, New York: Heritage, 1950.

Cuddy-Keane, Melba. "Inside and Outside the Covers: Beginnings, Endings, and Woolf's Non-Cooercive Ethical Texts." *Woolfian Boundaries: Selected Papers from the Sixteenth Annual International Conference on Virginia Woolf* (2007): 172–79.

———. "The Rhetoric of Feminist Conversation: Virginia Woolf and the Trope of the Twist." In *Ambiguous Discourse: Feminist Narratology and British Women Writers,* edited by Kathy Mezei, 137–61. Chapel Hill: North Carolina University Press, 1996.

Culler, Jonathan. *Structuralist Poetics: Structuralism, Linguistics, and the Study of Literature.* Ithaca, NY: Cornell University Press, 1975.

Doughan, David, and Peter Gordon. *Women, Clubs and Associations in Britain.* London: Routledge, 2006.

DuPlessis, Rachel Blau. *Writing Beyond the Ending: Narrative Strategies of Twentieth-Century Women Writers.* Bloomington: Indiana University Press, 1985.

Ellis, Havelock, and John Addington Symonds. *Sexual Inversion: A Critical Edition.* Edited by Ivan Crozier. New York: Palgrave Macmillan, 2008.

Flint, Kate. *The Woman Reader, 1837–1914.* Oxford: Clarendon Press, 1993.

Forster, E. M. *Commonplace Book.* Edited by Philip Gardner. Stanford, CA: Stanford University Press, 1985.

———. *The Feminine Note in Literature*. Edited by George Piggford, Bloomsbury Heritage Series. London: Cecil Woolf, 2001.

———. *Howards End*. Edited by Oliver Stallybrass. Abinger ed. London: Edward Arnold, 1973.

———. "Me, Them and You." In *Abinger Harvest*, 26–30. New York: Harcourt Brace, 1936.

———. *A Room with a View*. Edited by Oliver Stallybrass. Abinger ed. London: Edward Arnold, 1977.

———. *What I Believe*. London: Hogarth Press, 1939.

Friedman, Susan Stanford. "The Return of the Repressed in Women's Narrative." *The Journal of Narrative Technique* 19, no. 1 (1989): 141–56.

Furbank, P. N. *E. M. Forster: A Life*. 2 vols. New York: Harcourt Brace Jovanovich, 1978.

Golden, Catherine. *Images of the Woman Reader in Victorian British and American Fiction*. Gainesville: University Press of Florida, 2003.

Goldman, Jane. "Forster and Women." In *The Cambridge Companion to E. M. Forster*, edited by David Bradshaw, 120–37. Cambridge: Cambridge University Press, 2007.

Goodlad, Lauren M. E. "Where Liberals Fear to Tread: E. M. Forster's Queer Internationalism and the Ethics of Care." *Novel: A Forum on Fiction* 39, no. 3 (2006): 307–36.

Graham, Kenneth. *Indirections of the Novel: James, Conrad, and Forster*. Cambridge: Cambridge University Press, 1988.

Haycraft, Howard. *Murder for Pleasure: The Life and Times of the Detective Story*. New York: D. Appleton-Century Company, 1941.

Herman, David. "Narrative Theory and the Intentional Stance." *Partial Answers* 6, no. 2 (2008): 233–60.

Herman, Luc, and Bart Vervaeck. "The Implied Author: A Secular Excommunication." *Style* 45, no. 1 (Spring 2011): 11–28.

Hite, Molly. "Tonal Cues and Uncertain Values: Affect and Ethics in *Mrs. Dalloway*." *Narrative* 18, no. 3 (2010): 249–75.

Hogan, Patrick Colm. "The Multiplicity of Implied Authors and the Complex Case of *Uncle Tom's Cabin*." *Narrative* 20, vol. 1 (2012): 25–42.

Irwin, John T. "Mysteries We Reread, Mysteries of Rereading: Poe, Borges and the Analytical Detective Story." In *Detecting Texts: The Metaphysical Detective Story from Poe to Postmodernism*, edited by Patricia Merrivale and Susan Elizabeth Sweeney, 27–54. Philadelphia: University of Pennsylvania Press, 1999.

Kenney, Catherine. "Detecting a Novel Use for Spinsters in Sayers's Fiction." In *Old Maids to Radical Spinsters: Unmarried Women in the Twentieth-Century Novel*, edited by Laura L. Doan, 123–38. Urbana: University of Illinois Press, 1991.

Kent, Susan Kingsley. *Sex and Suffrage in Britain, 1860–1914*. Princeton, NJ: Princeton University Press, 1987.

Kermode, Frank. *Novel and Narrative*. Glasgow: University of Glasgow, 1972.

Kettle, Arnold. *An Introduction to the English Novel*. Vol. 2: *Henry James to the Present Day*. 2d ed. London: Hutchinson University Library, 1967.

Kindt, Tom, and Hans-Harald Müller. *The Implied Author: Concept and Controversy*. Berlin: Walter de Gruyter, 2006.

Knight, G. Wilson. "Powys and the Kundalini Serpent." In *Visions and Vices: Essays on John Cowper Powys*, edited by John D. Christie, 98–120. London: Cecil Woolf, 1990.

Langland, Elizabeth. "Gesturing toward an Open Space: Gender, Form, and Language in E. M. Forster's *Howards End*." In *Out of Bounds: Male Writers and Gender(ed) Criticism*, edited by Laura Claridge and Elizabeth Langland, 252–67. Amherst: University of Massachusetts Press, 1990.

Lanser, Susan Sniader. *Fictions of Authority: Women Writers and Narrative Voice*. Ithaca, NY: Cornell University Press, 1992.

———. "The Implied Author: An Agnostic Manifesto." *Style* 45, no. 1 (2011): 153–60.

Leaska, Mitchell A. *The Pargiters: The Novel-Essay Portion of* The Years. New York: Harvest, 1977.

———. "Virginia Woolf, the Pargeter: A Reading of *The Years*." *Bulletin of the New York Public Library* 80, no. 2 (1977): 172–210.

Leavis, F. R. "E. M. Forster." In *Forster: A Collection of Critical Essays*, edited by Malcolm Bradbury. Englewood Cliffs, NJ: Prentice-Hall, 1966.

Lee, Hermione. "Introduction." In *The Years*, by Virginia Woolf, xii–xxxii. Oxford: Oxford University Press, 1992.

Mao, Douglas, and Rebecca L. Walkowitz. "The New Modernist Studies." *PMLA* 123, vol. 3 (May 2008): 737–48.

Markley, A. A. "E. M. Forster's Reconfigured Gaze and the Creation of a Homoerotic Subjectivity." *Twentieth Century Literature* 47, no. 2 (2001): 268–92.

Martin, Robert K. "'It Must Have Been the Umbrella': Forster's Queer Begetting." In *Queer Forster*, edited by Robert K. and George Piggford Martin, 255–73. Chicago: University of Chicago Press, 1997.

Martin, Robert K., and George Piggford. *Queer Forster*. Chicago: University of Chicago Press, 1997.

McGann, Jerome. *A Critique of Modern Textual Criticism*. Chicago: University of Chicago Press, 1983.

———. "Impossible Fiction; Or, The Importance of Being John Cowper Powys. In *The Scholar's Art: Literary Studies in a Managed World*, 175–89. Chicago: University of Chicago Press, 2006.

———. *Textual Criticism and Literary Interpretation*. Chicago: University of Chicago Press, 1985.

McGregor, Robert Kuhn, and Ethan Lewis. *Conundrums for the Long Week-End: England, Dorothy L. Sayers, and Lord Peter Wimsey*. Kent, OH: Kent State University Press, 2000.

McNees, Eleanor Jane. "Introduction." In *The Years*, by Virginia Woolf, xli–lxxxiii. Orlando: Harvest, 2008.

Middleton, Victoria. "*The Years*: 'A Deliberate Failure.'" *Bulletin of the New York Public Library* 80, no. 2 (1977): 158–71.

Miller, D. A. *The Novel and the Police*. Berkeley: University of California Press, 1988.

Moffat, Wendy. *A Great Unrecorded History: A New Life of E. M. Forster*. New York: Farrar, Straus and Giroux, 2010.

Nash, Katherine Saunders. "John Cowper Powys's '*Great New Art*': Intermental Influence in the Lecture Career." *Powys Journal* 18 (2008): 38–66.

Nünning, Ansgar F. "Deconstructing and Reconceptualizing the Implied Author." *Anglistik: International Journal of English Studies* 8, no. 2 (1997): 95–116.

———. "Reconceptualizing Unreliable Narration: Synthesizing Cognitive and Rhetorical Approaches." In *A Companion to Narrative Theory*, edited by James Phelan and Peter J. Rabinowitz, 89–107. Malden, MA: Blackwell, 2005.

Palmer, Alan. *Fictional Minds*. Lincoln: University of Nebraska Press, 2004.

———. *Social Minds in the Novel*. Columbus: The Ohio State University Press, 2010.

Parrish, S. M. "The Whig Interpretation of Literature." *Text: Transactions of the Society for Textual Scholarship* 4 (1988): 343–50.

Phegley, Jennifer. *Educating the Proper Woman Reader: Victorian Family Literary Magazines and the Cultural Health of the Nation*. Columbus: The Ohio State University Press, 2004.

Phelan, James. *Experiencing Fiction: Judgments, Progressions, and the Rhetorical Theory of Narrative*. Columbus: The Ohio State University Press, 2007.

———. *Living to Tell about It: A Rhetoric and Ethics of Character Narration*. Ithaca, NY: Cornell University Press, 2005.

———. *Reading People, Reading Plots: Character, Progression, and the Interpretation of Narrative*. Chicago: University of Chicago Press, 1989.

———. "Rhetoric, Ethics, and Narrative Communication: Or, from Story and Discourse to Authors, Resources, and Audiences." *Soundings* 94, no. 1/2 (2011): 55–75.

Powys, John Cowper. *Autobiography*. New York: Simon and Schuster, 1933. Reprinted with an introduction by J. B. Priestley and a note on writing the autobiography by R. L. Blackmore. Hamilton, NY: Colgate University Press, 1967. Page references are to the 1967 edition.

———. *A Glastonbury Romance*. Woodstock, NY: Overlook Press, 1996.

———. *Letters to Henry Miller*. London: Village Press, 1975.

Prince, Gerald. *A Dictionary of Narratology*. 2d ed. Lincoln: University of Nebraska Press, 2003.

Rabinowitz, Peter J. "'The Absence of Her Voice from that Concord': The Value of the Implied Author." *Style* 45, no. 1 (Spring 2011): 99–108.

———. "Truth in Fiction: A Reexamination of Audiences." *Critical Inquiry* 4, no. 1 (1977): 121–41.

Radin, Grace. "'Two Enormous Chunks': Episodes Excluded During the Final Revisions of *The Years*." *Bulletin of the New York Public Library* 80, no. 2 (1977): 221–51.

———. *Virginia Woolf's* The Years: *The Evolution of a Novel*. Knoxville: University of Tennessee Press, 1981.

Reynolds, Barbara. *Dorothy L. Sayers: Her Life and Soul*. New York: St. Martin's Press, 1993.

Richardson, Brian. "The Implied Author: Back from the Grave or Simply Dead Again?" *Style* 45, no. 1 (2011): 1–10.

Rimmon-Kenan, Shlomith. *Narrative Fiction: Contemporary Poetics*. 2d ed. London: Routledge, 2002.

Roof, Judith. *Come As You Are: Sexuality and Narrative*. New York: Columbia University Press, 1996.

Rorty, Richard. *Contingency, Irony, and Solidarity*. Cambridge: Cambridge University Press, 1989.

Rosecrance, Barbara. *Forster's Narrative Vision*. Ithaca, NY: Cornell University Press, 1982.

Sayers, Dorothy L. "Are Women Human?" In *Unpopular Opinions*, 129–41. New York: Harcourt, Brace, 1947.

———. "The Detective Story." *The Bookmark and Everyman* (Autumn 1936): 8–10.

———. "Detectives in Fiction." 6 pp in 6 lvs. with revisions. Wheaton, IL: The Marion E. Wade Center, Wheaton College, n.d.

———, and Robert Eustace. *The Documents in the Case*. New York: Harper & Row, 1930.

———. *Five Red Herrings.* New York: Harper & Row, 1931.

———. *Gaudy Night.* New York: HarperCollins, 1936.

———. "Gaudy Night." In *Titles to Fame*, 75–95. London: Nelson, 1937.

———. *Have His Carcase.* New York: Harper & Row, 1932.

———. *Strong Poison.* New York: Harper & Row, 1930.

———. "Strong Poison." 371 pp in 371 lvs. with revisions, signed. Wheaton, IL: The Marion E. Wade Center, Wheaton College, n.d.

———, ed. *Great Short Stories of Detection, Mystery and Horror.* 3 vols. London: V. Gollancz, 1935.

Schmid, Wolf. "Implied Author." In *The Living Handbook of Narratology*, edited by Peter Hühn et al. Hamburg: Hamburg University Press, http://www.lhn.uni-hamburg.de/article/implied-author (accessed 2 July 2013).

Scholes, Robert. "The Orgastic Pattern of Fiction." In *Fabulation and Metafiction*, 26–28. Urbana: University of Illinois Press, 1979.

Serpell, Namwali. Discussion during the NEH Seminar "Narrative Ethics," directed by James Phelan at The Ohio State University, June 20, 2008.

Shaw, Harry E. "Loose Narrators: Display, Engagement, and the Search for a Place in History in Realist Fiction." *Narrative* 3, no. 2 (1995): 95–116.

———. *Narrating Reality: Austen, Scott, Eliot.* Ithaca, NY: Cornell University Press, 1999.

Showalter, Elaine. "*A Passage to India* as 'Marriage Fiction': Forster's Sexual Politics." *Women & Literature* 5, no. 2 (1977): 3–16.

Silver, Brenda. "Periphrasis, Power, and Rape in *A Passage to India*." *Novel: A Forum on Fiction* 22, no. 1 (1988): 86–105.

———. "Textual Criticism as Feminist Practice: Or, Who's Afraid of Virginia Woolf Part II." In *Representing Modernist Texts: Editing as Interpretation*, edited by George Bornstein, 193–222. Ann Arbor: University of Michigan Press, 1991.

Sontag, Susan. "Against Interpretation." In *"Against Interpretation" and Other Essays*, 3–14. New York: Farrar, Straus, and Giroux, 1961.

Spacks, Patricia Meyer. *Boredom: The Literary History of a State of Mind.* Chicago: University of Chicago Press, 1995.

———. *Desire and Truth: Functions of Plot in Eighteenth-Century English Novels.* Chicago: University of Chicago Press, 1990.

Sperber, Dan, and Deirdre Wilson. *Relevance: Communication and Cognition.* 2d ed. Oxford: Blackwell, 1995.

———. "Rhetoric and Relevance." In *The Ends of Rhetoric: History, Theory, Practice*, edited by David Wellbery and John Bender, 140–55. Stanford, CA: Stanford University Press, 1990.

Spilka, Mark. "New Life in the Works: Some Recent Woolf Studies." *Novel: A Forum on Fiction* 12, no. 2 (1979): 169–84.

Squier, Susan. "A Track of Our Own: Typescript Drafts of *The Years*." In *Virginia Woolf: A Feminist Slant*, edited by Jane Marcus, 198–211. Lincoln: University of Nebraska Press, 1983.

Stewart, Garrett. *Dear Reader: The Conscripted Audience in Nineteenth-Century British Fiction.* Baltimore: Johns Hopkins University Press, 1996.

Trilling, Lionel. *E. M. Forster.* Norfolk, CT: New Directions, 1943.

Van Dine, S. S. "Twenty Rules for Writing Detective Stories." In *The Art of the Mystery Story: A Collection of Critical Essays*, edited by Howard Haycraft, 189–93. New York: Simon and Schuster, 1946.

Vanderham, Paul. *James Joyce and Censorship: The Trials of* Ulysses. New York: New York University Press, 1998.

Wald, Gayle F. "Strong Poison: Love and the Novelistic in Dorothy Sayers." In *The Cunning Craft: Original Essays on Detective Fiction and Contemporary Literary Theory,* edited by Ronald G. Walker and June M. Frazer, 98–108. Macomb: Western Illinois University, 1990.

Walsh, Richard. *The Rhetoric of Fictionality: Narrative Theory and the Idea of Fiction.* Columbus: The Ohio State University Press, 2007.

Warhol, Robyn. *Gendered Interventions: Narrative Discourse in the Victorian Novel.* New Brunswick, NJ: Rutgers University Press, 1989.

Wimsatt, W. K., and Monroe C. Beardsley. "The Intentional Fallacy." In *The Verbal Icon: Studies in the Meaning of Poetry,* by W. K. Wimsatt, 1–18. Lexington: University Press of Kentucky, 1946.

Winnett, Susan. "Coming Unstrung: Women, Men, Narrative, and Principles of Pleasure." *PMLA* 105 (1990): 505–18.

Woolf, Virginia. "Character in Fiction." In *The Essays of Virginia Woolf,* edited by Andrew McNeillie. Vol. 3, *1919–24.* San Diego: Harcourt Brace Jovanovich, 1988.

———. "Modern Fiction." In *The Common Reader,* edited by Andrew McNeillie. Orlando: Harcourt Brace, 1984.

———. "Modern Novels." In *The Essays of Virginia Woolf,* edited by Andrew McNeillie. Vol. 3, *1919–24.* San Diego: Harcourt Brace Jovanovich, 1988.

———. *A Writer's Diary.* Edited by Leonard Woolf. San Diego: Harvest, 1982.

———. *The Years.* Edited by Eleanor Jane McNees. Annotated ed. Orlando: Harcourt, 2008.

———. "[The Years] The Pargiters; a Novel-Essay Based Upon a Paper Read to the London National Society for Women's Service." M42 volumes 1–8: The Berg Collection of English and American Literature, New York Public Library, Holograph, unsigned, dated 11 Oct. 1932–15 Nov. 1934.

Wyatt, Jean. "*Love*'s Time and the Reader: Ethical Effects of *Nachträglichkeit* in Toni Morrison's *Love.*" *Narrative* 16, no. 2 (2008): 193–221.

Young, Iris Marion. "Asymmetrical Reciprocity: On Moral Respect, Wonder, and Enlarged Thought." In *Intersecting Voices: Dilemmas of Gender, Political Philosophy and Policy,* 38–59. Princeton, NJ: Princeton University Press, 1997.

Zunshine, Lisa. *Why We Read Fiction: Theory of Mind and the Novel.* Columbus: The Ohio State University Press, 2006.

ᖇ INDEX

Page numbers for definitions are in boldface.

THEORY AND INTERPRETATION OF NARRATIVE

James Phelan, Peter J. Rabinowitz, and Robyn Warhol, Series Editors

Because the series editors believe that the most significant work in narrative studies today contributes both to our knowledge of specific narratives and to our understanding of narrative in general, studies in the series typically offer interpretations of individual narratives and address significant theoretical issues underlying those interpretations. The series does not privilege one critical perspective but is open to work from any strong theoretical position.